Redefining the Political Novel

Redefining the Political Novel

AMERICAN WOMEN WRITERS,
1797–1901

Edited by

Sharon M. Harris

The University of Tennessee Press • Knoxville

Sandra A. Zagarell's "Expanding 'America': Lydia Sigourney's *Sketch of Connecticut,*
Catharine Sedgwick's *Hope Leslie*" originally appeared in *Tulsa Studies in Women's Litera-*
ture 6, no. 2 (1987): 225–46. Nina Baym's "Reinventing Lydia Sigourney" originally appeared
in *American Literature* 62 (1990): 385–404 and has been revised for this collection. Both
articles are reprinted by permission.

Library of Congress Cataloging-in-Publication Data

Redefining the political novel: American women writers, 1797–1901 / edited by
 Sharon M. Harris. — 1st ed.
    p.   cm.
  Includes bibliographical references and index.
  ISBN 0–87049–869–X (cloth: alk. paper)
   1. Political fiction, American—Women authors—History and criticism. 2. Politics and
literature—United States—History—19th century. 3. Feminism and literature—United
States—History—19th century. 4. Women and literature—United States—History—19th
century.   5. American fiction—19th century—History and criticism. I. Harris, Sharon M.
   PS374.P6R44   1995
   813.009'358'082—dc20   94-28331
                                                                        CIP

Contents

Introduction: Literary Politics
and the Political Novel

Sharon M. Harris

The Critical Tradition

Studies of the American political novel have a long history, beginning in the 1920s when American literature was admitted to academic study. To trace this history, however, is also to study the politics of literary criticism; critical definitions of "political" and "the political novel" have, wittingly or unwittingly, acted (like the law and society at large) to exclude recognition of women's contributions, most often by distinguishing the "social" from the "political" novel. One of the earliest full-length studies to include American works was Morris E. Speare's *The Political Novel: Its Development in England and America* (1924). Speare's definition of the genre cited prose in which the focus was on legislation and the government, though he acknowledged that "the drawing-room is frequently used as a medium for presenting the inside life of politics" (ix). Further, Speare insisted that a political novel "leans rather to 'ideas' than to 'emotions'" (ix).

Over the next two decades, critics from Parrington to Trilling offered varied definitions of political writings. It was in the late 1950s, however, that three major studies devoted to the American political novel appeared; the influence that each has wielded—or failed to wield—tells us as much about today's critical atmosphere as it does about these studies themselves. In 1955, Joseph Blotner published *The Political Novel*; although he expanded on Speare's study in several ways, he asserted that the criteria for inclusion in this genre was that a work "*directly* describes, interprets or analyzes political phenomena" (2; emphasis added). While Blotner's definition thus narrows the focus of the political novel from a text that "leans" toward legislative or government machinations as plot to an insistence on explicit description and analysis of those machinations, he interestingly elides a definition of the political. "Political" had acquired a definition understood among the small school of critics working within the field at the time of Blotner's study. This passage into elision rather than definition was to be repeated two years later by the genre's most notable critic, Irving Howe. And it is Blotner's and Howe's works that have continued to be voices of renown in critical studies of the genre.

The third major study of the American political novel written during the late 1950s was never published, and, although many of its author's concepts were included in later publications, her work has had little lasting impact on studies of the political novel. Jean O. Johnson, who early took her place as one of the few female critics of the genre, argued in her 1958 doctoral dissertation that "efforts to create rigid classifications to distinguish the political novel from the economic, the social, the proletarian, and other related types are likely not only to be unsuccessful but to detract from an understanding of the development of the novel rather than to add to it" (qtd. in Milne 5).[1] Johnson extended her criteria for studies of the political novel in her 1959 introduction to Hamlin Garland's *Crumbling Idols*. It is notable that, while she was one of the few early voices calling for a recognition of the synthesis of the social and the political, she erred in believing that studies which ignored this conjunction would lack success. She was, however, painfully correct in asserting that our understanding of the genre would be limited until such conjunctions were acknowledged and analyzed.

The most successful and influential study, the standard that all subsequent analyses have had to address, is Irving Howe's *Politics and the Novel* (1957), which denies the impact of the political on the social; the study most often forgotten or ignored is Johnson's attempt to integrate under the rubric of "political" such facets of American life as economics, class structure, and social realities. The lasting success of Howe's criteria—a success that exposes the gendered nature of critical studies in academia then and today—recalls the similar process outlined by Nina Baym in her classic study, "Melodramas of Beset Manhood: How Theories of American Fiction Exclude Women Authors" (1981). In terms of the political novel, exclusionary critical practices extend back to the nineteenth century, when, for example, Henry James's definition of the business tycoon managed to exclude the writings of most women political novelists of his time. In 1898—long after numerous female and lesser-known male authors had published political novels before the Civil War, challenged political notions of the effects of the Civil War, and exposed the political nature of the reconstitution of society in postbellum America—James lamented that the American business tycoon never had been attempted as a subject by American novelists. His description of the tycoon, however, is revealing: in James's terms, this character is understood as

> an epic hero, seamed all over with the wounds of the market and the dangers of the field, launched into action and passion by the immensity and complexity of the general struggle . . . driven above all by the ex-

traordinary, the unique relation in which he for the most part stands to
the life of his lawful, his immitigable womankind. (Qtd. in Berthoff 36)

James's assertion that no one had addressed the business tycoon in
American novels was not merely an oversight on his part; he knew well
the works of early political novelists such as Rebecca Harding Davis and
Elizabeth Stuart Phelps, both of whom were concerned with the consequences of industrial capitalism.[2] Davis's first novel, *Margret Howth* (1862),
includes the character of Stephen Holmes, a rising young manufacturing
tycoon;[3] and James had reviewed Davis's political novel of the Civil War,
Waiting for the Verdict, when it appeared in 1868. As a reviewer, he also
undoubtedly knew of *John Andross,* her acclaimed study of political corruption during the Grant administration.[4]

But it is James's *definition* of the business tycoon—his politicized
definition—that allows him to ignore all predecessors. It is a highly romanticized vision of the tycoon, a vision at odds with those of authors
who sought to expose corruption within the newly emergent capitalist
society and its rippling effects throughout the political and social arenas
of American life. Ironically, a similar romanticization of the political novel
has supported the continued exclusion of so many American women's
writings from studies of the genre. The irony is double-edged: in spite of
this critical romanticization, women's political novels often have been
termed "romantic" or "sentimental" and therefore considered outside the
realm of the political novel genre.

Although Howe asserts in his initial chapter, "The Idea of the Political Novel," that "labels, categories, definitions . . . do not here concern
me very much" (17), he devotes several pages to a delineation of termi-
nology for inclusion, ultimately concluding:

> By a political novel I mean a novel in which political ideas play a domi-
> nant role or in which the political milieu is the dominant setting—though
> again a qualification is necessary, since the word 'dominant' is more than
> a little questionable. Perhaps it would be better to say: a novel in which
> *we take to be dominant* political ideas or the political milieu, a novel
> which permits this assumption without thereby suffering any radical dis-
> tortion and, it follows, with the possibility of some analytical profit. (19;
> emphasis Howe's)

It is notable that in Howe's statement, however, "political" is defined, as
it was for Blotner, only in self-referential terms and never outside the

assumption of finite meaning; indeed, it is "dominant" and not "political"
that Howe feels the need to define at length.

It is precisely in Howe's emphasized phrase—"*we take to be dominant*"—that the control over genre definition occurs. Not only is the
seemingly inclusive "we" questionable today, but also Howe's emphasis
upon definition through the recognition of the political as *dominant*
within a text ironically aligns itself with a *dominant-culture* definition,
especially in its separation of the social from the political. Nor is Howe
any less aware of his elimination of the social novel (most often, although not exclusively, the term applied to women's novels) than was
James of his restrictions on literary definitions; Howe simply sees the
genesis of the novel as hierarchically evolving in complexity—that is, as
having evolved from the picaresque novel through the nineteenth-century social novel to the more highly evolved political novel:

> Once . . . bourgeois society began to lose some of its élan and cohesion,
> the social novel either declined into a sediment of conventional medi-
> ocrity . . . or it fractured in several directions. The most extreme and
> valuable of these directions were the novel of private sensibility . . .
> and the novel of public affairs and politics. (21)

That this fracturing is also along lines of an author's sex is implicit in the
examples Howe employs: "The ideal social novel had been written by Jane
Austen" (21), while "the greatest of all political novels [was Dostoevsky's]
The Possessed" (24). That Austen's novels of "private sensibility" are less
"valuable" than male-authored political novels is made explicit. After
praising Austen's work, Howe writes:

> But soon . . . the novelist's attention had necessarily to shift from the
> gradations within society to the fate of society itself. It is at this point . . .
> that the kind of book I have called the political novel comes to be writ-
> ten—the kind in which the *idea* of society, as distinct from the mere un-
> questioned workings of society, has penetrated the consciousness of
> the characters in all of its profoundly problematic aspects, so that there is
> to be observed in their behavior, and they are themselves often aware of,
> some coherent political loyalty or ideological identification. . . . [T]hey
> rally to one or another embattled segment of society; and they do so in
> the name of, and under prompting from, an ideology. (21)

Howe is correct in asserting that the critic's perspective is crucial in defining a political novel. Today, for instance, many feminist critics would

argue, in direct opposition to Howe's assertion, that Jane Austen was not writing about "the mere unquestioned workings of society," but instead writing novels whose characters, as well as their author, explicitly addressed "the *idea* of society." In Howe's own terms, then, Austen wrote political novels.[5]

Late-twentieth-century criticism has continued to accept traditional definitions of the term "political" in studies of the political novel. The exclusion of women's writings from a subgenre that is understood specifically as an engagement with the history of ideas is once again to relegate women to the emotional, while preserving for men the rational—and the means to power. But, as the following discussion will reveal, the essentialist nature of these categorizations is belied by a close examination of the literary and critical traditions of the American political novel. I asserted at the beginning of my discussion of Howe's definition of the political novel that, like James's, his view is ironically romanticized; the irony lies in Howe's emotional tone as well. A rather long passage will illustrate this point:

> Like a nimble dialectician, the political novelists must be able . . . to grasp the way in which ideas *in the novel* are transformed into something other than the ideas of a political program. . . . At its best, the political novel generates such intense heat that the ideas it appropriates are melted into its movement and fused with the emotions of its characters. . . . one of the supreme challenges, for the political novelist: to make ideas or ideologies come to life, to endow them with the capacity for stirring characters into passionate gestures and sacrifices . . . so that they themselves—those abstract weights of idea or ideology—seem to become active characters in the political novel. . . . His task is always to show the relation between theory and experience, between the ideology that has been preconceived and the tangle of feelings and relationships he is trying to present. This he does in a number of ways: diseased and intimate emotion twisting ideology into obsessional chimeras . . . ; ideology fortifying emotion for an heroic martyrdom . . . ; ideology pure and possessed strangling emotion pure and disinterested . . . ; and emotion fatally sapping the powers of ideological commitment. (23–24)

Not only does Howe create—I emphasize this verb—a hierarchy that maintains the oppression or denigration of "emotion," but he does so, ironically, in a context of emotionally defended assertions of "heroic martyrdom" and "pure" ideologies. Thus, as Howe would have it, the political novelist himself is engaged in heroic battles: because of the "imper-

sonal claims of ideology to the pressures of private emotion, the political novel must always be in a state of internal warfare. The political
novelist . . . must pit himself against the imperious presence of the necessary" (24–25). But Howe carries this notion even further; he has,
through his own celebratory, impassioned prose, created the *critic* of
the political novel as an equally romantic, "heroic," and emotional figure.

As Daniel T. O'Hara has noted in his studies of modern theory, there
is a long tradition of signifying "critical creation" as equal to, if not surpassing, imaginative creation:

> More often than not now . . . the romance of interpretation is a revi-
> sionary way for a critic to imagine his relationship to society, tradition,
> "primary" literature, history, or language—whatever is being strongly
> misread as "natural" but is in fact a distorted representation of the means
> and forces of critical production effective at the time. The romance
> of interpretation is thus a deliberately perverse ideology of literary
> study, which does little positive to make reforms in the institution. . . .
> (*Romance* 5)

This statement, in many ways, captures the history of criticism of the
political novel, culminating in Howe's romantic representation of the political novelist *and* his critic, but also continuing into the present.

When Howe turns, after a study of James (whom he treats as an
English author), to "Some American Novelists," he asserts:

> Political ideas in America have never been as crystallized as in Europe. . . .
> In [de Tocqueville's] tantalizing little chapter ["Why Americans Have
> Never Been So Eager as the French for General Ideas in Political Af-
> fairs"] he points to those "social conditions" which have prompted
> the French to a passion for ideology, and the absence of which has
> allowed the Americans to make the suspicion of ideology into some-
> thing approaching a national creed. (163)

Ironically, however, Howe himself has passionately perpetuated his own
ideology: that "social conditions" relative to political ideologies are ab-
sent in American culture. Equally ironic is the fact that Howe follows
this assertion by stating that "one of the most striking facts about American life and literature is the frequency with which political issues seem
to arise in nonpolitical forms. . . . [P]olitics in America has often appeared in the guise of religious, cultural and sexual issues" (165). Thus it
is Howe's distinction between social and political novels, far more than

his pre-postmodernist attitudes toward ideology, that makes his analysis of the political novel unsatisfying for late-twentieth-century theories of the genre.

It is this fallacy of separation that feminist theorists have explored and that offers the bases for the challenges to traditional studies of the genre put forward in the present volume. In some ways, however, the issues of literary criticism are more complex, and one significant point must be emphasized. Perhaps it is easiest to discuss if we turn to a recent study of political principles and novels, Catherine H. Zuckert's *Natural Right and the American Imagination* (1990). Like most studies of the political novel since the 1950s that exclude women's contributions to the genre, this one includes a disclaimer concerning the narrowness of the selections: "because they all depict a withdrawal from civil society as well as some kind of return," they must engage "the characteristically American motif that—I argue—parallels and recasts the movement of thought in the 'classic' statement of American political principles in the Declaration of Independence" (x). This explanation of the exclusion of women's and minority male authors' writings is inadequate, since natural right—the central issue in Zuckert's study—and the parallel practices of political philosophers and novelists that she designates as requisite to her discussion are at the heart of most marginalized authors' political discourse. Catherine Macaulay and Judith Sargent Murray would have balanced the political philosophies of Rousseau and Jefferson; novels, from Hannah Webster Foster's *The Coquette* to Charlotte Perkins Gilman's *Herland,* would have balanced Zuckert's literary criteria. In fact, however, the problem runs much deeper and cannot be laid entirely at Zuckert's feet; at heart is the long-standing failure of a nation to recognize women's thought *as* political philosophy. As Catharine MacKinnon has observed, "The pursuit of consciousness becomes a form of political practice" (qtd. in Humm 120).

Feminist Reconceptions of the Political

In a stratified society all literature is engaged politically and morally.

—Marge Piercy

The political literature that some women writers have begun to create is so revolutionary that no wonder many critics are scared. Women are questioning the set of values that has sustained human society.

—Isabel Allende

Not surprisingly, then, virtually all of the classic studies of the political novel, and contemporary studies as well, either address only texts written by white male authors or address women's contributions to the genre marginally. In O'Hara's criticism of "the romance of interpretation," he juxtaposes the creative-critic with a "visionary criticism" that both exposes the former's presumptions and, at its best, evaluates "the rhetorical operations of this ideology of romance in modern and postmodern literary theory" (*Romance,* 5). Although O'Hara ignores feminist theorists,[6] they, in fact, are engaged in some of the most rigorous visionary criticism being formulated today, criticism that exposes and evaluates the hubris and exclusion of the dominant culture's critical system.

Feminist theorists in many fields—history, literature, philosophy, political science, sociology, among others—have challenged assumptions underlying narrow definitions of the political. In the field of political science, Louise A. Tilly and Patricia Gurin, editors of *Women, Politics, and Change* (1990), have made significant contributions toward redefining "politics" to include women as members of the polity. However, they exclude "power struggles in the family" from their definition of politics, "which is limited to the arena of the state or collective units within it . . ." (6). While their revised definition offers significant insights into how we can reconsider the idea of politics and the political, their exclusion of the family is disturbing for two reasons. First, while they do include collectivism within the broad framework of the political, they denote it as "protopolitical" (7). Second, their exclusion fails to recognize the family *as* a collective unit. I would argue not only that the family is a collective unit but also that, in political terms, the family, in its patriarchal structure and values, is a microcosmic representation of "the state."[7] To exclude the family from the political, especially in studies of pre-twentieth-century America, is to deny that arena in which women have most experience and from which their knowledge of the need for change most often has been drawn.

Political scientist Suzanne Lebsock, a contributor to *Women, Politics, and Change,* makes a significant point concerning definitions of the political. Discussing the increased activity of women in "formal politics" during the period 1880–1920, Lebsock denotes the power of definitions:

> Most men would not have used the term "politics" to describe what women were doing. Instead they called it "philanthropy" or "service" or, in a few cases, "disorderly conduct." Politics was *by definition* something men did; and as feminists intensified their demands for admission into the formal political community of voters, some men and women inten-

sified their insistence that politics was no business for ladies. Metaphors of filth abounded: politics was a sewer, a cesspool, a slimepit. (35, emphasis added)

Lebsock's observations confirm the importance of language as a means of dismissing women's political actions, such as those noted above, and the importance of that dismissal as integral to the critical tradition of the political novel. Lebsock's statement recognizes, too, the dominant culture's long-standing reliance on the ideals of True Womanhood to oppress women.[8] However, we must not forget that many women writers, in early America as well as in the nineteenth century, used the power of language to retaliate against such dismissal; they did this by writing novels that exposed their society's exclusionary practices and oppressive political systems.

Other political scientists today have posited a broader definition of the political. As Kathleen B. Jones and Anna G. Jónasdóttir have observed, feminist political scientists now assert that

to consider gender as an analytic category in political theory—that is, to perceive gender as at least an analytically distinct set of social relationships—re-defines and enlarges the scope of politics, the practice of citizenship and authority, and the language of political action, as well as recognizes the political dimensions of sexuality. (9)

It is this broader definition, brought to bear upon feminist literary theories of the political, that offers us the most viable bases for understanding how women novelists before the twentieth century engaged the political and redefined it in terms that appropriated women's experiences through an understanding of gender politics.

When we turn to feminist literary theories of the political, we are, of course, engaging in an act that brings aesthetics into alliance with the political. As we seek to redefine the criteria for a genre such as the political novel, we are not merely engaging in an act of adding works by women authors to the genre's canon; rather, we are, as Mary Devereaux, a philosopher of aesthetics, has asserted, demanding "a conceptual revolution" (339). This was the process that Jane Tompkins followed in her seminal 1985 reassessment of sentimental fiction, *Sensational Designs: The Cultural Work of American Fiction 1790–1860*. Sentimental fiction traditionally has been charged, Tompkins noted, with a failure "to deal with the brute facts of political and economic oppression" (160). In contrast, Tompkins exposes the "automatic prejudice" of critics themselves against sentimental writers; it was the critics, Tompkins demonstrates, who failed "to perceive that the great subject of sentimental fiction is preeminently a social issue" (160). Tompkins's example of a conceptual revolution offers the greatest opportunities to feminist theorists of the political novel: we must not merely reconceptualize its canon; we must interrogate the precepts upon which that canon is based. Such a reconceptualization recognizes the political—the social, the sexual, and the legislative—as intimately linked with the literary, and it also recognizes the bond between, on the one hand, gender, race, and class, and, on the other, our most basic conceptions of the valuation of literature and of aesthetic experience as it relates to that literature.

Josephine Donovan, in editing *Feminist Literary Criticism,* has explored this theoretical territory as well. "I believe," she asserts, "the ethics and the aesthetics of a text are congruent. In part this is because the formal devices we have come to see as 'aesthetic'—style, form, figurative language, etc.—are themselves ideologically determined, and therefore political" (ix–x). While this leads us directly to feminist revisionist definitions of the political, it is notable that we have accomplished more in terms of theorizing the politics of aesthetics than we have in utilizing such theories to reevaluate the novel as a genre. This is even more true, again somewhat ironically, when we look at the specialized designation of the political novel.

At this point some readers must be asking themselves: if we are to acknowledge the conjunction of the social and the political, and view the self as politicized, how then can we talk about "political novels" as a genre? It is a valid question, one that might be answered most succinctly by defining the political novel so as to include works that recognize the social consequences of political processes and the political consequences of social processes. But in answering this question—and the present collection is only an initial contribution toward such an enterprise—the fact that we cannot narrow this genre to a small, finite canon should neither disturb nor deter us. In fact, I embrace Piercy's assertion that it is precisely the stratifications of patriarchal society that make an end to exclusionary canons essential. This is especially true in the 1990s, when progressive feminist attitudes are under increasing attack from entrenched—and increasingly powerful—conservative ideologies, under the influence of which we are witnessing the increased acculturation of our young people to patriarchal structures and ideals.

While some postmodern feminists have belittled studies of women's literary traditions, I would argue that it is precisely such traditions, at first highly dependent upon the norms of patriarchal literary standards but later significantly challenging those norms, that have paved the way for us as twentieth-century feminists to abandon essentialist visions and to break with the literary valuation systems of male-centered criticism. Twentieth-century feminist theories did not emerge out of the ashes like a phoenix, nor did they evolve simply from the work of Freud and Lacan, or from any other series of theoretical systems. The literature of our collective past had as much to do with the evolution of theory as did any psychological, sociological, or linguistic movement. To reevaluate the political novel, then, is to reevaluate the politicized nature of literary criticism itself. Marge Piercy has asserted about her own writing of political novels, "I'm responsible to many people with buried lives: people who have been rendered as invisible in history as they are powerless in the society their work creates, populates, cleans, repairs and defends" (120). This equally well describes the purposes and processes of the women novelists whose works are analyzed in this collection—writers who sought to expose and record a variety of "invisible histories" in their own eras and who, like the contributors to this volume, understood that to do so was to begin the process of recovering power over one's own life, to assist others in doing so, and to acknowledge the collective history of such literary activities.

The epigraphs in this section are significant for the ways in which they expose the alignment of contemporary political novelists with the attitudes of nineteenth-century American women political novelists. But one failure of feminist explorations of the political has been to assume that, in terms of the novel, little in the way of examining the implications of the political was attempted in this genre by women writing before the twentieth century. For instance, Carolyn Heilbrun notes that Teresa de Lauretis's work in cinema theory has applications for literature. "What she is recommending," Heilbrun observes, "is the 'practice by which the relations of the subject in social reality can be rearticulated from the historical experience of women' (*Alice Doesn't* 186). To put it simply, we must begin to tell the truth, in groups, to one another" (45). Both de Lauretis and Heilbrun are offering provocative means of bringing theory and practice into conjunction; my concern here is with the implication of Heilbrun's statement—that we are only now beginning "to tell the truth, in groups, to one another." The women novelists surveyed in this collection, and many others like them, had begun the process long before the women's movement and feminism were revitalized in the twentieth century. Their works constitute political novels precisely because they recognize the social and the sexual as political. If, as de Lauretis suggests, we must honor and articulate "the historical experience of women," we must do so with a recognition that it is not just a contemporary sense of "historical" experience.

Concerns recently raised by Nancy Fraser as to the significance of change as a defining element of feminist studies serve as a means of historically extending the assertions of Piercy, Heilbrun, and de Lauretis. In arguing that, for feminists, Saussurian structuralism "evacuates social agency, social conflict, and social practice," while Lacan's theory of discourse ultimately results in "an ironclad determinism" that inscribes "women's subordination . . . as the inevitable destiny of civilization" (87, 88–89), Fraser suggests that feminists must seek alternative theories of discourse that enable us better to understand "how people's social identities are fashioned and altered over time . . . [and] how the cultural hegemony of dominant groups in society is secured and contested" (83). For Fraser, such alternative theories should, finally, "shed light on the prospects for emancipatory social change and political practice" (83).

It is notable that the novelists surveyed in the essays contained in *Redefining the Political Novel* were interested in exploring the many avenues by which, overtly or covertly, the political both synthesized and dictated the social, especially in terms of women's lives. These works bring to the forefront debates by women novelists on the nature of political orders (both macrocosmically and in their microcosmic representations of family and social structures), the suppression of classes and races that are not part of the dominant culture in American society, and the means by which women's art forms have been controlled and defined under patriarchy.

The contributors to this book are acting in accord with Fraser's demands: they have recognized the ways in which women novelists have consciously politicized the genre of the novel, beyond merely attending to overt political machinery. This book's chapters explore ways in which these novelists have exposed, satirized, addressed, and challenged unspoken political ideologies in art, in the workplace, in all facets of existence under patriarchy.

In the first essay, I attempt to bring the theoretical points raised in this introduction into practice through an analysis of Hannah Webster Foster's *The Coquette* (1797), a critique of political limitations for women in late-eighteenth-century America. Foster explicitly understood the means by which language was being manipulated to inculcate political ideologies into the social milieu, especially dominant-culture ideologies that barred women from positions of autonomy and authority. Whereas my essay analyzes a well-known and readily accessible work, Christopher Castiglia's examination of Susanna Rowson's *Reuben and Rachel* (1798) calls attention to a little-known early American novel, one that not only challenges our conceptions of early women's writings but also forces us to reexamine the political nature of Rowson's oeuvre. As Castiglia argues, *Reuben and Rachel* inverts official histories of the nation's heroic founding in conquest and suppression, by measuring American prosperity in terms of race and gender—that is, in terms of Native American resistance to colonization and of white women's escape from the confinements of both British tyranny and domestic tyranny.

Sandra A. Zagarell's essay, "Expanding 'America,'" reveals how early-nineteenth-century authors such as Lydia Sigourney and Catharine Maria Sedgwick extended these ideas by confronting in their novels, *Sketch of Connecticut* (1824) and *Hope Leslie* (1827), respectively, a major political topic of their day: the nature of the American nation. As Zagarell perceives, not only did Sigourney and Sedgwick redefine the prevailing definitions of the nation to recognize the potential for inclusiveness and communitarianism, but they also reshaped genre classifications in the process. Nina Baym's essay, "Reinventing Lydia Sigourney," follows Zagarell's lead and exposes the misrepresentation of Sigourney as predominantly a pious poet and reestablishes her place in American literary history to include recognition of Sigourney as a political author.

Baym's article concludes with a call for a reconsideration of women's antebellum writings, and Kristie Hamilton heeds this call when she evaluates the means by which writers such as Sara Payson Parton ("Fanny Fern") are freed from their traditional critical classifications when they are studied in conjunction with working-class women's writings, which were more readily accorded the definition of political texts. In *Ruth Hall* (1854), Parton traverses dominant antebellum constructions of the political and the literary by creating a collective model of social existence that foregoes the utopian idealism of later writers. Similarly, Mary Bortnyk Rigsby reexamines Louisa May Alcott's post–Civil War novel *Work* (1872–73), demonstrating how Alcott redefines traditional concepts of strength and independence and challenges the value structures of American capitalism, heroic individualism, and the role assigned to women in patriarchal society. Both Hamilton and Rigsby denote these authors' interest in moving away from a masculine model of individualism to one that is exclusively (Fern) or equally (Alcott) woman-identified and (for both) communitarian in nature.

Mary E. Bradley Lane explores even more radical and subversive means of redefining the political nature of social constructions in her 1880–81 utopian novel, *Mizora*. The politically subversive nature of Lane's vision of an all-female society is revealed in Duangrudi Suksang's analysis of *Mizora*'s uncompromising insistence upon the destruction of both patriarchy and the dual-gendered nature of society, as the only means by which women could gain the liberty historically afforded their male counterparts. In this, Lane anticipates Charlotte Perkins Gilman's twentieth-century separatist feminist utopian tradition.

Dorothy Berkson's essay on Mary Wilkins Freeman's novel, *The Portion of Labor* (1901), examines Freeman's engagement with class labor issues and women's sexuality (acceptable female bonding and the love between two women that begins to threaten cultural "norms" of "womanliness"). When the tension between the issues of labor and "genteel womanhood" emerges in the novel, Berkson argues, "Freeman's undeniable sympathy with and attraction to socialist ideology about labor becomes evident."

The collection concludes with Claire Pamplin's essay, "'Race' and Identity in Pauline Hopkins's *Hagar's Daughter*" (1901). As Pamplin demonstrates, Hopkins's novel confronts turn-of-the-century political debates on the ambiguities of racial identity. By reconstructing the popular nineteenth-century fiction formulas of disguises and double identities, Hopkins critiques contemporary efforts to realign race and legal status, which had been separated through the Emancipation Proclamation. As Pamplin recognizes, Hopkins understood the social implications of these political maneuvers; rather than merely critiquing conservative efforts to reestablish social constructs of separation, however, Hopkins in her fiction deliberately attempted to proffer another notion: that there could be an "American race."

The eighteenth- and nineteenth-century authors examined in these essays conflated the political and the domestic to expose the false constructions of the political that have separated the so-called public and private spheres. The manner in which these earlier authors negotiated the tensions between exposing the gendered ideologies of their eras and the struggle for cultural change says much, not only about the particular authors' political consciousnesses but, cumulatively and equally, about that of the nation itself.

As the essays in this book demonstrate, feminist analyses of American women's novels of the eighteenth and nineteenth centuries are reshaping our understanding of specific authors' works and ideologies. In addition, these analyses are redefining the boundaries of genres (see especially the essays by Zagarell and Baym) and insisting upon a realignment of the social and the political. Rather than accepting literary definitions, the authors of these essays interrogate the political nature of literary criticism itself.

Notes

1.   Gordon Milne, writing in 1966, asserts that Johnson's point is "sensible" and that he has "chosen to follow her pattern of avoiding very inflexible stratification" in defining the political. However, his inclusiveness is limited; he asserts that "the economic, social protest, proletarian, and utopian areas . . . have already received the careful attention of such scholars as Walter Taylor, Vernon Parrington, Jr., and Walter Rideout" and therefore

need not be reintroduced in his analyses (5–6). Thus, once again, the social (even in this limited context) is eliminated from discussions of the
political. It should be noted, however, that Milne is one of the rare critics
working in this area before 1970 who at least names and briefly discusses
a few women writers of the genre.

2.   This is true of Phelps's early works only. For Davis, it was a lifelong com-
       mitment to expose abuse of the working class under capitalism, begin-
       ning with her first novel, *Margret Howth* (1862).

3.   See also Yellin's excellent introduction to *Margret Howth* in the recent
       Feminist Press edition.

4.   See Sharon M. Harris, *Rebecca Harding Davis and American Realism,* for
       discussions of Davis's novels, especially *Margret Howth* and *John Andross.*

5.   For discussions of these issues in Austen's novels, see Poovey and Kirk-
       ham.

6.   Indeed, O'Hara's *The Romance of Interpretation,* which is intended as a
       study of modern criticism from Pater to de Man, contains not a single ref-
       erence to a woman critic or author, let alone to feminist theories. This is
       unfortunate, since O'Hara otherwise is one of our most interesting and
       challenging postmodern theorists, especially in terms of his interests in
       "the relation between theory and politics" and in the self as "an ever-pro-
       visional, mobile effect of specific rhetorical acts" ("Mask Plays" 129, 131),
       issues that abound in the essays in this volume.

7.   Certainly there are alternative family structures in America today, as there
       were to a lesser extent in earlier eras; but the fact that they always are
       considered distinct by comparison to the traditional family model under
       patriarchy makes them as much an element of the political as is the tradi-
       tional family model.

8.   Just how enduring is the tradition of depicting politics as "nonfeminine"
       is implied when Trilling defines the conjunction of literature and politics
       as a "dark and bloody crossroads" (11).

Works Cited

Alcott, Louisa May. *Work: A Story of Experience.* 1872–73. New York: Schocken,
       1977.

Allende, Isabel. "Writing as an Act of Hope." Zinsser 39–63.

Baym, Nina. "Melodramas of Beset Manhood: How Theories of American Fic-
       tion Exclude Women Authors." *The New Feminist Criticism.* Ed. Elaine
       Showalter. New York: Pantheon, 1985. 63–80.

Berthoff, Warner. *The Ferment of Realism: American Literature, 1884–1919.*
       New York: Cambridge UP, 1965.

Blotner, Joseph L. *The Political Novel.* Garden City, NY: Doubleday, 1955.

Davis, Rebecca Harding. *John Andross*. New York: Orange Judd, 1874.

————. *Margret Howth: A Story of To-Day*. Boston: Ticknor & Fields, 1862.

————. *Waiting for the Verdict*. New York: Sheldon, 1867.

de Lauretis, Teresa. *Alice Doesn't: Feminism, Semiotics, Cinema*. Bloomington: Indiana UP, 1984.

————, ed. *Feminist Studies/Critical Studies*. Bloomington: Indiana UP, 1986.

Devereaux, Mary. "Oppressive Texts, Resisting Readers and the Gendered Spectator: The *New* Aesthetics." *Journal of Aesthetics and Art Criticism* 48 (Fall 1990): 337–47.

Donovan, Josephine, ed. *Feminist Literary Criticism: Explorations in Theory*. 2nd ed. Lexington: U of Kentucky P, 1989.

Foster, Hannah Webster. *The Coquette; or, The History of Eliza Wharton*. 1797. Ed. Cathy N. Davidson. New York: Oxford UP, 1986.

Fraser, Nancy. "The Uses and Abuses of French Discourse Theories for Feminist Politics." *boundary 2* 17 (Summer 1990): 82–101.

Freeman, Mary Wilkins. *The Portion of Labor*. Ridgewood, N.J.: Gregg, 1967.

Harris, Sharon M. *Rebecca Harding Davis and American Realism*. Philadelphia: U of Pennsylvania P, 1991.

Heilbrun, Carolyn G. *Writing a Woman's Life*. New York: Ballantine, 1988.

Hopkins, Pauline. *Hagar's Daughter: A Story of Southern Caste Prejudice*. In *The Magazine Novels of Pauline Hopkins*. 1901–2. New York: Oxford UP, 1988. 3–284.

Howe, Irving. *Politics and the Novel*. New York: Avon, 1957.

Humm, Maggie, ed. *Modern Feminisms: Political, Literary, Cultural*. New York: Columbia UP, 1992.

Johnson, Jean O. Introduction. *Crumbling Idols,* by Hamlin Garland. Cambridge: Belknap P of Harvard UP, 1959–60.

————. "The American Political Novel in the Nineteenth Century." Diss. Boston U, 1958.

Jones, Kathleen B., and Anna G. Jónasdóttir, eds. *The Political Interests of Gender: Developing Theory and Research with a Feminist Face*. London: Sage, 1988.

Kirkham, Margaret. *Jane Austen: Feminism and Fiction*. New York: Methuen, 1986.

Lane, Mary E. Bradley. *Mizora: A Prophecy*. 1890. Boston: Gregg, 1975.

Lebsock, Suzanne. "Women and American Politics, 1880–1920." *Women, Politics, and Change*. Eds. Louise A. Tilly and Patricia Gurin. New York: Russell Sage Foundation, 1990. 35–62.

Milne, Gordon. *The American Political Novel*. Norman: U of Oklahoma P, 1966.

O'Hara, Daniel T. "Mask Plays: Theory, Cultural Studies, and the Fascist Imagination." *boundary 2* 17 (Summer 1990): 129–54.

————. *The Romance of Interpretation: Visionary Criticism from Pater to de Man*. New York: Columbia UP, 1985.

Parrington, Vernon Louis. *Main Currents in American Thought*. 2 vols. New York: Harcourt Brace & World, 1927.

Parton, Sara Payson Willis [Fanny Fern]. *Ruth Hall and Other Writings*. Ed. Joyce W. Warren. New Brunswick: Rutgers UP, 1986.

Piercy, Marge. "Active in Time and History." Zinsser 89–123.

Poovey, Mary. *The Proper Lady and the Woman Writer: Ideology as Style in the Works of Mary Wollstonecraft, Mary Shelley, and Jane Austen*. Women in Culture and Society Series. Chicago: U of Chicago P, 1984.

Rowson, Susanna Haswell. *Reuben and Rachel; or, Tales of Olden Times*. 2 vols. London: Minerva, 1798.

Sedgwick, Catharine Maria. *Hope Leslie; or, Early Times in the Massachusetts*. New York: Harper & Bros., 1842.

[Sigourney, Lydia Howard Huntley.] *Sketch of Connecticut, Forty Years Since*. Hartford, Conn.: Oliver D. Cooke & Sons, 1824.

Speare, Morris E. *The Political Novel: Its Development in England and America*. New York: Oxford UP, 1924.

Tilly, Louise A., and Patricia Gurin, eds. *Women, Politics, and Change*. New York: Russell Sage Foundation, 1990.

Tompkins, Jane. *Sensational Designs: The Cultural Work of American Fiction 1790–1860*. New York: Oxford UP, 1985.

Trilling, Lionel. *The Liberal Imagination*. New York: Viking P, 1950.

Yellin, Jean Fagan. Introduction. *Margret Howth*. New York: Feminist P, 1991.

Zinsser, William, ed. *Paths of Resistance: The Art and Craft of the Political Novel*. Boston: Houghton Mifflin, 1989.

Zuckert, Catherine H. *Natural Right and the American Imagination*. Savage, Md.: Rowman & Littlefield, 1990.

CHAPTER 1

Hannah Webster Foster's

The Coquette:

Critiquing Franklin's America

Sharon M. Harris

Crime has no sex and yet to-day
    I wear the brand of shame;
Whilst he amid the gay and proud
    Still bears an honored name.

Can you blame me if I've learned to think
    Your hate of vice a sham,
When you so coldly crushed me down
    And then excused the man? . . .

           Frances E. Watkins Harper,
           "The Double Standard" (1895)

[Women] are so overloaded with precepts by guardians, who
think that nothing is so much to be dreaded for a woman as
originality of character, that their minds are impeded by doubts till
they lose their chance of fair, free proportions.
    Margaret Fuller, *Woman in the Nineteenth Century* (1845)

Before women gained the vote in 1920, the suppression of women's political voices was not only a legal and civic silencing but was equally
prevalent in the literary arts, where women's writings often were reclas-
sified as "regional" or "domestic" and thereby marginalized in studies of
the political novel.[1] To exclude women's writings from a genre that is
understood specifically as an engagement with the history of ideas is
once again to relegate women to the emotional, while preserving the
rational—and the means to power—for men. Of particular interest to me
in the following discussion is the way in which critical assumptions continue to place women's political commentaries on the sidelines by cat-

egorizing their novels as "sentimental"—a critical stance that thrives despite the seminal work in this area by Jane Tompkins and others. This categorization seems especially to have been applied to the earliest novels by women in America; while the literature of the eighteenth century is rife with debates about the new political order, about the "rights of man," and about what it means to be an American, women's novels of this era are rarely recognized as other than social commentaries. Cathy N. Davidson, whose studies of the rise of the American novel have significantly advanced our understanding of that literary movement, has made initial steps toward changing our attitudes about the earliest fiction by women. For instance, she argues that, as an eighteenth-century sentimental novel, Hannah Webster Foster's *The Coquette; or, The History of Eliza Wharton* (1797) is "ultimately about silence, subservience, and stasis (the accepted attributes of woman as traditionally defined) in contradistinction to conflicting impulses toward self-expression, independence, and action (the ideals of the new American nation) . . ." (Introduction xix). This formulation juxtaposes the social and the political and, although Davidson does not classify *The Coquette* as a political novel, she does recognize that juxtaposition and the resulting sidelined position of women's writings as political.

Davidson asserts that Foster fails to extend the connections between the social and the political: "The problem arises because the form itself—or the writer—cannot imagine a life beyond her society's limitations without violating the essential social realism on which sentimental fiction (contrary to the usual critical clichés) is ultimately based" (Introduction xix). I agree with Davidson that sentimental novels are based on social realism and that they are, therefore, based on the "silence, subservience, and stasis" typical of most eighteenth-century women's lives. And I agree that Foster places the responsibility for considering this reality on the reader.

I would argue, however, that Foster indeed does imagine alternative lifestyles for women. The plot outline of *The Coquette* follows the patterns of the early sentimental novel: a headstrong young woman follows her own inclinations rather than the advice of parents and friends; her actions lead to her "downfall," pregnancy, separation from society, and death. The narrative style of Foster's novel, however, does not adhere to the usual pattern of the didactic novel, in which, as Susan K. Harris has noted, "the narrator always makes her presence felt, addressing a female consciousness she perceives as extremely susceptible to whatever error her tale is designed to prevent" (45). By using a true epistolary format (in contrast to many early American epistolary novels which merely allude to epistolarity), Foster eliminates the overt authorial intrusion commonly aligned with didacticism.

By recognizing and satirizing, first, the political systems that create women's social realisms and, second, the language used to convey those systems to the broader culture, Foster exposes the sexist bases of the new nation's political ideologies. Most pointedly, she reveals the ways in which Franklinesque maxims—what I shall call "the rhetoric of the republic"[2]—acculturize the new nation's citizens to its patriarchal political system and the social constructs of that system. Prior to the publication of *The Coquette,* of course, there had existed a long history of conduct literature that presented "straightforward, prescriptive injunctions: 'do not learn to romp,' 'obey your husband,' and so forth" (Newton 140).[3] Foster, however, does not merely critique rules of conduct; she also exposes the political agenda encoded in the rhetorical strategies by which rules of conduct were passed down from America's political leaders, especially in the form of Franklin's often humorous maxims.

The French feminist Claudine Herrmann has articulated the danger of axiomatic "playfulness": "Proverbs are full of charm. For example, 'You bind oxen with cords and men with words'" (xiii). As Herrmann implicitly recognizes, this "proverb" itself is problematic, for it is the discourse of the dominant culture that has bound women into silence and submissive lifestyles, while here suggesting that men are the victims of words beyond their control. Thus the maxim—in content, certainly, but equally so in form or genre—elides men's traditional discursive power over women at the same time that it appropriates their victimization. In *The Coquette,* Foster explicitly challenges the "truth" of patriarchal structures established to guide—and to control—women's lives, by satirizing the Franklinesque use of maxims. As Foster recognizes, maxims, presumably crafted as moral suasion, in fact often are used to inculcate gender differences; that is, she illuminates the political ideology of excluding women from citizenship and systems of power that is fostered in the social milieu.

In contrast to Davidson, then, I propose that, by revealing the social as a political construct, Foster denies the necessity of stasis. Davidson views *The Coquette* as a novel that emphasizes "the marital possibilities facing later eighteenth-century women of the middle- or upper-middle classes . . ." but "does not openly challenge the basic structure of patriarchal culture." I am arguing, however, that the novel has precisely the opposite emphasis: Foster is far less concerned with the issue of marriage than with the political system of the new republic that can envision that institution as the only opportunity for its female "citizens."

In the opening letter of this epistolary novel, Eliza Wharton acknowledges that "both nature and education had instilled into my mind an implicit obedience to the will and desires of my parents" (5), an obedience that is extended to all figures of authority in society. The emphasis upon "nature *and* education" is perpetuated throughout the novel. As

Davidson has observed, Foster's emphasis upon women's education is un-
paralleled in early American fiction (*Revolution* 78). But Foster intends far
more than conventional definitions of education. By linking "nature and
education," she acknowledges the double-edged oppression of women that
Judith Sargent Murray had exposed in her 1790 essay, "On the EQUALITY
of the SEXES": denied a formal education and thereby denied the development of their *natural* intellectual abilities, women were educated only to
what Murray called "*second nature*"—that is, social custom (1033–34).

The Coquette is a very densely textured political novel; at the heart
of the novel is Foster's recognition of the numerous levels on which the
new republic perpetuates a double standard for men and for women. In
an era when Franklin's almanacs and *Autobiography* served as a model
for constructing oneself as a hard-working, productive American citizen
who thereby could reap the benefits of "industry and frugality," young
women were being told that their place was strictly domestic seclusion,
not independence, nor citizenship, nor a public voice in the shaping of
the new nation.

Eliza's nature is not easily categorized. Foster does not depict her as
innocent of complicity in her seduction and "fall." She is a character
whose thoughts and actions frustrate readers as often as they charm us,
but, as Marge Piercy has observed:

> Writing politically, writing as a feminist, writing as a serious woman,
> doesn't mean . . . creating impossible, good, heroic, pure, strong, healthy,
> no-fault, no-ulcers women who run around in seven-league boots, right-
> ing wrongs before breakfast. Writers aren't in the business of fulfilling
> anyone's fantasies, even those of the oppressed. . . . Our writers must tell
> us stories and create us characters that have more truth in them than
> wishes—stories that have enough grit and power to wound as well as to
> please. (118–19).

What we must interrogate in Foster's novel, then, is why the author has
Eliza act as she does. What forces, personal and social, shape this character's
actions and her understanding of her opportunities in late-eighteenth-century American society? Why is Eliza's nature so appealing and yet so
unacceptable to that society? And what is meant by "education" in an
era when formal study for women was extremely limited?

What is Eliza's "nature," then, as presented in the novel? This may
be understood, at least in part, as Eliza's desire to make her own choices
and decisions in life; it is this attitude and her discovery that such ideas
must be repressed that, as much as anything, lead to her downfall. She
is repeatedly defined as a woman of lively mind and personality; even
Selby, whose accounts of Eliza's activities contribute to Reverend Boyer's

rejection of her,[4] observes that everyone is drawn to Eliza because her "fund of useful knowledge, and extensive reading, . . . the brilliancy of her wit, the fluency of her language, the vivacity and ease of her manners, are inexpressibly engaging" (L24, 46).[5] In a man, similar traits would make their possessor a national leader. Eliza herself asserts, "Social converse . . . is the true zest of life" (L14, 30). This assertion is important on several levels: it occurs immediately after she has rejected Reverend Boyer's first proposal of marriage; it suggests her desire for a sphere of activity wider than the domestic domain; and it is one of Eliza's earliest attempts to create a discourse that embraces her own definitions of a viable future for herself.

The novel opens with Eliza's sense of liberation after the death of Mr. Haly, her fiancé in an arranged marriage: "An unusual sensation possesses my breast; a sensation, which I once thought could never pervade it on any occasion whatever. It is *pleasure*; pleasure, my dear Lucy, on leaving my paternal roof!" (L1, 5). When friends and suitors first propose that she again consider marrying, Eliza tries to avoid the discourse of marriage. When Boyer begins to pursue her in earnest, she writes, "I studiously avoided every kind of discourse which might lead to this topic. I wish not a declaration from any one . . ." (L5, 12). If marriage and family constitute a microcosmic representation of patriarchy's political structure,[6] it is little wonder that Eliza rejects Boyer's "declaration"; the political Declaration of Independence had done her no service, either. She notes that Boyer's conversation is remarkably similar to that of the man her parents had first selected for her. Her assertion of a desire for "social converse" is not merely an attempt to avoid Boyer's stylized rhetoric; it evolves into a desire to find another "language" that is appropriate to women like herself.

What Eliza is arguing against are the voices coming at her from all sides that insist she must "resign [her] freedom" (L14, 30). It is the act of silencing that Eliza resists: "I must write to you the impulses of my mind," she tells Lucy, "or I must not write at all" (L3, 8). Late in the novel, when Eliza comes to believe that society's dictates will prevail, she abandons her writing as futile, recognizing that there is no place in late-eighteenth-century American society for her opinions. It is the recognition of this fact that constitutes Eliza's true loss of innocence, and in the novel the numerous deaths of infants (the Richmans' daughter, Nancy Sanford's stillborn son, Eliza's own child) act as reverberations of the death of innocence. In many ways, the novel's structure is the unfolding of Eliza's growing awareness of this social truth.

Behind many of Eliza's actions lies a frustration with social customs. At the beginning of the novel, she asserts that "the absurdity of a custom" that is to be followed "for no other reason, than a compliance with fashion is to be treated in a manner, which the laws of humanity forbid" (L3, 9). Arguing that she has just escaped the "shackles" of proposed matrimony through the death of Mr. Haly, Eliza rejects Mrs. Richman's intervention on Boyer's behalf by imploring, "Let me then enjoy that freedom which I so highly prize" (L5, 13). She knows that the Richmans, like her parents, wish her to "sacrifice" her freedom in accordance with their "authority" (L5, 13). Eliza argues for an opportunity to participate in "those pleasures which youth and innocence afford" (L5, 13). This statement is followed by the first maxim Foster uses in the novel. In detailing his own youthful errors, Benjamin Franklin had suggested that, if an erring youth sincerely repented and desired to repair any damage done to another person, the youth should be accepted back into the social fold. Franklin's own "youthful errors" (his "Errata") were not minor: he kept money for himself that was due another, he abandoned his fiancee, and he tried to seduce his friend's mistress. His *Autobiography* is a detailed account of restitution, of being accepted again by society, and of rising to such heights that, to all subsequent generations, he has come to represent the American Dream. While Franklin had argued astutely for the possibility of correcting the errors of youth, Mrs. Richman employs the novel's first maxim to caution Eliza against expecting this outcome for herself: "The round of fashionable dissipation is dangerous" (L5,13). Eliza's hardest lesson will be that, for women in America, there is no freedom, no equality, and no "second chance."

Seven years before Foster's novel appeared (and two years before Mary Wollstonecraft's *Vindication of the Rights of Woman*), the American essayist Judith Sargent Murray published "On the EQUALITY of the SEXES." In this essay, she argued against the traditional education for women that "limits and confines," noting that

> after we have from early youth been adorned with ribbons, and other
> gewgaws . . . ; after, I say fifteen years thus spent, we are introduced
> into the world, amid the united adulation of every beholder. . . . It is
> expected that with the other sex we should . . . triumph over the machi-
> nations of the most artful. We must be constantly upon our guard; pru-
> dence and discretion must be our characteristicks; and we must rise
> superior to, and obtain a complete victory over those who have been
> long adding to the native strength of their minds, by an unremitted study
> of men and books. (1036–37)

More importantly, Murray notes that "the smallest deviation in our conduct" leads to "infamy" (1037). As Gérard Genette observed in a discussion of Madame de Lafayette's *La princesse de Clèves*: "Real or assumed, [public] 'opinion' is quite close to what today would be called an ideology, that is a body of maxims and prejudices which constitute both a vision of the world and a system of values" (qtd. in Donovan, *Feminist* xv). It is this kind of false and potentially destructive "education," inculcated in the populace most notably through maxims and codes of conduct, that Hannah Webster Foster recognizes as political in origin as well as in consequence and that she denounces in *The Coquette.*

It can be argued that Eliza's failure to heed Mrs. Richman's advice leads to her downfall, but it is Mrs. Richman herself who reveals both the duplicity of maxims and the paradoxical necessity of obeying all such counsel. "Even the false maxims of the world must be complied with in a degree," she intones (L9, 20). In Foster's relatively short novel, more than thirty maxims appear, many drawn directly from Franklin's writings. For every action that Eliza, Boyer, Lucy, Sanford, or any other character in the novel wishes to take, there is a maxim arguing for such action and an equally handy one exposing the dangers of doing so. No one in Eliza's social circle counsels her, however, on how to know which maxims are false and which to follow. "A reformed rake makes the best husband" is a common adage, Eliza notes, but so, too, is "A man, who has been dissolute before marriage, will seldom be faithful afterwards" (L26, 53; L51, 111). Thus maxims become, in the rhetoric of the republic, the discourse of disguise; they epitomize the deception of social discourse.

Like Franklin, Eliza does not want to marry until she has "sowed all [her] wild oats" (L34, 68). She knows what is necessary for marriage, as she observes with seriousness at Lucy's wedding: "The consonance of their dispositions, the similarity of their tastes, and the equality of their ages are a sure pledge of happiness" (L36, 70). All her counselors (and there are many) repeatedly tell her that her disposition must be altered so as to fit Boyer's, even though she herself recognizes that they have "such a disparity of dispositions" (L38, 74). It is her failure to conform her own personality and actions to Boyer's "disposition" that leads to his censure of her when they are in Boston. As Michel Foucault has observed, docility was a crucial element in the evolving eighteenth-century political machinery's recognition of "the body as object and target of power. . . . A body is docile that may be subjected, used, transformed and improved" (136). The rise of conduct literature in eighteenth-century America and its integration into everyday aspects of "acceptable" female behavior led to a conviction that docility was the proper demeanor for women. While Eliza's outgoing personality initially is attractive to Boyer, he would not countenance the same if she were his wife; for that role, Boyer asserts, there must be "discretion sufficient" for the "regulation" of "a gay disposition" (L4, 10). Eliza resents his censure, recognizing his comments as "the censure of my own heart" (L38, 74). She draws specifically on one of Franklin's maxims to support her preference for the company of Sanford: "Pleasure is now diffused through all ranks of the people, especially the rich," she observes; "and surely it ought to be cultivated, since as the wisest of men informs us, that 'a merry heart doth good like a medicine'" (L41, 86). But Franklin's maxims advocating pleasure and independence cannot apply to Eliza or to any other young woman of her social standing.

While Lucy and Mrs. Richman place a veil of pleasantry over the confinements of marriage, Sanford openly observes that, if Eliza marries Boyer, she will become "the property of another" (L18, 35). Sanford is not only a master of seduction; he is also adept at understanding social customs and recognizes Eliza's nature as one that will be stifled in conforming to social constructs. Thus his words, framed to meet her own desires, begin to carry an unwarranted weight with her. While Franklin's model of citizenry suggests the means to become a property owner, Sanford exposes the limitations for women of being nothing more than property itself, socially and legally.[7] Eliza's fascination with imagination and fancy thus becomes an instrument of escape from the life of "constraint and confinement" (L14, 29); she increasingly views the social role she is destined by her sex to play as little more than slavery, often echoing similar images employed by Phillis Wheatley. In "On Imagination," Wheatley suggests that "silken fetters" and "soft captivity" can only be escaped mentally, by "leav[ing] the rolling universe behind" (24), and then only temporarily. Eliza's imagination "paints, in alluring colors, the charms of youth and freedom, regulated by virtue and innocence. Of these, I wish to partake" (L14, 29). Marriage to Boyer, on the other hand, offers the scene of captivity. Thus she writes to Boyer:

> I recoil at the thought of immediately forming a connection, which must confine me to the duties of domestic life, and make me dependent for happiness, perhaps too, for subsistence, upon a class of people, who will claim the right of scrutinising every part of my conduct. . . . I would not have you consider me as confined to your society, or obligated to a future connection. (L14, 29)

What Eliza desires is to be left "to the exercise of my free will" (L14, 29).[8]

Because Eliza's acculturation comes mostly through other women, she finds herself falling deeper and deeper into an intellectual quagmire, in which friendship acts to stifle her with the language and customs of patriarchy. The fact that, in the novel, it is mostly women who enforce these codes of Womanhood makes some feminist critics uncomfortable; but it is not an issue we should shy away from. Women's participation in perpetuating the dictates of patriarchy has been part of the process of acculturation from Foster's time through Virginia Woolf's to our own, and it is less often encountered in the blatant form of a Phyllis Schlafly than it is in the more subtle form of our mothers and women friends.[9] As Foster understood, the acculturation process cannot be altered until it is openly acknowledged. Almost every page of *The Coquette* is imbedded with confirmations of this process; Foster thus creates an atmosphere in which we as readers begin to feel as oppressed by the system as does Eliza.

We are, however, afforded another voice within the text, one that satirizes the dictates of a political system presenting itself as a democratic republic while harboring very old ideals of patriarchy. It is no easy task, in an epistolary novel, subversively to express ironic discord and disruption. Mimicry of Franklinesque maxims is, in many ways, a dangerous technique to undertake; as Toril Moi has argued, "Mimicry . . . cannot be rejected as unsuitable for feminist purposes," but it also runs the risk of becoming little more than "just a woman speaking like a man" (142–43). Foster bridges this danger with acumen and grace. As Moi acknowledges, "It is the *political context* of such mimicry that is surely always decisive" (143).

The following examination of *The Coquette* will reveal, then, both how Foster presents the voices of accommodation that seek to educate Eliza to the ways of patriarchy under the new political system and her own satirical narrative pattern that seeks to disrupt the system.[10] Lucy Freeman, Mrs. Richman, and later Mrs. Wharton and Julia Granby all voice opinions about "woman's place" as advocated by the dominant culture; as Kristie Hamilton notes, they "are the spokeswomen for republic ideology" (141). These women do not voice such opinions out of malicious intent. Rather, they believe that their counsel is offered for Eliza's own good. Such an assumption in itself recalls the hierarchy inherent in America's new political order, which was formed not as a democracy but as a republic precisely because of the Federalist belief that the majority of American citizens could not judge what was in their own best interests. When James Sullivan suggested the possibility that men without property should have the vote, John Adams recoiled: "It is dangerous to open so fruitful a source of controversy . . . there will be no end of it. New claims will arise; women will demand a vote . . . every man who has not a farthing, will demand an equal voice with any other, in all acts of state. It tends to confound all distinctions, and prostrate all ranks to one common level" (931). What Adams objects to, of course, is the creation of a political order based on equality for all members of society.

It is Lucy Freeman who becomes the dominant culture's voice, supporting limited freedom for women. She insists that Eliza holds too tenaciously to her ideas of freedom: "Freedom . . . is a play about words" (L15, 31). Indeed, it is; and Foster exposes through Eliza's life exactly how, for women, the American construction of a seemingly democratic society has been little more than "a play about words." Eliza, according to Lucy's counsel, must be satisfied with a "modest freedom" (L13, 27). Eliza might have been better able to judge the value of Lucy's advice if it had been as consistent as these first examples suggest. But all of Eliza's advisors reflect the discursive pattern of the maxims when they counsel opposing actions or proffer advice that society's actions discount. Franklin himself had humorously acknowledged the power of the maxim as a means to justify a person's doing what "one has a mind to do" (844). Not surprisingly, Major Sanford adheres to this pattern, too, when he admits that he is interested in Miss Lawrence only for her money. "Necessity," he intones, imitating Franklin, "is the mother of invention" (L18, 34). But Lucy also joins, unwittingly, in this discursive pattern. For instance, she insists that "a man of a vicious character cannot be a good member of society" (L15, 31). This in itself is a play about words. She does not say that he cannot be a member of society, but simply that he cannot be a *good* member. Sanford's acceptance by society in Hartford and Boston discredits any idea that propriety—"virtue"—is requisite for a man's social acceptance. Nor would impropriety eliminate Sanford from political power, since he has the opportunity to work at a "lucrative office in the civil department" (L32, 65). He chooses to marry for money instead.

Lucy also counsels Eliza against any mannerisms that might be construed as those of a coquette; rather, be reserved in manner, she urges. Yet, when she herself decides that she has met the "swain" whom she intends to marry, she asserts, "What folly then would it be to affect reserve and distance, relative to an affair in which I have so much interest?" (L15, 31) And while Eliza is warned away from Sanford's seductive ways, she realizes that Boyer is attempting to "seduce me into matrimony" (L33, 66), and he has the encouragement of all of her friends in doing so. Thus the duplicity of the advice Eliza receives begins to pervade the novel as the true "rhetoric of the republic."[11]

Foster satirizes Lucy's unwitting duplicity first through her ironic name: Lucy *Freeman*. The name reflects the gendered nature of freedom in eighteenth-century America and also suggests that Lucy loses even the "modest freedom" she has when she marries and becomes Mrs. Sumner. But Foster exposes the dangers of patriarchy for women in a much more serious way. While Eliza is admonished for fearing that "marriage is the tomb of friendship" (L12, 24), Lucy's subsequent actions reveal that, in many ways, Eliza's maxim is truer than all the protestations against it. As Eliza explains:

> [Marriage] appears to me a very selfish state. Why do people, in general, as soon as they are married, centre all their cares, the concerns, and pleasure in their own families? former acquaintances are neglected

or forgotten. The tenderest ties between friends are weakened, or dissolved; and benevolence itself moves in a very limited sphere. (L12, 24)

This statement often has been cited as reflecting Eliza's selfishness, but Lucy's actions prove Eliza's fears well-founded. As Eliza becomes increasingly steeped in despair and she relates her mental anguish to Lucy, her friend's "benevolence" does indeed move in "a very limited sphere."

Before her marriage, Lucy's letters constitute four long texts and a significant portion of the novel; after her marriage, only three short epistles are sent to Eliza. Lucy's last letter as "Miss Freeman" is rife with maxims emphasizing the double standard for men and women. The maxim "Place and honors have been bought for gold, / Esteem and love were never to be sold," leads to the idea that "In spite of all the virtue we can boast, / The woman that deliberates is lost" (L31, 62–63).

Ironically, Lucy also notes that, although she will not socialize with Sanford, "he has been called up and welcomed by most of the neighboring gentry" (L31, 62). In fact, when Sanford visits Eliza at her mother's home, he comes in the company of Mr. Stoddard (L34, 67). No one in eighteenth-century New England would have failed to make the appropriate associations with such a renowned name as Stoddard—a name that epitomized piety and propriety. Public opinion thus seems to render Lucy's and Mrs. Richman's advice stuffy and out of step with the "common fame."

Also embedded in Lucy's heated attack upon remaining single is Foster's exposure of the legal perpetuation of double standards. "I look upon the vicious habits, and abandoned character of Major Sanford," Lucy says, "to have more pernicious effects on society, than the perpetrations of the robber and the assassin. These, when detected, are rigidly punished by the laws of the land," while "the assassin of honor . . . is received and caressed" by the society that passes such laws (L31, 63). However, while Lucy wishes women "would more generally espouse their own cause," she has been sending Eliza letter after letter advocating woman's role as anything but overt espousal of "their cause"; rather, she advocates for Eliza domestic seclusion and the subjugation of her will to a husband's.

As Eliza's mental state deteriorates, so does the quality of Lucy's friendship. Where Lucy had once admonished Eliza for her outgoing personality, she now chides her for being melancholy, tells her that she must revive her "animated . . . engaging" style (L49, 107), and laments her "indulgence of melancholy" (L52, 112). As Sarah Emily Newton has discovered, advice against disobedience and misery was "a kind of 'natural law' in conduct literature" of the eighteenth century (145). Lucy sets the pattern for advice offered by all the women in the novel who voice the duplicitous social and political traditions of patriarchy. Having earlier urged docility upon Eliza, the women now frown on her melancholy. Mrs. Wharton, Mrs. Richman, and Julia Granby all deny Eliza's right to respond to her situation with melancholy. In the code of True Woman-hood,[12] a pleasant and cheerful demeanor is the only emotion accept-able in a lady. Further, after Sanford's marriage, when Eliza is just begin-ning to recover her sense of self, Sanford calls upon her. She does not want to see him, but her mother remains passive and Julia advises, "I see no harm in conversing with him" (L55, 117). In Julia's account of the situation to Lucy, however, she asserts, "I hope she will not diverge too far from her present sedateness and solidity" (L56, 121).

This contradictory exchange reveals how deeply acculturated these young women are and how closely their letters follow the discursive patterns of the rhetoric of the republic. One of the most persuasive texts of the late eighteenth century was Thomas Paine's *Crisis* paper No. 1. After noting that "these are the times that try men's souls," Paine em-ploys the technique of cataloguing maxims, usually in groups of three: "Yet we have this consolation with us, that the harder the conflict, the more glorious the triumph. What we obtain too cheap, we esteem too lightly; it is dearness only that gives every thing its value" (946). Lucy's last admonition against "indulgence" replicates Paine's discursive pattern by presenting three maxims, tacked back to back upon her "concern" for Eliza's health: "It is by surmounting difficulties, not by sinking under them, that we discover our fortitude. True courage consists not in flying from the storms of life; but in braving and steering through them with prudence. Avoid solitude. It is the bane of a disordered mind, though a great utility to a healthy one" (L52, 112). Nowhere is the rhetoric of the republic's reliance upon emotionally empowering but psychologically simplistic solutions so evident.

Perhaps most painful to Eliza, however, is Lucy's failure to visit her when she is desperately in need of a friend. Lucy sends Julia Granby in her place, since she herself now must focus upon her husband's needs. The manner in which Lucy's benevolence—her "modest freedom," we might call it—is thus limited is most evident when later we are told that Lucy insists, in spite of Eliza's request to the contrary, that Julia stay in Boston with her rather than return to be with Eliza. Further, Lucy herself later chooses to travel to the country rather than visit her old friend. Thus, marriage has, as Eliza predicted, become the tomb of friendship for these once close and supportive friends. Lucy has been so fully accul-turated under the ideals of patriarchy in the new republic that she no longer can find a language in which to communicate with the divergent Eliza.

Ironically, Mrs. Richman, who seems the perfect example of a woman who synthesizes the demands of marriage with concern for friends and self-satisfaction,[13] in reality also acts to acculturate Eliza into patriarchy and fails her in much broader terms than Lucy does. Mrs. Richman tells Eliza that Major Sanford's "rank and fortune . . . procure him respect" (L7, 16) but that he is "deficient in . . . virtue" (L9, 20). Yet Mrs. Richman's initial reactions to Sanford are much less clear. Although she and her husband do not approve of the major, he is always admitted to their home when he calls; the Richmans practice a discourse of deception through their long silences. While Eliza senses the Richmans' hesitation concerning her companion, the source of their hesitation remains "incomprehensible" to her because it is not articulated until Eliza is already deeply involved with Sanford. Indeed, Mrs. Richman tells Boyer that she does not want Eliza to associate with the major before she tells Eliza herself (L7, 17). Further, Mrs. Richman excuses her slowness in revealing Sanford's true character to Eliza with the rationalization that "we thought it best to protract your enjoyment as long as possible, not doubting but your virtue and delicacy would, in future, guard you against the like deception" (L9, 20). Again, Mrs. Richman assures Eliza that "by no means" does she need to "become an avowed prude and refuse [Sanford] admission, if he call"; she insists that Eliza must forbid Sanford's pursuit of her, but she must do so "without any breach of the rules of politeness," since he is an accepted member of society (L9, 20). Even later, when General Richman wanders into the garden and stumbles upon Sanford kissing Eliza's hand, he "cheerfully" greets Sanford, and Mrs. Richman "politely" receives him; when Sanford leaves, Eliza is scolded for *her* actions (L19, 37–38). It is not until letter 26, one-third of the way through the novel, that Mrs. Richman speaks openly to Eliza about Sanford's reputation; it is little wonder, then, that Eliza finds her friend's early counsel "incomprehensible."

Foster offers several episodes that reveal Mrs. Richman as a voice of patriarchy who not only perpetuates the double standard for men and women but, indeed, portrays that system's ideals in a manner that continues to be incomprehensible. The implication is that the rhetoric of deception *intends* to create a sense of imbalance and to make it impossible for any young woman to decipher what actions are socially acceptable or will be personally rewarding. Nothing is more conducive to subservience than the shattering of an individual's confidence in her own judgment. Mrs. Richman begins this process by suggesting to Eliza that women need to be protected. Marriage, she tells her, is a state in which women "can repose in safety" (L12, 24). Eliza, however, has not been afraid of the world; she thrives on its diversity and its challenges.

In truth, Mrs. Richman agrees with Eliza's assertion that marriage is the end of friendship; a woman's husband becomes her only friend. In fact, Mrs. Richman reveals a sinister facet to her advice. Advice is offered only to her cousin Eliza; when her neighbor, Miss Lawrence, erroneously assumes (as Eliza had) that Sanford is well-off financially and that "he is a very fine gentleman," Mrs. Richman "smiles rather contemptuously" and publicly informs neither Eliza nor Miss Lawrence of her true opinion (L30, 61). This same social silence will also condemn Nancy to the horrors of her marriage to Sanford. In no figure is the internalization of patriarchal ideals so sadly evident as in Mrs. Richman and her discourse of omission. When the gentlemen at one of the gatherings praise her for voicing ideas that are "truly republican" (L23, 44), Foster's irony comes full circle.

Eliza's mother also espouses the new republic's patriarchal values. In creating Mrs. Wharton, Foster explicitly exposes the ways in which women have been excluded from the new political order even though every facet of their lives is controlled by it. Trying to assuage Eliza's concerns about the limited freedom of marriage, Mrs. Wharton specifically uses the rhetoric of the republic: "With regard to [marriage] being a dependent situation," she observes, "what one is not so? Are we not all links in the great chain of society, some more, some less important; but each upheld by others, through the confederated whole?" (L21, 41). Rather than envisioning society as a democracy advocating equality, this vision of the "great chain of society" recalls more closely the hierarchical social order of John Winthrop's "A Modell of Christian Charity," in which he asserts that God "soe disposed the Condicion of mankinde, as in all times some must be rich some poore, some highe and eminent in power and dignitie; others meane and in subjeccion" (191).

In an episode that follows soon after Mrs. Wharton's proclamations, Foster explicitly reveals the social system by which women are educated to believe that they should be silent supporters, the ones to uphold others and not those who have a voice in the public and political policies of the republic. The scene takes place, not surprisingly, at the Richmans' home. When politics arises as a topic of conversation, the women participate "judiciously, yet modestly," as Selby reports to Boyer (L23, 44). This observation is rife with irony. American politics do not admit women's participation "judiciously" or in any other manner; and the repetition of the word "modestly" recalls Lucy's advocacy of women's "modest freedom." Further, it is only Mrs. Richman and Eliza who participate, even in such a limited manner; the other women, Selby approvingly notes, "amused themselves" elsewhere. Mrs. Lawrence, like Mrs. Wharton, intones the rhetoric of the republic when she insists "that she never meddled with politics; she thought they did not belong to ladies" (L23, 44). It is, as much as anything else, this recognition of the duplicitous nature of society that leads to Eliza's death.

When Eliza learns that Sanford, the novel's overt symbol of duplicity, is married, she begins the fatal process of devaluing her own opinions. "What a dreadful thing it is," she observes, "to be afraid of one's own reflections" (L54, 115). It is, ironically, in adhering to the republic's political silencing of women that Eliza sets out on an entropic path of so-called "self"-destruction.[14] This process might best be understood in terms of the Foucauldian panoptic. "Historically," Foucault argues,

> the process by which the bourgeoisie became in the course of the eighteenth century the politically dominant class was masked by the establishment of an explicit, coded and formally egalitarian juridical framework, made possible by the organization of a parliamentary, representative regime. But the development and generalization of disciplinary mechanisms constituted the other, dark side of these processes. . . . The contract may have been regarded as the ideal foundation of law and political power; panopticism constituted the technique, universally widespread, of coercion. (222)

While Eliza does not confront a tangible structure like the Panopticon (an architectural structure that "induce[s] in the [prison] inmate a conscious and permanent visibility that assures the automatic functioning of power" [201]), the social panoptic of everyone observing and commenting on her actions also produces what Foucault terms "homogenous effects of power" (222). Patriarchy's objectification of women creates the formula, the "anatomy," for the constant observation and criticism of every aspect of women's lives. As Foucault notes:

> The efficiency of power, its constraining force have, in a sense, passed over to the other side—to the side of its surface of application. He who is subjected to a field of visibility, and who knows it, assumes responsibility for the constraints of power . . . he becomes the principle of his own subjection. By this very fact, the external power . . . tends to the non-corporal; and, the more it approaches this limit, the more constant, profound and permanent are its effects. (202–3)

The social as political is nowhere so astutely rendered by Hannah Webster Foster as in her extended damnation of women's limited spheres in the new republic. Momentarily, Eliza tries to reject society's concern for appearances because "it is an ill-natured, misjudging world" (L57, 123), but too many forces work against her; she cannot sustain this pose of defiance. She stops writing, literally slipping into silence, and the acculturated voices of her friend Julia and her lover Sanford begin to relate Eliza's own story for her.[15] Eliza's rejection of both the suitors and the social options presented to her constitutes what Nancy K. Miller has recognized (in analyzing Virginia Woolf's critique of a George Eliot heroine) as a "demand of the heroine for something else . . . the extravagant wish for a *story* that would turn out differently" (352). In one of Eliza's last letters, she remarks upon the bleak picture of the future that such a "misjudging world" forecasts for her:

> The world is to me a desert! If I indulge myself in temporary enjoyment, the consciousness or apprehension of doing amiss, destroys my peace of mind. And, when I have recourse to books, if I read those of serious description, they remind me of an awful futurity, for which I am unprepared. . . . (L62, 135)[16]

The issue of being unprepared is at the heart of Foster's novel: eighteenth-century American society in no way prepared young women to take their rightful places in a democratic republic. Near death, Eliza writes to her mother: "In what words, in what language shall I address you?" (L68, 153) The rhetoric of the republic at last has educated Eliza to silence rather than to an independence of expression; under its tutelage, she can only define herself as "fallen" and "polluted" (L68, 153).

Benjamin Franklin had used a situation similar to Eliza's as a humorous episode in his *Autobiography*. As a youth with no money for his passage from Boston to New York, he, along with his friend Collins, concoct a story about Franklin's "being a young Acquaintance of [Collins] that had got a naughty Girl with Child, whose Friends would compel me to marry her"; thus he must flee the city (835). In his account, Franklin conveys the prevailing attitude that the woman is "naughty" and that the man needs to be saved from her and her friends. This "story" is so culturally acceptable that Franklin does not even classify it as one of the "Errata" he needs to rectify later in life. Foster suggests that, for young women, Franklin's America offers no such opportunities for escape, nor the possibility of restitution through a rectification of "errata." That Eliza's final destination is Salem, the symbolic place of persecution, should not be overlooked. The fallen Eliza's fate differs from that of the "witches" only in the manner of death. The finger has been pointed, and society willingly listens to her accusers. Foster extends the painful irony of this allusion by including Eliza, who has now internalized her society's values, as one who joins in the process, damning herself. She thus personifies the panoptic principle that when an individual is not only subjected to, but also recognizes herself as subject to a "field of visibility," she is compelled by the efficiency of the political anatomy to participate in the exercise of her own subjection.

As Josephine Donovan observes in "Women and the Rise of the Novel":

> Women were uniquely situated to contribute to the development of a hybrid, "unofficial," polyvocal form like the novel because of their historical grounding in use-value production, which provided them with the basis both for an aesthetic theory and a perspective or standpoint from which to criticize the increasingly dominant ethos of commodity exchange. (443)

The very literal loss of the "devalued" Eliza Wharton at the conclusion of *The Coquette* thus constitutes a condemnation not of one young woman but of an entire society that viewed marriage-aged women as commodities for exchange and that failed to teach its young people the sociopolitical truths of early American political ideology. While Franklin had proffered his autobiographical text as a model for developing young people capable of rising to positions of leadership in American politics and society, Foster's depiction of Eliza's death represents the elimination of women from positions of autonomy and authority in post-Revolutionary America.

Had Foster ended her novel on this note, we could agree with Cathy Davidson's assertion that Foster was incapable of imagining "a life beyond her society's limitations" (Introduction xix). But Eliza's death is not the only tragedy depicted in Foster's novel. The other, equally devastating tragedy is that the rhetoric of disguise, employed throughout the new republic, acts to veil the power of women's communities such as the one that emerges after Eliza's death. In attending to the power of a women's community, Foster certainly does not "violat[e] the essential social realism" of her time. As Davidson has discovered, while the dominant culture sought to project the real woman Elizabeth Whitman, on whom Eliza Wharton is based, as a symbol, "an object lesson on the dangers of female rights and female liberty" (Introduction ix), numerous young women later made pilgrimages to Whitman's grave (*Revolution* 149). Foster chooses to emphasize in her conclusion the community of young women who do not abandon their friend in death. Eliza's death acts as a powerful "object lesson" in its own right, but not as community leaders had intended. Importantly, the lesson is not codified into a short maxim which would be open to misappropriation.

While Lucy continues to intone the maxim-ideals of True Womanhood, "To associate, is to approve; to approve, is to be betrayed!" (L73, 168), Foster captures in the novel's final scene another possibility: the potential of community to overcome the rhetoric of oppression that pits woman against woman and that perpetuates the ideals of patriarchy. The final word is not Lucy's but Julia Granby's. Writing to Eliza's mother, Julia impresses upon Mrs. Wharton the *actions* taken by the young women. Seeking to eradicate the horrifying vision of a future without change that devastates Eliza in her last days and, equally, seeking to replace the traditional view of a women's community that works to support and perpetuate patriarchal ideals, Foster ends with an image that suggests a potentially different future. Foster suggests through this final image of community, through Julia's "exertions of friendship" (L74, 169), that the rectification of "errata" could become possible for young women.

Notes

1.   Judith Fetterley and Marjorie Pryse's introduction to *American Women Regionalists* has gone a long way toward reclaiming regionalism as a valued and distinct art form.

2.   See Kerber, *Women of the Republic,* for numerous other manifestations of the new republic's patriarchal ideology.

3.   Although Newton does not discuss *The Coquette,* she argues persuasively for a reassessment of Foster's later novel, *The Boarding School,* as covertly conveying "the empowerment of women through motherhood and the ability of women to control their own destinies" (145).

4.   See Shuffleton for a discussion of Selby's role as a part of the "brotherly watch" that Eliza seeks to escape by leaving her paternal home.

5.   Documentation of quotations from *The Coquette* will, for readers' convenience, note the numbers of both letter and page.

6.   The introduction to this volume discusses the family as a microcosm of patriarchy's political structure.

7.   On women's legal status in late-eighteenth-century America, see Kerber and Salmon.

8.   See Hamilton on Foster's exploration of free will versus predestination in *The Coquette.*

9.   The social reality of this process for upper-class American women's lives (or for the woman seeking to rise to the upper class) is revealed in the similarity of Lily Bart's explanation, in the opening pages of Edith Wharton's *The House of Mirth,* of her frustration with social axioms that rule a young woman and yet fail to provide true guidance. Lily explains to Lawrence Selden that he should not make love to her:

> Don't you see that there are men enough to say pleasant things to me and that what I want is a friend who won't be afraid to say disagreeable ones when I need them? . . . You

don't know how much I need such a friend. My aunt is full
of copy-book axioms, but they were all meant to apply to
conduct in the early fifties. . . . (11)

Eliza's friends, unlike Lily's, are not simply social conveniences, but even
they rely upon "copy-book axioms," and conflicting ones at that. Although
written more than a century after *The Coquette,* Wharton's novel reveals
that little had changed in terms of expectations for upper-class women's
lives. Lily's understanding of what is expected of her parallels Eliza's situation in the eighteenth century: "I've been about too long," Lily observes,
"people are getting tired of me; they are beginning to say I ought to marry"
(11).

10.   One of the most disturbing features of feminist studies to date has been
      the antagonistic split between "Anglo/American feminism" and "French/
      postmodern feminism," a split that, I argue, far too often is rooted in ig-
      norance rather than intellectual difference. Although the split often is de-
      picted as a failure of the factions' willingness to engage in critical debates
      over differences, that depiction shrouds the real cause of disruption: the
      failure—of both sides—to learn the discursive histories and theories of
      the opposing side. Too many "Anglo/American feminists" broadly reject
      postmodernist feminist theories and, far too often, postmodernist feminist
      theorists are ignorant of English and American literary and critical histo-
      ries. Since, in the present text, I am dealing with an American novel, let me
      use it as an example. Distinguishing between French and Anglo/American
      feminisms in "The Question of the Canon," Verena Andermatt Conley
      asserts that, "In a French tradition, letters and politics are seldom sepa-
      rated, and letters are usually thought to be on the side of subversion"
      (11), implying that the same is not true in the American tradition. But this
      is relevant only if one does not move outside the American *canon*; as
      soon as one does, the politics of race, class, and gender enter letters pre-
      cisely through subversion, as is evident in Foster's novel and many other
      American women's epistolary novels, from the late eighteenth century to
      twentieth-century resurrections of this noncanonical literary tradition through
      works such as Alice Walker's *The Color Purple.* The following discussion
      suggests the synthesis of "letters" (in all its meanings) and politics in *The
      Coquette.*

11.   As the late Cynthia S. Jordan argued, "Franklin, Brackenridge, and Brown,
      writing in the wake of the Revolution, which granted authority to new
      Fathers, believed with varying degrees of optimism that language could
      be used to maintain a patriarchal social order in the new nation" (x).

12.   Barbara Welter's now classic essay on the rise of True Womanhood ar-
      gues for its origins in the nineteenth century; as literature of the earlier
      period has received increased critical attention, it has become apparent

that the origins of True Womanhood extend back at least to the mid-eighteenth century.

13. Cathy Davidson believes that the Richmans' marriage "exemplifies the Wollstonecraftian ideal of a partnership of equals" (*Revolution* 143). As the following discussion reveals, I find Mrs. Richman's characterization much more complex and disturbing.

14. This destruction is "so-called" because it is induced by the political machinations of Eliza's society; on the other hand, however, these machinations act literally to destroy Eliza's sense of self. Through the letters written by Eliza, which vary according to her audience, and through letters by various others about Eliza, Foster captures the fluidity and multiple facets of Eliza as subject/self. The multifaceted self is lost, however, when Eliza succumbs to the patriarchal ideology of Woman, which seeks to deny diversity and uniqueness among women. This loss constitutes one of the tragic themes of Foster's novel.

15. It is on this crucial point that I disagree with Cynthia Jordan's otherwise astute study of "second stories" in early American literature. As Jordan notes, the early "Fathers" silenced women's stories; but she argues that later writers, from Cooper to Melville, altered this pattern by having their central male characters relate women's stories as well. My contention is that to allow male characters to voice women's stories is little advancement; it still enacts a process of silencing and interpretation that elides women's participation in public expression. The patriarchal dominant culture remains, as Eliza notes, a "misjudging world" when it comes to interpreting women's lives. See Sharon Harris, "Review," for further discussion of this point.

16. This "awful futurity" most often is interpreted as Eliza's reference to an afterlife; but it should be understood as an equally true recognition of what her earthly life would continue to be under prevailing conditions of the time.

Works Cited

Adams, John. "Letter from John Adams to James Sullivan, May 26, 1776." Lauter et al. 931.

Conley, Verena Andermatt. *Hélène Cixous: Writing the Feminine*. Expanded ed. Lincoln: U of Nebraska P, 1984.

———. "The Question of the Canon." In Conley, *Hélène Cixous*, 10–13.

Davidson, Cathy N. Introduction. *The Coquette; or, The History of Eliza Wharton*. By Hannah Webster Foster. New York: Oxford UP, 1986. vii–xx.

———. *Revolution and the Word: The Rise of the Novel in America*. New York: Oxford UP, 1986.

Donovan, Josephine, ed. *Feminist Literary Criticism: Explorations in Theory.* 2nd ed. Lexington, U of Kentucky P, 1989.

———. "Women and the Rise of the Novel." *Signs* 16 (Spring 1991): 441–62.

Fetterley, Judith, and Marjorie Pryse. Introduction. *American Women Regionalists 1850–1910: A Norton Anthology.* Ed. Fetterley and Pryse. New York: Norton, 1992. xi–xx.

Foster, Hannah Webster. *The Boarding School; or, Lessons of a Preceptress to Her Pupils.* Boston, 1798.

———. *The Coquette; or, The History of Eliza Wharton.* 1797. New York: Oxford UP, 1986.

Foucault, Michel. *Discipline and Punish: The Birth of the Prison.* Trans. Alan Sheridan. New York: Viking, 1979.

Franklin, Benjamin. "From *The Autobiography.*" Lauter et al. 823–81.

Fuller, Margaret. *Woman in the Nineteenth Century.* 1845. New York: Norton, 1971.

Hamilton, Kristie. "An Assault on the Will: Republican Virtue and the City in Hannah Webster Foster's *The Coquette.*" *Early American Literature* 24, no. 2 (1989): 135–51.

Harper, Frances Ellen Watkins. "A Double Standard." 1895. Rpt. in Schockley 201–3.

Harris, Sharon M. Rev. of *Second Stories: The Politics of Language, Form, and Gender in Early American Fictions,* by Cynthia S. Jordan. *Pennsylvania Magazine of History and Biography* 116 (Jan. 1992): 90–92.

Harris, Susan K. *Nineteenth-Century American Women's Novels: Interpretive Strategies.* New York: Cambridge UP, 1990.

Herrmann, Claudine. *The Tongue Snatchers.* Trans. Nancy Kline. Lincoln: U of Nebraska P, 1989.

Jordan, Cynthia S. *Second Stories: The Politics of Language, Form, and Gender in Early American Fictions.* Chapel Hill: U of North Carolina P, 1989.

Kerber, Linda. *Women of the Republic: Intellect & Ideology in Revolutionary America.* New York: Norton, 1986.

Lauter, Paul, et al., eds. *The Heath Anthology of American Literature.* Vol. 1. Lexington, Mass.: D. C. Heath, 1990.

Miller, Nancy K. "Emphasis Added: Plots and Plausibilities in Women's Fiction." *The New Feminist Criticism: Essays on Women, Literature and Theory.* Ed. Elaine Showalter. New York: Pantheon, 1985. 339–60.

Moi, Toril. *Sexual/Textual Politics: Feminist Literary Theory.* New York: Methuen, 1985.

Murray, Judith Sargent. "On the EQUALITY of the SEXES." Lauter et al. 1032–39.

Newton, Sarah Emily. "Wise and Foolish Virgins: 'Usable Fiction' and the Early American Conduct Tradition." *Early American Literature* 25.2 (1990): 139–67.

Paine, Thomas. " From *The American Crisis.*" Lauter et al. 946–51.

Piercy, Marge. "Active in Time and History." *Paths of Resistance: The Art and Craft of the Political Novel.* Ed. William Zinsser. Boston: Houghton Mifflin, 1989. 89–123.

Salmon, Marylynn. *Women and the Law of Property in Early America.* Chapel Hill: U of North Carolina P, 1986.

Shockley, Ann Allen, ed. *Afro-American Women Writers, 1746–1933: An Anthology and Critical Guide.* New York: New American Library, 1988.

Shuffleton, Frank. "Mrs. Foster's *Coquette* and the Decline of the Brotherly Watch." *Studies in Eighteenth-Century Culture* 16 (1986): 211–24.

Welter, Barbara. "The Cult of True Womanhood: 1820–1860." *American Quarterly* 18 (Summer 1966): 151–74.

Wharton, Edith. *The House of Mirth.* New York: Scribner, 1905.

Wheatley, Phillis. "On Imagination." Schockley 23–25.

Winthrop, John. "A Modell of Christian Charity." Lauter et al. 191–99.

Wollstonecraft, Mary. *The Vindication of the Rights of Woman.* London, 1792.

CHAPTER 2

Susanna Rowson's *Reuben and Rachel:* Captivity, Colonization, and the Domestication of Columbus

Christopher Castiglia

> Great genius and the people of these states must never be demeaned to romances. As soon as histories are properly told there is no more need of romances.
>
> Walt Whitman,
> Preface, *Leaves of Grass*

Reprinted only once between 1720 and 1770, Mary Rowlandson's captivity narrative suddenly appeared in three editions in 1770, followed by three more printings before 1773. Rowlandson's narrative owed its renewed popularity in the 1770s, as Greg Sieminski demonstrates, to Revolutionary politics. As "the colonists began to see themselves as captives of a tyrant rather than as subjects of a king," Sieminski argues, the "image of collective captivity" (36) at the core of narratives such as Rowlandson's reflected colonial political rhetoric in crucial ways. The captivity story became effective as propaganda in part because it offered a model for forming identity through opposition. While contemporary narratives such as Daniel Boone's stressed assimilation into a culture perceived as "other" (in Boone's case, Indian culture), the reprinted Puritan narratives instead valorized resistance to acculturation. When a Puritan survived captivity, the resistance to the captors' culture affirmed her or his place in a community defined by what the captive—and by extension the entire community—does not believe, what rituals he or she will not perform (Sieminski 36). So, too, the colonists defined the new "American" culture in opposition to the British. The captivity narratives thus provided vehicles for affirming the essential "sameness" of all colonists held in captivity, and for defining a national character in opposition to the culture of British captors.

Despite the deployment of her story to espouse antityrannical ideals of inalienable freedom for all Americans, Rowlandson's gender would have precluded her from enjoying the liberties her narrative helped attain. Rowlandson is a more fitting figure, then, not for the common American destiny, but for the fate of American women who, despite their active involvement in the war, soon discovered the meaning of "home rule": as a rule, women in the new republic were kept at home. Historians have documented the disappointment women felt in the early Federal years, as the situation of women under democracy remained virtually unchanged from what it had been under British rule. There were slight improvements in women's legal and social rights—the British legal principle of coverture was less strictly adhered to, although by no means abandoned; divorce became easier to obtain in some states, although women were still largely denied access to courts.[1] These gains were counterbalanced, however, by an increased separation of public and private spheres after the war. No longer having England to define themselves against, American men turned their attention to gender rather than national identity, and enforced with renewed vigor the "essential" differences between men and women. Carroll Smith-Rosenberg argues that these asserted gender differences defined women so as to excise from "the feminine character" the very qualities—independence and virtue—necessary for public and civic duty. In the new republic, Smith-Rosenberg notes, "independence" came largely to mean the ability to earn one's living, while "virtue" implied modesty in regard to one's commercial success. Women, forbidden by law to earn their own living, instead were expected to become showcases for their husbands' prosperity. Required thus to be "elegant and nonproductive" ("Domesticating," 166), women of the early republic by definition were denied both independence and virtue, and hence access to the public sphere.

Smith-Rosenberg locates the cause of this betrayal in the need of middle-class American men to restore a lost legitimacy through the subjugation of women. Tracing the charges leveled by American men against women, Smith-Rosenberg notes their similarity to those the English gentry used to justify foreign rule. "As the gentry had accused middle-class men of venality and extravagance," she writes, "so middle-class men, depicting themselves as hardworking and frugal, harangued middle-class women for alleged extravagances in dress and household management" ("Domesticating," 166). Moreover, the English gentry had asserted that commercial men, "living in the fantastical, passionate, and unreal world of paper money, stocks, and credit," were incapable of civic virtue. Smith-Rosenberg notes that middle-class men turned this charge against women by characterizing them as unreliable and impractical "because they lived in another fantastical, passionate, and unreal world of paper— the world of the novel and the romance" ("Domesticating," 166).

Other historians have argued more generally that the vigorous reassertion of women's "proper role" was meant to limit the revolutionary zeal that threatened the stability of the newly formed United States govern-ment.[2] Betsy Erkkila, for instance, outlines postwar efforts "to silence and disembody women politically by depriving them of citizenship and legal rights under the terms of the Articles of Confederation and the Constitu-tion of the United States signed by the Congress in 1787" (198). For the Founding Fathers, Erkkila concludes, "the American Revolution became a kind of Pandora's box, releasing potentially violent and disruptive fe-male energies that would not and could not be controlled once the war was over" (190). Renewed domestic, economic, and legal constraints on women became the mode of control chosen by the new government, and eagerly carried out by a (male) society eager to attain prosperity within a stable state of "normalcy." Women, in the meantime, rather than enjoying the new liberties promised by the rhetoric of the Revolution, instead found themselves increasingly confined.

The significance of Susanna Rowson's novel *Reuben and Rachel; or, Tales of Olden Times* (1798) lies in its appropriation of the genres and metaphors of the Revolution to resist the forces that excluded women from the liberties promised by that rhetoric. *Reuben and Rachel* is strik-ing in scope, as it follows ten generations of women, from Christopher Columbus's wife Beatina to the colonial women who lived through the American Revolution. Historical accounts such as *Reuben and Rachel* were mainstays of Federal literature. Emory Elliott documents the efforts of Federal authors such as Philip Freneau and Timothy Dwight "to give America a vision of herself as a promised, New World utopia" (11). Like other post-Revolutionary writers, Rowson establishes in *Reuben and Rachel* an American past, a tradition that the present nation could live up to and complete.

More than a standard historical novel, however, *Reuben and Rachel* is a chronicle specifically of those most typically excluded from the "offi-cial story" of the nation. The denial to women of the privileges attendant upon public life in America entailed, too, their removal from the record of that sphere and of its past—in short, women were erased from America's history. Postwar literature that attempted to establish America's heroic past broadcast the courage of white men—Columbus, Washington—romanti-cized the conquest of the native population and ignored the achieve-ments of colonial women. (One might think, for instance, of Timothy Dwight's *The Conquest of Canaan* or Joel Barlow's *The Columbiad*.) In contrast, *Reuben and Rachel* reintroduces the courage of women and Indians into American history.

To tell her version of American history, Rowson turned to the cap-tivity narrative. Rowson's use of the captivity story in her generic hybrid of history and romance is logical, since women's personal narratives, as Kerber notes, were the only patriarchally sanctioned form of history that also contained women heroes (260). Rowson's choice also reflects the popularity of captivity narratives before and during the Revolution. However, unlike deployments of the captivity narrative that furthered a nationalistic zeal which ultimately disempowered women and people of color, Rowson used the captivity story to achieve for both groups liberties denied by more traditional stories of America's past. First, the captivity story got Rowson's heroines out of the home. *Reuben and Rachel* depicts women successfully adapting to the American landscape at a time when women were being separated, in literature if not in reality, from the wilderness where Rowson's heroines prosper and thrive. Second, the captivity narrative allowed Rowson to present a version of American history centered on the enforced helplessness of women and the violence directed towards Indians, but also celebrating the resistance and fortitude of both groups. As confinement becomes the experience not of a single woman but of ten generations of women, paralleling the development of the nation, captivity comes to be the defining trope of America itself. The new nation, in Rowson's novel, will do only as well as its women, as the strength of the American character becomes measured by the successful resolution of the captivity story. But a successful resolution for Rowson did not mean the butchery of Indians and the masculine rescue of helpless women that would soon fill frontier fictions written by men. In an inversion of the official tale of the nation's heroic founding, *Reuben and Rachel* doesn't measure America's prospects in terms of conquests and other male heroics directed against women and Indians. Rather, America's prosperity is measured by the ability of its natives to withstand violent colonization and of its women to endure and escape confinement imposed not only by British tyrants or Indian invaders, but also by their own husbands, fathers, and brothers.

By these standards, America's story—as rendered by Rowson— is not one of increasing democracy and liberty, but of growing misogyny and racism. As the American identity grows stronger, women and Indians become increasingly isolated and powerless, their captivities harder to escape. Explaining the popularity of the captivity story in Revolutionary America, Sieminski notes that the "captivity experience began and ended in freedom" (44), thereby prefiguring America's ultimate delivery from British tyranny. Rowson's captivity romance never achieves the closure that liberty brings in the conventional captivity narrative. Rather, generation after generation of American women must repeat their captivities, as release from one tyranny leads directly into another. *That,* Rowson implies, was the experience of American women, moving from restriction under British law to restriction under the new American government.

The economic and social losses of Indians and white women are signified by the generic change *Reuben and Rachel* undergoes towards its conclusion, as Rowson's history approaches the author's own lifetime. From a frontier romance featuring strong and independent women of both races, *Reuben and Rachel* becomes a sentimental novel, complete with abandonment by worthless lovers and a lovelorn suicide. The move from frontier romance to sentimental novel accurately reflects the experience of many American women, who witnessed their own transformation in the nation's perception of the ideal American woman from a brave and industrious fighter for liberty to a frail, overwrought, housebound, sentimental heroine. While *Reuben and Rachel* suggests that both history and romance contain prisons for women, Rowson also casts a critical eye on the models that women might choose to follow, offering her reader a history not only of confinement and victimization, but also of endurance and even resistance.

Written in two volumes, *Reuben and Rachel* contains four captivity stories framed by two narratives depicting the figurative and literal rape of a native population by Christian colonists. The volume begins with Columbus's settlement of Peru, where a native woman, Bruna, is raped by Columbus's deputy and kills herself rather than live as a reminder of Peru's subjection. Rowson's narration of the settlement and victimization of Peru is followed by a series of captivities endured and escaped by Columbus's descendants, beginning with his granddaughter, Isabelle Arundel, and her daughter Columbia. The widow of an executed Puritan, Isabelle is arrested by Sir James Howard, a spy for the Catholic Queen Mary. When Sir James arrives to arrest Lady Arundel, however, he falls in love with Columbia and consequently convinces Queen Mary to allow him to keep the women jailed in his house, where they remain until their escape shortly after Elizabeth's ascension to the throne.

This Richardsonian imprisonment is then translated into an American setting, as New Hampshire Indians capture Rachel and William Dudley, Columbia Arundel's great-great-grandchildren. William gains the favor of the Indian sachem, is named his heir, and marries the sachem's daughter, Oberea, while William's younger sister, Rachel, becomes engaged to an Indian warrior, Yankoo. But during an attack on an English settlement, Yankoo is about to kill an Englishman whom William recognizes to be his long-lost father. Throwing himself between his father and Yankoo's tomahawk, William is killed. Not long thereafter, during a retaliatory attack by the English, Yankoo too dies. William's widow returns with her grieving sister and mother-in-law to England.

The reader then follows Rowson's characters back to England, where in the next captivity story Jessy Oliver, best friend of Rachel Dudley (the first Rachel Dudley's niece), is locked up by her father until she agrees to marry the nobleman he has selected for her husband. But Jessy, whose affection belongs to Rachel's brother Reuben, is resolute. On the eve of her arranged wedding, Jessy escapes her father's prison and establishes herself as postmistress in a remote village, where one day she encounters her old friend Rachel. Together they set off to America to find Reuben. Meanwhile, Reuben has become the subject of Rowson's fourth captivity story; like his grandfather William, he has been taken hostage by Indians. With the help of an Indian princess, Eumea, Reuben escapes his captivity and returns to Philadelphia, where he is reunited with his sister and marries his beloved Jessy. The novel then ends as it begins, with the suicide of a native woman. Upon learning of his marriage to Jessy, Eumea, who loves Reuben desperately, drowns herself in the Schuylkill River.

The symmetrical structure of *Reuben and Rachel* makes two important claims about women's lives.[3] First, the balance of English Richardsonian imprisonments with New World Indian captivity narratives dehistoricizes the experience of constriction. Women in all generations, in all nations, Rowson implies, have been captives—of lovers, of warriors, of fathers. The manifest content may change, but the central image of a captured female remains the same. Second, the relationship between the central captivity tales and the framing stories of Bruna and Eumea suggests a similarity between the subjection of women and of Indians. Several captivity romances depict Indian culture as divided by the gender divisions that marked white culture. Later authors equated the oppression of white and Indian women—both are the victims of abusive husbands—but tended to ignore the violence that white men directed specifically at native women. Rowson is unique among early white novelists in depicting Indian women as the objects of a dual subjection, as she implies through the representation of their oppression by rape—an act of violence directed both by a colonist against a native and by a man against a woman. In so doing, Rowson not only correlates her analysis of racial and gender oppression, but subverts the image of native women as the promiscuous sexual objects of white men, a stereotypical mainstay of wilderness tales by men.[4] The very structure of the novel suggests its two primary thematic assertions: that captivity is metaphorically expressive of racial and gender subjection, and that, since the situations of white women and Indians of both genders under white male colonialism are equivalent, only through cooperation can these two groups escape their captivity.

The oppositions that the structure of *Reuben and Rachel* attempts to integrate—between whites and people of color, men and women—were particularly troublesome at the time of the novel's composition, as the Founding Fathers attempted to define the place of women, Indians, and blacks in a republic in which all men nominally were created equal. Rowson presents these racial and gender divisions as basic to the American character, having been brought to the continent by the nation's first ancestor, Christopher Columbus. Hardly a benign settler and heroic adventurer, Rowson's Columbus is naive and self-serving. When Columbus sees the political havoc his settlement of Peru has wrought on the native people, represented by the rape of Bruna, he exclaims, "I am innocent! I sought not new worlds for conquest, or for power; I felt, forcibly felt, the blessings of Christianity, the comforts resulting from a commercial intercourse with other nations" (1: 45). That Columbus has found nicer terms to express religious proselytizing and economic exploitation does not keep Rowson from depicting the harsher realities behind the words, exemplified by the turning of his "intercourse" into Bruna's rape. Columbus's wife, Beatina, offers an assessment of those who followed Columbus to the colonies that is more to the point: "Their idols were avarice, ambition, luxury, and lawless passion; to them they bend the knee, and on their altar did they sacrifice millions of innocent people" (1: 79).

In her treatment of Columbus, Rowson is also quick to show—again despite his protestations of innocence—the close relationship between geographical (racial) and domestic (gender) exploitation. In a letter to Beatina, Columbus writes, "Why, why, my beloved, are you not endowed with strength of frame, that your friendship might increase my fortitude in danger, and share the glorious triumph of unexpected success? Yet why should I wish you to lose the sweet feminine softness which first won, and still holds captive, my heart?" (1: 22). Despite his rhetoric to the contrary, it is Columbus who holds his wife, shown elsewhere in the novel to be as strong and courageous as her husband, captive in a rhetoric of feminine passivity, the rhetoric of post-Revolutionary "separate sphere ideology," which depicted women as soft, sweet, and delicate of frame. Columbus must assert women's weakness, which defines him as the strong, adventuring male and justifies him in leaving his wife and family behind, just as he must believe in the passivity and inferiority of the natives whose land he appropriates.

While Rowson thus presents colonial and domestic subjugation as central features of America's first father, she offers its first daughters as agents of equality and justice on both fronts. The split between Columbus and Beatina is healed by their great-granddaughter, Columbia, whose very name links her two ancestors and establishes her as representative of the ideally American character. Columbia, who accompanies her mother to what she considers certain death at Sir James's hands and wages verbal battle with Bloody Mary, is a successful hybrid of the rational and adventurous spirit of her great-grandfather and, in her devotion to her mother and to her girlhood friend Mina, a more traditionally "feminine" nature. Neither entirely "masculine" nor wholly "feminine," Columbia escapes her captivity precisely through her combination of traditional roles, becoming the ideal "human" of whom Rowson would write in *A Present to Young Girls*: "A woman who to the graces and gentleness of her own sex, adds the knowledge and fortitude of the other, exhibits the most perfect combination of human excellence" (Weil, 37).

Moreover, in her characterization of Columbia, Rowson stresses that the "knowledge and fortitude" needed to create the ideal woman are best instilled by other women. Living in an abandoned castle with her Peruvian maid, Cora; her best friend, Mina; and, most importantly, her mother, Isabelle, Columbia inhabits a world of women.[5] Columbia is particularly strengthened by her relationship to Isabelle, who was to her daughter "mother, sister, friend, every tender connexion combined in one" (1: 14). During their captivity in the home of Sir James, when Isabelle learns that Elizabeth is on the throne, she prepares Columbia for escape by redefining "femininity":

> We are women, it is true, and ought never to forget the delicacy of our sex; but real delicacy consists in purity of thought, and chastity of words and actions; not in shuddering at an accidental blast of wind, or increasing the unavoidable evils of life by affected weakness and timidity. (1: 189)

Ironically, in the lesson Isabelle gives to her daughter on the proper feminine character, "delicacy" comes to mean hardiness, assurance, bravery—exactly the opposite of its traditional meaning. While initially Isabelle tries to isolate Columbia, teaching her that "content builds her dwelling in solitude" (1: 191), she sees her female retreat as a nursery for more heroic characteristics. She states that her "happy obscurity" has allowed herself and her daughter "that liberty of conscience which calms and fortifies the soul, and fits it for all events" (1: 132). The truth of Isabelle's statement is borne out each time her daughter meets with danger. In the face of potential rape, Columbia is taught by her mother that "nothing is more pernicious to the health of mind or body, than indolence and inaction" (1: 189). And even when Columbia meets a milder threat to her independence in the form of Sir Egbert, whose affections Columbia returns, Isabelle urges her daughter to see the world before she settles down into romance. Through the companionship of strong friends and sisters, none of Rowson's heroines suffers patiently under her captivity, as Charlotte Temple does. Rather, participation in female community offers strength and resolution to Rowson's heroines, from Columbia Arundel to Jessy Oliver, who, encountering her friend Rachel after years of quiet country life, tells her, "I am weary of this dull sameness of scene, and you and I will now set out together in search of adventure . . . we will live together, my dear, Rachel in humble, but contented independence" (2: 278). Rowson's heroines thus reflect the experiences of many women of Rowson's generation who created strong and empowering friendships with other women as a partial resistance to the prescribed and enforced isolation of a domestic existence.

Columbia further heals the violent split between colonizers and indigenous people represented by her great-grandfather's settlement of Peru. Columbia's grandfather was Columbus's son, Ferdinando, who married a Peruvian princess, Orrabella. Thus Columbia physically combines both races. Columbia also is raised by a Peruvian woman, Cora, who teaches her that

> avarice had discovered this new world was an inexhaustible mine of wealth; and, not content to share its blessings in common with the natives, came with rapine, war, and devastation in her train! and as she tore open the bowels of the earth to gratify her insatiate thirst for gold, her steps were marked with blood. (1: 42)

Columbia also learns of the violence of male imperialism from Beatina herself, who indirectly enters the female community surrounding Columbia through a series of letters written to Isabelle in her youth and now read to Columbia by Cora. The word of the mother—Beatina's first-person narrative is longer than that of any other character in the novel—enables and educates the daughter, and in turn brings the mother into an empowering community.

The fusion Columbia effects is short-lived, however, as the situations of both women and Indians quickly deteriorate throughout the remainder of the novel. As the English colonies grow larger and more secure, Rowson's utopian solution to interracial strife becomes harder to maintain. The novel marks this decline through the increased difficulties faced by members of interracial couples. The first interracial marriage—between Christopher Columbus's son Ferdinando and the Peruvian princess Orrabella—is a relatively successful one. Although Orrabella lives to see Peru subjugated by Christian pirates and her family assassinated, Ferdinando shares her pride in Peru's native culture and her anguish at its colonization. Through the second interracial marriage, between William Dudley and Oberea, Rowson appears to suggest that Christians not only can be assimilated to Indian culture, but actually will benefit from the conversion. Although the interracial romances of William and Rachel Dudley end tragically, Rowson is unambiguous in assigning guilt for that tragedy to white colonial aggression, and in showing the enlightening and strengthening effect of "Indianization" on the two English children, particularly on the girl. The first Rachel Dudley, taken captive in the New Hampshire wilderness, is strengthened and cheered by her friendship with her Indian sister-in-law, Oberea. Rowson writes that, although Rachel was "naturally more timid" than Oberea, her nerves became "new-strung by affection" (1: 25). But when William's grandson, Reuben, himself is taken captive in Pennsylvania, he demonstrates how far he has come from the sympathies of his ancestors:

> Often would his thoughts revert to his grandfather, William Dudley,
> who was for many years in a situation somewhat similar. But Reuben
> had seen too much of savage men and manners to have a wish to re-
> main amongst them, even though he might have been elevated to the
> highest seat of dignity. (2: 202)

When *his* Indian princess, Eumea, falls in love with her English captive, he doesn't even notice her affection. Eumea nevertheless aids in Reuben's escape, devotedly following him back to Philadelphia. Reuben repays Eumea for her kindness by establishing her as a servant in a neighboring home, where she "assiduously endeavored to conform to the European dress, customs, and manners; but she pined at being separated from Reuben, and if more than two days elapsed without her seeing him, she would give way to the most violent affliction" (2: 288). Rowson here overlays the language of the sentimental abandonment plot (romantic affliction) with images of colonial exploitation and enforced conformity, reasserting the connection between the plights of Indians and of women. Eumea's story finally is as tragic as Charlotte Temple's: when Reuben marries an Englishwoman, Eumea, in a fit of despondency, drowns herself. Thus Rowson contrasts the positive results of the integration of a white woman into Indian society with the tragic results of the opposite transformation.

Significantly, indifference to the state of Indians coincides with the removal of white women from the wilderness. Beatina lives with the Peruvians; Rachel Dudley not only inhabits the New England wilderness, she agrees to marry a native warrior. But at the conclusion of *Reuben and Rachel,* white women are gone from the wilderness, returned to the domestic sphere and to their role as representatives of white "civilization." In the last wilderness tale of the novel, there are no women at all: William Dudley is taken captive with only a male companion. As long as women are permitted access to the wilderness, Rowson suggests, the possibility of interracial harmony exists. In *Reuben and Rachel,* when white women are farthest from the wilderness, native women are most sexually victimized. When white women are in the wilderness, on the other hand, relationships form based on love or friendship. With the "masculinization" of the American wilderness comes the end of interracial union and the progressive weakening of the Indians, particularly Indian women.

Just as Orrabella's courage eventually gives way to the forlorn lovesick-
ness and self-destruction of Eumea, so, too, do Columbia's female descendants, removed from the wilderness, lose the strength and determination
characteristic of her. As the novel progresses, there is less cooperation
among women, particularly between daughters and mothers, who less and
less serve as empowering models. While Isabelle enables Columbia's
independence, Rachel's mother ultimately restricts her daughter's freedom.
Following the attack on the English settlement, Mrs. Dudley returns to England with her daughter Rachel and her Indian daughter-in-law, Oberea,
and sees to it that both are properly Anglicized. The result of Mrs.
Dudley's removal of her daughters from the wilderness is the creation of
properly Christian, yet ultimately less happy and less active, women: "Her
own appearance and those of her daughters was always neat, always
respectable; and their countenances were serene, if not cheerful; but their
hands were constantly employed, and indolence and luxury were alike
strangers to their dwelling" (1: 279). Mrs. Dudley's benign conversion
results in the early death of Oberea, who is isolated from her native
culture, and the transformation of Rachel Dudley from a wilderness adventurer into a rather pathetic Old Maid, smiling and listening patiently
as her nephew, Reuben Dudley, spews stereotypes about his "savage"
mother, Oberea, and her heathenish race. Finally, while Mrs. Dudley
proves a poor model for her daughters, Jessy Oliver has no mother at
all; she is left solely at the mercy of an overbearing father who literally
imprisons her.

Rowson's removal of mothers from *Reuben and Rachel* might represent her reaction to what Linda Kerber has called the ideology of "Republican Motherhood." Demonstrating her patriotism through domestic
self-sacrifice, the Republican Mother enforced the division between the
public and private spheres:

> Women could be encouraged to contain their judgments as republicans
> within their homes and families rather than to bridge the world outside
> and the world within. In this sense, restricting women's politicization
> was one of a series of conservative choices that Americans made in the
> postwar years as they avoided the full implications of their own revolu-
> tionary radicalism. (Kerber 287)

By removing mothers from her novel, then, Rowson circumvents the
"conservative choice" and frees her heroines from a limited model of
womanhood. As Cathy Davidson writes, "A motherless daughter [in the
new Republic] is unguided, uneducated, unprotected, but also unencum-
bered" ("Mothers" 120). If the removal of mothers from the novels frees

Rowson's heroines on one hand, on the other it leaves them without any model of womanhood at all.

As women become more isolated, their captivity begins to seem more permanent, until, at the end of the novel, romance and marriage supplant adventure and community. The growing importance of romance in the heroines' lives—and the threat it poses to them—is represented by the increased prominence in the novel of the abandonment plot. As *Reuben and Rachel* progresses, the threat of abandonment encroaches both upon the lives of the heroines and the text of the novel, as *Reuben and Rachel* transforms from a frontier to a sentimental romance. Columbia's final success as an adventurous heroine is measurable by the contrast between her fate and that of her girlhood friend, Mina. While Columbia resists the temptations of romance, preferring instead to remain a prisoner with her mother, Mina surrenders to the seduction of Sir James Howard, who leaves her to die with her newborn son. In the novel's second volume, Rachel Dudley's life in the wilderness is paralleled by a second seduction plot, involving Mary Holmes, also left to die soon after giving birth to an illegitimate child. But the balance between the stories of Rachel Dudley and Mary Holmes is different from that between Columbia Arundel and Mina. Columbia's adventures ultimately are more successful than are Rachel's, while Mina's narrative receives relatively little space in the novel compared to Mary Holmes's, which develops into a narrative of some importance to the novel. While the adventure plot loses ground, then, the seduction plot gains momentum, registering a loss of female agency in the novel (and, by implication, in history). Yet, in the narratives of both Mina and Mary Holmes, Rowson shows that the seduction and ruin of women damages not only the particular woman, but America itself. The illegitimate children born of both women—Howard Fitz-Howard and Jacob Holmes—become primary villains in *Reuben and Rachel*; each man threatens to disturb the generational flow (and hence the narrative continuation) of the Columbian family. Jacob Holmes, using religious rhetoric to defraud Reuben Dudley of his rightful inheritance, especially signifies the corruption of American ideals of social justice. His illegitimacy represents the bastardization of colonial principles. He is also one of the most abusive husbands depicted in the novel, a fact that emphasizes the connection between the fate of America and that of its women.

The last pairing of a seduction and an adventure plot is the most telling as well as the most discouraging. While Jessy Oliver is held prisoner by her father and ultimately escapes in order to live her own life, the second Rachel Dudley's narrative closely resembles that of Charlotte Temple. Rachel has fallen in love with Hamden Auberry, who, because his family is from a social class higher than that of the Dudleys, at first refuses to marry Rachel. When he does marry her, he establishes Rachel in London under a false name, while he sets off to tour the Continent with his wealthy aunt, leaving his wife alone and pregnant. Rachel soon falls victim to rumors and is forced to move to increasingly less savory dwellings, without friends and finally without money. Only at the last moment, when at her most destitute she encounters Jessy Oliver in a rural post office and together they set off to America, does Rachel discover a newly humbled Auberry and gain a traditionally respectable marriage. In the relationship of Rachel and Auberry, Rowson again equates abandonment with a betrayal of American ideals. By settling into marriage, Auberry indicates his surrender of class distinctions and his acceptance of a democratic social arrangement. Each of Rowson's seduction plots is, significantly, set in England, suggesting that English inequality is countered by American conjugal happiness. Yet, despite the happy resolution suggested by the marriages that conclude *Reuben and Rachel*, by the end of the novel the abandonment plot, given relatively little space at the beginning of the novel, has moved to the forefront, while the adventure/captivity plot is given not to the heroine as it is in the first two instances, but to a secondary character.

With the growing prominence of seduction, as a closure both to the heroine's life and to Rowson's text, marriage begins to seem a relatively happy resolution, and certainly it is the ending Rowson chooses. The novel ends quite traditionally, with every character married to the proper partner, indicating Rowson's indebtedness to the forms of the sentimental novel. The virtue of good women rescues men from wayward paths, good women would rather go to prison than marry for other than love, and the virtue and happiness of good, domestic women reflect the virtue and happiness of the nation. America's destiny resides in the conjugal felicity of its inhabitants—the one man still unmarried, Lieutenant Courtney, must return to England at the end of the novel because he has been ruined by a false woman.

But the eventual marriages of Rachel Dudley and Jessy Oliver do not represent the progress of America, as Michael Bell argues happy marriages do in historical romances.[6] Rather, they signal the failure of the original spirit of adventure and equality represented by the American wilderness and by the American rhetoric of democracy and tolerance. When, at the end of the novel, Reuben Dudley declares America "a young country, where the only distinctions between man and man should be made by virtue of genius, and education" (2: 313), his representation of "democracy" is undermined by the novel's depiction of a society in which men are superior to women, the educated (i.e., wealthy) to the uneducated, whites to slaves and Indians. Rowson's final irony comes when Reuben, rejecting English titles and manners in favor of American equality and brotherhood, says that he is speaking for his sister and her husband as well as for himself. The opinions of his wife apparently are of little consequence.

Cathy Davidson describes the narrative options of colonial heroines as the Scylla and Charibdis of abandonment and marriage. Due to the high childbirth mortality rate and the *feme covert* status of women that gave control of policy and property entirely to husbands,[7] matrimony was a risky endeavor for colonial women. The seduction plot, Davidson argues, therefore served as a vivid analysis of how *not* to make a marriage, while simultaneously exposing the pressures and dangers faced by all colonial women, married or not. Thus, the best that can be said of the lot of married women is that it surpasses that of abandoned Charlotte Temples—just barely. The unsatisfactory options offered colonial women, fictional and real, are precisely those given at the conclusion of *Reuben and Rachel*. Yet the power of *Reuben and Rachel* lies in its effort to resist the narrative options characteristic of the sentimental novel. The choice between tragic abandonment and domestic tranquillity enters the novel only at its conclusion. Prior to the ending, the novel's "sentimental formula"[8] is complicated by its status both as a historical and as a captivity romance. Seduction and marriage are not the only options offered by Rowson to Columbia Arundel or to the first Rachel Dudley. As a historical romance, *Reuben and Rachel* suggests an alternative to the Federal society in which women are viewed only as potential wives or potential mistresses. In questioning those depictions of women, Rowson gives the lie to the ostensible inevitability or "naturalness" of those roles, showing them instead to be only two of many potential options available to women, and poor ones at that. Using a captivity plot, Rowson both literalizes the restrictions forced upon women by their roles in society, and provides a narrative in which constriction is escaped. The sentimental heroine, Davidson implies, eventually must either settle into marriage or die abandoned. Rowson offers a third alternative. Through their captivity, Columbia Arundel and Rachel Dudley paradoxically escape from narrative paths that in other novels appear inexorable. Bravery, adventurousness, and intelligence are characteristics not of Rowson's men only, but, in their ability to abide and even transcend their captivity, of her women as well.

Susanna Rowson wrote *Reuben and Rachel* at a crucial moment in American history. On March 31, 1776, Abigail Adams wrote to her husband John:

> I long to hear that you have declared an independency—and by the way in the new Code of Laws which I suppose it will be necessary for you to make I desire you would Remember the Ladies, and be more

generous and favorable to them than your ancestors. Do not put such unlimited power into the hands of the Husbands. Remember all Men would be tyrants if they could. If particular care and attention is not paid to the Ladies we are determined to foment a Rebellion, and will not hold ourselves bound by any Law in which we have no voice, or Representation. (*Adams Family* 370)

Abigail Adams expresses the hopes of many colonial women that the casting off of British rule might lead to a rejection of *all* subjugation, that the rhetoric of democracy in America might result in the reality of a truly equitable society in which women were recognized as the equals of men.

Reuben and Rachel initially shares Adams's optimism, employing the language of democracy and religious tolerance, embodied by Columbia Arundel, against political and religious tyranny. Rachel Dudley, through her first-hand experience of the American wilderness, becomes not bitter and fanatical but more open-minded and sympathetic. And in her discussion of religious sects, Rowson praises above all the Quakers, who not only were more tolerant of religious diversity, antiviolent, and pro-Indian than other groups, but were the first church to allow women to speak publicly. Above all, throughout *Reuben and Rachel,* Rowson pushes against traditional hierarchies by creating strong, independent women and by showing the injustices done to natives by "superior" Christians.

In response to his wife's threat of rebellion, John Adams wrote, "I cannot but laugh":

We have been told that our Struggle has loosened the bonds of Government every where. That Children and Apprentices were disobedient—that schools and Colledges [*sic*] were grown turbulent—that Indians slighted their Guardians and Negroes grew insolent to their Masters. But your Letter was the first Intimation that another Tribe more numerous and powerfull than all the rest were grown discontented. —This is rather too coarse a compliment, but you are so saucy I wont blot it out. Depend upon it, We know better than to repeal our Masculine systems. (*Adams Family* 382)

John made good on his promise to retain the power of men over women (as well as of owners over workers, parents over children, and whites over Indians and blacks) by supporting the Alien and Sedition Acts, in order to repress the very zeal Abigail hoped would free women from their matrimonial subjection. Even more disastrous for his wife's hopes than his flat rebuttal is John's subsequent argument, in which he turns women's domestic consignment from a restriction into an exalted position:

We Dare not exert our power in its full Latitude. We are obliged to go fair, and softly, and in Practice you know We are subjects. We have only the Name of Masters, and rather than give up this, which would completely subject Us to the Despotism of the Petticoat, I hope General Washington, and all our brave Heroes would fight. I am sure every good Politician would plot, as long as he would against Despotism, Empire, Monarchy, Aristocracy, Oligarchy, or Ochlocracy. (*Adams Family* 382)

Adams, in turning his wife's social disempowerment into a rhetorical "despotism" through the translation of the political into the domestic realm, mirrors the strategy of metaphoric compensation, echoed in Washington Irving's "Rip Van Winkle" and other works by male authors, that sought to content women with their disenfranchisement and lack of economic control by granting them "home rule."

The exchange between Abigail and John Adams reflects the expectations raised in women by the American Revolution, as well as their subsequent disappointment, as the rhetoric of separate spheres forced women into even more limited roles. The nonimportation and domestic production movements, designed to loosen Britain's hold on the American economy, brought a momentous, if temporary, change in American attitudes towards the home. Suddenly domestic acts—what women made, what they bought, whose products they purchased—gained enormous political importance. In order to persuade women to support these movements, men discussed politics and government with their wives and daughters for the first time on a national scale. Suddenly interested and involved in the public sphere, women dared to take a more active role in the Revolution.

Yet the political importance assigned to the home, as well as the relative freedom allowed women prior to the war, was short-lived. Rather than becoming equal participants in the new democracy, women found themselves returned to their "proper sphere." In Philadelphia, for instance, women began a Ladies Association, which they hoped would become the first national women's organization. The women of the association went from door to door, collecting $300,000 for the war effort.[9] Yet when the Ladies Association sent its funds to George Washington with suggestions about how the money should be spent, Washington acted, as John Adams hoped he would, by forcing women back into the home. Washington insisted that the money be spent on shirts for the soldiers, which the women should sew themselves. The women of the Ladies Association thus were forced from the streets back into a sewing circle (Norton 185–88). The official governmental reassertion of women's domestic nature is evident in Washington's letter of gratitude: "It embellishes the American character with a new trait; by proving that the love of country is blended with those softer domestic virtues, which have always been allowed to be more peculiarly *your own*" (qtd. in Norton 187).

Race as well as gender provided a locus for rhetorical and legal stabilization after the war. Michael Paul Rogin, tracing governmental policy affecting the Indians from the Revolution through the presidency of Andrew Jackson, reveals a pattern of rhetorical liberation and political subjection strikingly similar to that experienced by postwar American women. Having manipulated a rhetoric of opposition to slavery to justify the American revolt against England, American leaders then took great pains to control the "republican nightmares" that people of color represented (27).[10] Noting the widening gap between egalitarian rhetoric and oppressive social policy after the Revolution, Rogin comments that "republican leaders were imprisoned in racial patterns to which they did not want to consent and which their revolution would not alter" (28).

It is tempting to read in the captivity stories of *Reuben and Rachel,* then, resentment that the Revolutionary rhetoric of equality failed to better the lives not only of women but of people of color as well. The attraction of the captivity narrative as a fictional source perhaps lay partially in its necessary generic concern with both race and gender. Rowson's captivity romance becomes a gauge of America's failed rhetoric and of the fatal consequences of that failure for American women and Indians. As the dust from the Revolution settled, it became unmistakably clear, as Davidson writes, that women "had virtually no rights within society and no visibility within the political operations of government, except as a symbol of that government—Columbia or Minerva or Liberty" (*Revolution,* 120). The power of Rowson's novel is that her Columbia is not at all a mute symbol of a repressive and misogynistic government, but a lively reminder of the potential strength and ability of women. The tragedy of the novel is its realistic mirroring of the dwindling of that potential as the Republic forced women into the very limiting choice of marrying or being abandoned—a sad perversion of the revolutionary call to live free or die.

Notes

1.   See Kerber and Norton.

2.   See, e.g., Kerber 47, or Erkkila 190.

3.   In arguing for an organic and significant structure in *Reuben and Rachel,* I am taking issue with Henri Petter, the only critic to consider the composition of the novel, who dismisses Rowson as a mere sensationalist:

> Her Indian chapters are insufficiently coordinated with the
> more usual parts of the novel; they read like an element
> deliberately introduced to give the story a dash of the un-
> common and are not so much a part of the narrative as a
> picturesque feature, rather like the Columbus material in
> the opening chapters. *Reuben and Rachel* is clearly not a
> historical novel but a poorly organized book, setting fash-
> ionable plots against a sketchy background of historical
> fact. (35–36)

4.   On the sexualization of Indian women, see Barnett and Herzog. See es-
     pecially the excellent discussion by Dawn Lander, who writes, "In the
     wilderness, the 'otherness' of sexual opposites, of male-female polarity, is
     reinforced or even replaced by polarities of class or race. In fact, the for-
     eignness of class or race is an indispensable component of eroticism in
     the wilderness" (201).

5.   On the formation and importance of female community in nineteenth-cen-
     tury America, see Cott and Smith-Rosenberg, particularly the latter's chap-
     ter, "The Female World of Love and Ritual: Relations between Women in
     Nineteenth-Century America."

6.   Bell, for instance, writes that Catharine Sedgwick's *Hope Leslie* expresses its
     author's optimism "by means of a conventional romantic narrative plot,
     found again and again in historical romance, in which historical progress
     becomes identified with the romantic attachment of hero and heroine"
     (214).

7.   For detailed accounts of the origins of and changes in the *feme covert*
     status of married women in eighteenth-century America, see Salmon and
     Kerber. Both note the connection between political and domestic hierar-
     chies in the *feme covert* laws. As Salmon puts it:

> In English practice, "Baron and Feme" was the law of do-
> mestic relations. The very wording implies a political rela-
> tionship: lord and woman, not husband and wife. One party
> had status as well as gender, the other had only gender. As
> "baron," husband stood to wife as king did to baron. (119)

Given the antimonarchical rhetoric of the Revolution, women hoped that
the symbolic legal kingship of husbands might be renounced as well. But
Kerber details the ways in which the "first half-century of the Republic
was a time when it became even harder for married women to control
their own property" (155).

8.   The phrase is used by Brown to encapsulate the entire Richardsonian narrative of seduction and abandonment.

9.   Both Kerber and Norton discuss the "domestication" of Revolutionary politics. Both also include accounts of the Philadelphia Ladies Association.

10. Erkkila notes the similar effects the metaphors of the Revolution had on women and blacks in America. The rhetoric of justifiable revolt, Erkkila writes, led to "a certain openness and indeterminacy in black/white relations during the revolutionary era" (210), an openness Erkkila reads in Phillis Wheatley's poems. Yet, just as the freedoms granted women during the war were undermined by renewed emphasis on "proper" domesticity, so racial "indeterminacy . . . would begin to close and rigidify once the war was over and slaves were written into the Constitution as three-fifths human" (210). And, while the situations of slaves and of Indians in postwar America of course differed significantly, Rogin notes that, in the imaginations of those seeking to restore social hierarchy, all people of color in America posed a similar metaphorical political threat. The letter from John Adams to his wife, quoted above, is one example; another is Tom Paine's charge in *Common Sense* that England was "that barbarous and hellish power which hath stirred up the Indians and the Negroes to destroy us" (qtd. in Rogin 27). Yet, while critics have noted the connections in official rhetoric between women and slaves and between slaves and Indians, none that I have encountered has drawn the connection between Indians and women. Critics have noted the sympathy—even empathy—between female and Indian characters in the captivity romances. But none has accounted for that sympathy by examining the cultural rhetoric that made the experience of women and of Indians analogous.

Works Cited

Adams Family Correspondence. Vol. 1: Dec. 1761–May 1776. Ed. L. H. Butterfield, Wendell D. Garrett, and Marjorie E. Sprague. Cambridge: Harvard UP, 1963.

Barnett, Louise. *The Ignoble Savage: American Literary Racism, 1790–1890*. Westport, Conn.: Greenwood P, 1975.

Bell, Michael Davitt. "History and Romance Convention in Catharine Sedgwick's *Hope Leslie*." *American Quarterly* 22 (1970): 213–21.

Brown, Herbert Ross. *The Sentimental Novel in America, 1789–1860*. Durham, N.C.: Duke UP, 1940.

Cott, Nancy F. *The Bonds of Womanhood: "Woman's Sphere" in New England, 1780–1835*. New Haven: Yale UP, 1977.

Davidson, Cathy N. "Mothers and Daughters in the Fiction of the New Republic." *The Lost Tradition: Mothers and Daughters in Literature*. Ed. Cathy Davidson and E. M. Broner. New York: Frederick Ungar, 1980. 115–27.

———. *Revolution and the Word: The Rise of the Novel in America*. New York: Oxford UP, 1986.

Elliott, Emory. *Revolutionary Writers: Literature and Authority in the New Republic, 1723–1810*. New York: Oxford UP, 1986.

Erkkila, Betsy. "Revolutionary Women." *Tulsa Studies in Women's Literature* 6 (1987): 189–223.

Herzog, Kristin. *Women, Ethnics, and Exotics: Images of Power in Mid-Nineteenth-Century American Fiction*. Knoxville: U of Tennessee P, 1983.

Kerber, Linda. *Women of the Republic: Intellect & Ideology in Revolutionary America*. Chapel Hill: U of North Carolina P, 1980.

Lander, Dawn. "Eve Among the Indians." *The Authority of Experience: Essays in Feminist Criticism*. Ed. Arlyn Diamond and Lee Edwards. Amherst: U of Massachusetts P, 1977. 194–211.

Norton, Mary Beth. *Liberty's Daughters: The Revolutionary Experience of American Women, 1760–1800*. Boston: Little, Brown, 1980.

Petter, Henri. *The Early American Novel*. Athens: Ohio State UP, 1971.

Rogin, Michael Paul. *Fathers and Children: Andrew Jackson and the Subjugation of the American Indian*. New York: Knopf, 1975.

Rowson, Susanna Haswell. *Reuben and Rachel; or, Tales of Olden Times*. 2 vols. London: Minerva, 1798.

Salmon, Marylynn. *Women and the Law of Property in Early America*. Chapel Hill: U of North Carolina P, 1986.

Sieminski, Greg. "The Puritan Captivity Narratives of the American Revolution." *Journal of American Culture* 2 (1980): 575–82.

Smith-Rosenberg, Carroll. *Disorderly Conduct: Visions of Gender in Victorian America*. New York: Knopf, 1985.

———. "Domesticating Virtue: Coquettes and Revolutionaries in Young America." *Literature of the Body: Essays on Populations and Persons. Selected Papers from the English Institute, 1986*. Ed. Elaine Scarry. Baltimore: Johns Hopkins UP, 1988. 160–84.

———. "The Female World of Love and Ritual: Relations between Women in Nineteenth-Century America." *Signs* 1 (1975): 1–29.

Weil, Dorothy. *In Defense of Women: Susanna Rowson (1762–1824)*. University Park: Pennsylvania State UP, 1976.

Whitman, Walt. Preface. *Leaves of Grass*. Ed. Sculley Bradley and Harold W. Blodgett. New York: Norton, 1973.

CHAPTER 3

Expanding "America":
Lydia Sigourney's *Sketch of Connecticut,*
Catharine Sedgwick's *Hope Leslie*

Sandra A. Zagarell

Feminist critics have shown that antebellum American women writers had much to say about the public life of the country, but generally such critics have assumed that, from Sedgwick to Stowe, women's point of departure was the domestic sphere: women wanted to reform the world by making it more like the home.[1] As literature by women continues to reemerge, however, it is becoming clear that, as early as the 1820s, not all writing was as directly informed by domesticity as, for example, what Nina Baym calls woman's fiction. In some cases, women turned a sharply analytical eye on public matters, and, while they wrote from a consciously female viewpoint and drew on values of antebellum women's culture, their writing was concerned quite directly with the foundations and organization of public life.

In *Sketch of Connecticut* (1824) and *Hope Leslie; or, Early Times in the Massachusetts* (1827), Lydia Sigourney and Catharine Maria Sedgwick addressed a major political topic of the day, the nature of the American nation.[2] These works explored formative moments in the nation's history—the time just following the Revolution and early Puritan settlement, respectively—to criticize restrictive, masculinist policies that became institutionalized in the course of the nation's founding. Both writers exhibited a daring that is at once political and literary. Sigourney expanded a developing genre, the village sketch, to represent a locality with a diverse population as a microcosm of the nation at its founding; Sedgwick negotiated among conventions of the historical romance and other popular genres to portray the state the Puritans founded as one that exterminated Indians and oppressed women. Together the two authors demonstrate that, during the take-off decade of American literature, some women deliberately extended official definitions of the nation to imagine an America grounded in inclusiveness and communitarianism.

In *Sketch of Connecticut,* Lydia Sigourney focuses on the United States at the time of its transformation into a nation. *Sketch* takes place in the early months of 1784, just as ratification of the peace treaty with the British made the country's nationhood official. The author evokes in a single stroke the nation's birth and its infant precariousness: "The British Colonies of America were numbered among the nations. The first tumults of joy subsiding, discovered a government not organized, and resting upon insecure foundations" (15).[3] Sigourney poses this question: how do groups largely excluded from the formal structures of the polity— white women, Indians, and blacks of both sexes—fare within the nation's borders? Her choice of genre is audacious. Whereas other contemporary forms of narrative (novel, historical romance, frontier romance) depicted (white) heroines and heroes in love and/or adventure stories and included members of marginal groups in minor roles, if at all, the village sketch's concentration on one community allows Sigourney to focus on a racially and socially diverse population. Despite the scope of this project, *Sketch* is almost totally unknown today. Both its anonymous publication and, with few exceptions, critics' lack of familiarity with Sigourney's prose account in part for this obscurity;[4] the common assessment of the sketch as a trivializing, often nostalgic genre also has played a role. The sketch's capacity to accommodate significant tension is beginning to attract critical attention, however, and feminist scholars are focusing on ties between village sketch literature by women and nineteenth-century women's culture, with its emphasis on the relational and on the material life.[5] A major impetus for many sketches by women appears to lie in the wish to capture the life of a particular village or locale, for which purpose women like Sigourney drew specifically on the stationary quality of women's lives, their concentration on domestic detail their commitment to the ideal of interdependence. In the sketch, these authors fashioned a genre that featured daily life and local culture and history as compelling literary subject matter.

As *Sketch* shows, the genre also could both accommodate racial and ethnic tensions and generalize their significance to the country at large. Sigourney presents local life in considerable detail, while casting that life in a national and explicitly political light. She portrays the Connecticut town of N—— (modeled on Norwich, where she grew up) as the nation in miniature: N——'s residents include Mohegan Indians, former slaves and free blacks, an impoverished white widow with dependent children, hardy Farmer Larkin (a representative of the agricultural class, which would provide the nation's official citizenry), clergymen of various stripes, children, the dying widow of a British soldier, officers and soldiers from the Revolutionary army, and the local aristocracy. As we shall see, *Sketch* suggests that the nation, as a formal, political entity, ignored the existence of many of these groups. The text further suggests that all could be accommodated within a communitarian mode of life based on New Testament principles of charity and empathy. These principles, in Sigourney's day, were becoming identified as the particular virtues of women, and she exemplifies them in a matriarchal figure named Madam L——.

In contrast to the nation, N—— (which, as *Sketch's* title suggests, stands for all of Connecticut) has no public male figures. Nor is it plagued, like the nation at large, by an absence of unifying institutions. For Madam L—— presides over N——, and her policies embody values of antebellum women's culture within a hierarchically organized community to make the town a potential model for the former "British Colonies of America" (15). Herself the beneficiary of the patronage of an elite Connecticut family, Sigourney saw the wealth of Connecticut's "aristocracy" (a word she uses frequently) as a community resource acquired "through an [industriousness] which impoverished none" by those "intent . . . upon becoming illustrious in virtue" (4). In a country still without a central government, aristocratic and compassionate Madam L—— alone can develop a comprehensive public policy. She extends a "sympathy with those who mourned" (14), propounds Christian ethics at length, disburses charity, and includes all N——'s residents in her realm. Taking up the issue of the poor, who are depicted as being dependent on private alms, she creates a plan for institutionalizing charity that will provide domicile, work, medical care, and education. One chapter describes her concept of education; two others show her managing with skill her relations with her tenant, Farmer Larkin, taking an interest in the well-being of his family and counseling him in religious tolerance. She sets an example for the nation's policy towards new immigrants by paying the road toll of a recalcitrant Irishman, and, while her presence is weaker in chapters that feature blacks and Indians, the narrative voice and tone carry forward her ethic of justice and inclusiveness.

To suggest that, if the model nation is communal, the ideal public leader is a woman, Sigourney amalgamates heterogeneous, culturally resonant images of leadership. She maneuvers carefully within conventional conceptions of womanhood to create a figure who, while retaining her feminine qualities, acquires public authority. Madam L—— is dissociated from motherhood and domestic life, for, in the second decade of the nineteenth century, thinkers like Sigourney's friend Catharine Beecher had not yet infused women's conventional roles with political resonance by giving motherhood the moral task of reforming the public sphere. The ideology of separate spheres, asserting that "home *is* [women's] world," as articulated in Sarah Hale's *Lady's Magazine* in 1830, still officially restricted women's activities to a narrowly defined domestic life (qtd. in Woloch 101). Thus Sigourney prunes the kin networks with

which, in her autobiography, *Letters of Life,* she surrounds her own benefactress and Madam L——'s prototype, Mrs. Lathrop (10–11, 43–48, 74–
96). Like Mrs. Lathrop's, the widowed, seventy-year-old Madam L——'s
children have predeceased her, but, unlike the historical figure, Madam
L—— has no visible social peers and only one relative, a younger brother-
in-law, Dr. L——, whose major function is to attest to her wisdom. A
woman of wealth and social status, Madam L—— is shown almost exclusively in the context of her public concerns, and, in contrast to Grandmother Badger, the matriarch of Stowe's *Oldtown Folks,* she is seen only
in her parlor, never in the kitchen. The regal connotations of "Madam"
are extended by several references to her as "the Lady"; even when she
is likened to "our first mother," she is shown walking in a garden whose
mixture of elegant and "personified" flowers makes it an emblem of the
heterogeneous realm over which she governs. Here, unhindered by the
presence of any Adam, she engages in aristocratically managerial activities: she "amuse[d] herself by removing whatever marred [the garden's]
beauty, and cherish[ed] all that heightened its excellence" (7).

If Sigourney takes pains to dissociate Madam L—— from the domestic, she does anticipate Beecher, Stowe, and others in granting this character status in the one area in which women's participation in the public
life was acceptable, religion.[6] Though nominally respectful towards the
clergy, *Sketch* suggests that Madam L—— is a far more Christian religious leader than most clergymen. It stresses the narrow sectarianism of
two religious leaders, the Congregationalist minister Dr. S—— and the
Jesuit Father Paul, and attributes to both a thoughtless and sometimes
destructive enthusiasm for military matters that links institutional religion
with an America founded on exclusionary principles. Madam L——'s religion, on the other hand, is spiritual and all-embracing. She "looked
upon the varying sects of Christians, as travellers pursuing different roads
to the same eternal city" (9). In a strategy that anticipates Stowe's feminization of Christ in *Uncle Tom's Cabin,* she is explicitly identified with the
savior. A description of her spiritual peace (the serenity of "one whose
'kingdom is not of this world'" [8]) draws on scriptural description of the
peace of Christ. When the narrator, alluding to Madam L——'s death,
promises to render thanks to the widow ("where the righteous hear the
words, 'Inasmuch as ye have done good unto one of the least of these,
ye have done it unto me'"), the ambiguous "me" merges the Messiah
with Madam L—— (104).

Finally, Sigourney underscores Madam L——'s importance as an icon
of public governance by associating her with the most highly respected
male public figure of the day, George Washington. The connection is
made in a sequence in which Madam L—— is visited by a veteran soldier of the Revolutionary War and two officers. The officers devote their

visit to recounting a story about a brother officer, which illustrates what public leadership means for them—patriotism, honor, male camaraderie. Though they greet the disabled, impoverished veteran in a warmly military manner, all they can share with him are war memories. Only Madam L——, who "felt a deep interest in those soldiers who had borne the burdens of our revolution" (181), conceives and enacts a policy for integrating veterans into the community. "[E]xtend[ing] her unwearied friendship," she disburses medicine and food "with that judgment which accompanies a discriminating mind" (182). These acts ally her with Washington, whose "fatherly compassion" and principled "firmness" in dealing with his troops the officers commemorate (224). Because *Sketch* evokes Washington in the past tense, repressing allusions to the Constitutional Congress and the federal government that he soon would head, it casts the widow as the general's political successor. *Sketch* represents the public space this heroic figure occupied as a void that only a Madam L—— can fill.

Juxtaposing the nation as it really was in 1784 with this idealized, and monitory, communitarian model, *Sketch* dramatizes the economic and cultural consequences that living in the American colonies had for those among N——'s population who were not factored into the concept of the "national character." Sigourney exploits the openness of the sketch form to call into question the assumption that an America subsumed within so monolithic a term does, or should, exist. As she and other women developed it, the sketch frequently embraces a proto-ethnographic conception of character. Characters in *Sketch* cannot be described in terms we usually draw on for discussing fiction—"round" or "flat," psychologically or morally conceived, "protagonist" or "minor." In fact, the term "characterization" scarcely seems accurate at all: *Sketch* brings to life residents of N—— who in drama-based, conventionally plotted narratives would have been relegated to cameo appearances or tertiary roles, and it presents them as members of the community. It does so by destabilizing prevalent conceptions of Indians, blacks, and poor white women, juxtaposing the stereotypes according to which members of these groups were conventionally perceived with portrayals that try to capture their actual experiences. Sigourney cannot, of course, transcend her cultural moment, and *Sketch* often reproduces racist and culturally biased stereotypes uncritically. But because it develops other ways to give life to the experiences of the marginalized, it also casts stereotypes as cultural constructions that overlay and obscure the actuality of those they purport to represent. Particularly with regard to the representation of the Mohegans of N——, Sigourney practices the kind of sympathetic hermeneutics prominent, in varying ways, in female authors such as Sedgwick, Stowe, and Jewett. She scrutinizes the silences and erasures of highly regarded written sources (the Puritan histories, which were enjoying a revival in the 1820s), reading daily life as an eloquent source of information. She thus becomes at once historiographer of how whites have represented Indians and creator of a revisionary political and cultural history.[7]

Sigourney's approach entails pushing beyond the contemporary flurry of literary interest in America's Indians that, as Richard Slotkin indicates, attended their diminishing status as a threat to American life and tended to reify them. Generally, literature in the 1820s sympathetic to Indians placed them in the past tense, often also celebrating in them qualities white civilization was thought to repress (Slotkin 356–57). Eulogizing Indians as a noble race swept away by the onward progress of history was a particularly common attitude, and *Sketch* is not exempt from it. Numerous passages, as well as the epigraphs that precede several chapters, invoke the "red man" "roaming" in "his" natural setting in the days before European contact; they also present the Indians as beings closer to nature than culture and naturalize their demise, in the era's favorite image, as the end of a day.

Yet *Sketch* also recuperates for the Mohegans an extended and periodicized history, which, Sigourney reveals, is inadvertently documented in the Puritan historical narratives themselves. Like a few other writers of the era, among them Irving and Sedgwick, Sigourney reverses the self-justifying intent of Puritan historians in order to reveal the Indians' actual experiences. She produces a chronology that reinstates the causes of demise erased by the natural imagery and traces the sequence of a hundred years of steady cultural and political loss. While her account never explicitly identifies the causes of the Mohegans' decline, the details on which she concentrates link this history irrevocably to the whites' formation of their nation. She connects the Puritans to America in 1784, calling them "our ancestors" and terming their narratives "our national annals," emphasizing both the Mohegans' importance to Connecticut's early settlement and the fact that the Puritans "have been careful to give us [a] reverse" picture of the reliability of the Mohegan chief Uncas (39, 42). Further, she shades the information the annals contain to connect implicitly the friendship that Uncas and his son Oneco display towards the whites with the Indians' loss of cultural integrity and of power. Uncas's submission to the whites' "greater wisdom" in determining how to deal with the captured Pequod chief Minantonimoh, and Uncas's modification of Indian practices for executing an enemy emerge as a precarious effort to balance white and Indian culture; while Oneco's loyalty during the war with King Philip results in what she shows to be the loss of approximately half the Mohegans' able-bodied male population. Sigourney also shows that the steady degradation of the tribe is tied to its submission to a deracinating Christianity, which Uncas, as she sympathetically reports, rejected as a rationalization of genocide. She registers the later decline of the tribe in terms of its gradual acceptance of Christianity and submission to white demands for land; after Oneco, the chiefs of the Mohegans bear Old Testament names—Joshua, Benjamin, and Samuel. The annals note the "peaceful" Joshua only for "executing deeds for the conveyance of lands to the English" (46); Samuel "adopted a military dress, and was fond of the customs and conversation of the whites" (47). Her account concludes with Uncas's last descendant, Isaiah Uncas, who was educated into white ways at a Christian seminary and does not "inherit either the intellect, or enterprise, which distinguished the founder of that dynasty" (48). The saga of cultural annihilation, ceded lands, and population decimation explains this "weakness" as the result of genocide.

Sketch carries this reinstatement of the repressed to the point of America's official arrival as a nation by turning a sympathetically interpretive eye on details of Indian life in N—— in 1784. The book reads assimilation—which a few writers, including Joel Barlow, the late-eighteenth-century producer of nationalistic epic poems, had briefly entertained as the only possible protection against Indians' degeneration[8]—as white domination and interprets the Indians' experience of Christianity as metonymic of cultural and political decline. Using a device common in village sketch literature (one generally employed, however, only in connection with bona fide citizens), *Sketch* devotes an entire chapter to thumbnail portraits of five Indian men, distinguishing them primarily in terms of the degree to which they have accepted Christianity. The most detailed treatment is that of John Cooper. His Anglo-Saxon first and family names announce an assimilationist embrace of Christianity, while his cultivation of crops, signifying his acceptance of white ways, makes him prosperous. The portrait concludes by testifying to his alienation from his tribe and the impossibility of his achieving an identity that keeps the two cultures in balance. The Indians criticize him, saying that "they 'never saw an Indian so eager after both worlds'" (55).

Another proto-ethnographic technique common in village sketch literature, the reproduction of community members' interpretations of their own experience, underscores even more powerfully the alliance between white hegemony and Christianity. *Sketch* includes an extended conversation between the Mohegan's chief, Roger Ashbow, and an Indian missionary, the Reverend Samuel Occom, on the eve of the emigration of half the Mohegan tribe to a location further west. Reflecting an empathy reminiscent of Madam L——, the narrative presents the conversation (which occurs in Madam L——'s parlor) without commentary, so the Indian leaders' words stand on their own. These words reveal the Mohegan experience of Christianity to be as irredeemably problematic in 1784 as in the seventeenth century. Ashbow, who "suffered his reasoning powers to be perplexed with the faults, the crimes of Christians" despite his admiration for Christ's sacrifice for all of humanity, insists on the hypocrisy of Christian ideology (52). His argument takes the form of a passionate deconstruction of the self-serving character of the ideology; his speech recalls, in its thrust, Sigourney's own earlier deconstruction of the Puritan annals: "Why are those . . . who expect an inheritance in the skies, so ready to quarrel about the earth, their mother? Why are Christians so eager to wrest from others lands, when they profess that it is *gain,* for them to leave all, and die?" (160, emphasis Sigourney's). Occom's response exemplifies the Christian minister's counseling of acceptance. He maintains that "all men, all nations of men, have sinned. In this world retribution is not perfect. It becomes not us to contend with Him, who dealeth more lightly with us than our iniquities deserve" (160–61). Coming after a historical reconstruction that locates the answers to Ashbow's questions in white self-justification and expansionism, such pieties expose institutional Christianity as more the handmaiden of political and cultural interests than the expression of a spiritual creed.

Far-reaching as it is, *Sketch* finally gives way under the strain of historical actuality and the limits of genre. It cannot show a transformed nation, for the nation did not in fact transform itself. The characteristic ending of the village sketch (life remains unchanged, and the narrator either remains in the village and bids farewell to the reader or leaves and bids farewell to the village) would vitiate N——'s status as the microcosm of a troubled nation. Registering the irresolvable characters of its own dilemmas, *Sketch* disintegrates into a hodgepodge of popular genres—captivity narrative, adventure story, the sentimental tale of the death of a young woman—as it suddenly becomes highly plotted, narrating the story of the final months of the life of Oriana, the young widow of a British soldier, with her adopted Mohegan parents, Zachary/Arrowhamet and Martha.

Yet shards of Sigourney's vision of a reconstructed nation surface. The white/Indian family stands as an alternative to assimilation *qua* annihilation, which *Sketch* had so eloquently exposed. It entails a type of miscegenation different from, but, for an antebellum America whose ideology celebrated the family, as powerful in its way as interracial marriage. Cultural differences are honored—Zachary/Arrowhamet's double name betokens his retention of white and Indian identity, and he prays both to his native God and to the Christian one. And Sigourney's communitarianism deepens to include intense personal bonds. The three repeatedly name each other "mother," "father," and "daughter"; Oriana says she has found "joy" with her new parents. Physical contact between the races, avoided by many white writers, is highlighted in the affectionate ministrations these parents perform for Oriana and in the hands she extends to them as she dies. Christianity as political ideology is purged, and only a genuinely spiritual Christianity remains. Oriana, like Madam L——, embraces an inclusive religion that extends to the Indians while honoring their distinctive histories; in a letter that she leaves for her minister, she urges him, too, to acknowledge their spiritual equality.

Thus, though *Sketch* replaces the nation-as-community with a purely domestic vision and preaches a change of heart rather than continuing to focus on public policy, it continues its principled challenge to the temper of those actually in charge of the nation. For, in 1825, President Monroe would ask Congress to plan all Indians' (unforced) removal beyond the Mississippi because, in historian Richard Drinnon's paraphrase, "'experience has shown' the impossibility of whites and Indians becoming one people in their present state" (115). Dismissals of Sigourney like that in the *Literary History of the United States*—though she "knew something of the humanitarian movements of the day, all . . . she did for Negroes, Indians, the poor, and the insane was to embalm them in the amber of her tears" (McDowell 289)[9]—thus constitute a radical, if inadvertent, censorship of what the nation has meant to its writers. Perpetuating ignorance about certain modes of representing the nation, such pronouncements contribute to the sort of monolithic definitions of the national culture to which Sigourney herself so strongly took exception.

Like *Sketch of Connecticut, Hope Leslie* perceives common ground between white women and native Americans. Taking race and gender as its primary points of departure, *Hope Leslie* characterizes the first major historical period in the nation's history, the solidification of the Massachusetts Bay Colony, as being grounded in a legalistic patriarchy in which domestic and external policy—masculine dominance in the home, obliteration of the Indians—are two sides of the same coin.[10] Like Sigourney, Sedgwick pushes at literary boundaries, implying that existing conventions often serve specific ideological interests. But whereas *Sketch* interrogates dominant stereotypes and official ideologies within a developing communitarian-based genre, *Hope Leslie* negotiates within established narrative structures—Puritan histories, the frontier romance, the historical romance.[11] It has its share of conventional formulas and stereotypes: it pays homage to the Puritan fathers as courageous founders of the country; it often presents Indians as noble savages and occasionally attacks them as demonlike; its Pequod heroine, Magawisca, declares dramatically that white and Indian cannot be reconciled. Most fundamentally, however, *Hope Leslie* casts light on the collusion between established narrative structures and racist, patriarchal definitions of the nation. It is on this that I shall focus.[12]

By situating Indian brutality within Puritan expansionism, *Hope Leslie* strongly challenges the ways in which several popular narrative modes repressed the fundamental connections between white settlement and conflicts with the Indians. The downplaying of historical connection was conspicuous in the Puritan histories that Sedgwick researched to write *Hope Leslie* and in the frontier romances popular earlier in the nineteenth century. In both genres, Indians tend to be depicted as innately malevolent, their violence against whites unprovoked. The typical narrative line of both highlights Indian provocation and violence and concludes with a white victory that often involves extermination of Indians and the forward movement of white settlement. By the 1820s, frontier romances, like other literature, did portray some Indians as noble savages; the best-known examples are Chingachgook and Uncas in James Fenimore Cooper's *The Last of the Mohicans* (1826), a partial exception to many of the formulas of frontier romances, and, as we shall see, a work much on Sedgwick's mind when she wrote *Hope Leslie*.[13] But even "good" Indians are as much inherently good as the "evil" ones are inherently bad, and they too are almost always dead at the narrative's conclusion. *Hope Leslie* can make the links most other works conceal because it sees in Puritan expansionism the wrongful dispossession of Indians. The early chapters depict the settling of Springfield in 1636 as such a displacement ("the wigwams which constituted the village . . . gave place to the clumsy, but more convenient dwellings of the Pilgrims" [1: 18]), and although this particular settlement is not violent, it is juxtaposed with the Puritans' brutal massacre of the Pequod Indians in 1637—a victory that marked an essential step towards Puritan dominance in the New World.

The narrative insists, moreover, that the Puritans' policies set into motion a complex chain of events that could not be captured in the polarization into good and bad with which historical and frontier romance, as well as Puritan narrative, tended to explain the course of history. Focusing on the family of William Fletcher, whose disenchantment with Puritan repressiveness leads him to build his home outside the Springfield compound, *Hope Leslie* demonstrates that even men with the best intentions cannot exempt themselves from the consequences of their government's policies. John Winthrop, first governor of the Massachusetts Bay Colony, sends to Fletcher as servants the captured children of the Pequod chief Mononotto, fifteen-year-old Magawisca and her younger brother Oneco. Carefully establishing the bonds of affection Magawisca develops for Mrs. Fletcher and her son Everell, *Hope Leslie* problematizes the good Indian–bad Indian formula by showing that personal ties cannot negate past history. Magawisca herself soon recounts the events of the Pequod massacre, and this lesson in history is followed by a grisly scene in which Mononotto and two Mohawks murder Mrs. Fletcher and her daughters. One of the Mohawks "dashes" the family baby against the door-stone, in a rewriting of a similar scene in *The Last of the Mohicans* in which a Huron "savage," thwarted in his desire for a white woman's shawl, "dashed the head of [her] infant against a rock, and cast its quivering remains to her very feet." (Cooper 226). The acts of Cooper's Indian have nothing to do with the whites' policies; he is intrinsically malevolent, and the murder he commits touches off a wanton massacre of the English. *Hope Leslie*'s narrative structure, however, situates its analogous and undeniably horrifying act as part of a chain of white-initiated historical events. Furthermore, it highlights the Indians' view of the murders as political retribution. Calling an end to the violence while two whites still live, Mononotto says to his companions, "We have had blood enough . . . you have well avenged me, brothers" (1: 93–94).

At the same time that *Hope Leslie*'s dramatization of this causal chain rejects the simplistic moral dichotomies of much popular writing, the novel challenges the official history of original settlement by exposing the repositories of the nation's early history, the Puritan narratives, as justifications of genocide.[14] Occasionally, Sedgwick allows the Puritans to speak for themselves, as in the epigraph to the chapter devoted to the Puritan massacre of the Pequods: she quotes the famous lament of pastor John Robinson after the slaughter of eight friendly Indians: "It would have been happy if they had converted some before they had killed any" (1: 56). Following a strategy somewhat similar to Sigourney's, she also incorporates the Indians, who to the Puritans were nonhuman or devilish, into the nation's history. The massacre is described from the victims' viewpoint, narrated by Magawisca—both an Indian and a woman. The Puritan accounts cast the attack as a military event, the victorious siege of a "fort," and barely register the presence of Indian women and children. One of Sedgwick's main sources, the account by the Reverend William Hubbard, relies heavily on the record of John Mason, a leader of the attack, and is told in the first person. Hubbard's account strongly emphasizes the Lord's guidance in military decisions, depicts the Indian men as subhuman, and, ignoring the presence of women and children, contains a terse description of the massacre that focuses on Mason's bravery; it concludes: "Being very hot and dry, we could very hardly procure any Water." This rendition and that of Benjamin Trumbell, another Sedgwick source, give the Pequods only two words: "Owanux, Owanux" ("Englishmen, Englishmen") (Hubbard 2: 126).[15]

"[P]utting the chisel into the hand of truth, and giving it to whom it belonged" by having Magawisca recount this history, Sedgwick fills the gaps around these two words (1: 76). The Puritans are mass murderers, while the Pequods feel fear, agony, and outrage and exhibit great courage. The noise that Hubbard ignores and Trumbell barely mentions becomes a multidimensional language: Magawisca describes the guns of the English "that we had never heard before," the Indians' battle yell, the "piteous cries of the little children—the groans of our mothers," and the silence of the dead (1: 68). Hubbard's account erases the history of white-Indian contact and valorizes Mason's assertions of heroism: "entering one of their wigwams, I took a Firebrand . . . and suddenly kindled a Fire in the Mats wherewith [the Pequods] were covered, and fell to a Retreat, and surrounded the Fort" (126). Magawisca portrays the same act as the conscious destruction, not of a "fort," but of what she maintains the Puritans knew from firsthand experience to be a village with families: "Then was taken from our hearth-stone, where the English had been so often warmed and cherished, the brand to consume our dwellings . . . . Thus did the strangers destroy, in our own homes, hundreds of our tribe" (1: 69).

Though many contemporaneous historical romances were critical of the Puritans' repressiveness, they tended to honor the Puritan era as the nation's founding moment and to conceive of the nation's development in a linear fashion, as a decline from that initial moment or an improvement on it.[16] Like Lydia Child's *Hobomok,* however, *Hope Leslie* refuses to see history as a matter of progress or regression; in fact, it pays little attention to the movement of history at all. Its interest is in problematizing the Puritan founders' beliefs and policies. In particular, it elucidates their attitudes towards white women as the domestic analog of their views of Indians. This was a most radical perspective for the 1820s, when the complete separation of the domestic and public spheres was seen as natural and good. *Hope Leslie* is doubly subversive because it develops this position most powerfully with regard to John Winthrop, whom historical romances typically idealized in a way Michael Bell finds reminiscent of popular idealization of George Washington (*Hawthorne* 21). Reporting Winthrop to have "been a model of private virtue, gracious and gentle in his manners," the narrative adds, in describing his private conduct, that "the only divine right to govern, which [our ancestors] acknowledged, was that vested in the husband over the wife" (1: 212). "[D]ivine right" elides the rule of kings, the rule of husbands, and the valor in massacring Indians that William Hubbard thought was divinely sanctioned; for *Hope Leslie* consistently suggests that, to Winthrop and other Puritan authorities, white women and Indians are threats to the social order and must be forcibly controlled. Thus, to such men, both white women and Indians are like animals. Madam Winthrop is "a horse easy on the bit" (1: 213); hoping to reduce the spirited Hope Leslie to the same state of subordination by marrying her off, Winthrop says to Fletcher, "[I]f I may use the sporting language of our youth, I am impatient to put jesses on this wild bird of yours, while she is on our perch" (1: 229). The Indians are seen as more bestial, more inimical to civilization than white women, a view that justifies their extermination; Fletcher himself initially refers to the Pequods as "this wolfish tribe" (1: 25), a favorite metaphor of Cotton Mather (another of Sedgwick's sources).

The Puritan authorities' equation of difference with chaos also achieves expression in the desire to dictate the clothing of white women and Indians.[17] Sedgwick allows Puritan gynophobia and the disguised desire to imprison women to speak for themselves, quoting one man's self-revealing pronouncement that it breaks his heart "to see [the women] imprisoned in French cages, peeping out of their hood-holes for some men of mercy to help with a little wit . . . . If I see any of them accidentally, I cannot cleanse my phansie of them for a month after" (1: 36). With regard to the Indians, she shows that gynophobia gives way to genocide. *Hope Leslie* repeatedly registers both the efforts of Puritans to force the Indians into English clothing and the Indians' resistance to these efforts. Magawisca's defense when she is unjustly tried for sedition against the Puritans links cultural and political annihilation and registers respect for the Indians' claims to autonomous nationhood: "Her national pride [was] manifest in the care with which, after rejecting with disdain the governor's offer of an English dress, she had attired herself in the peculiar costume of her people" (2: 157). That dress, which Sedgwick describes with respect and in detail, becomes the sartorial analog of Magawisca's proclamation to Winthrop: "I am your prisoner, and you may slay me, but I deny your right to judge me. My people have never passed under your yoke; not one of my race has ever acknowledged your authority" (2: 164). Finally, while white women are kept in close quarters in the home, Indians within the Puritan state live in literal servitude, like Magawisca and Oneco, or are actually consigned to jail. Magawisca herself is incarcerated in the Boston prison; and when an old Pequod woman, Nelema, is imprisoned in Springfield (again, on false charges), home and jail are revealed to be one: Springfield not yet having an official prison, she is locked in the cellar of the home of the settlement's leader, Mr. Pynchon.

Going beyond establishing parallels between the Puritans' treatment of white women and Native Americans, Sedgwick also revises the prevalent tendency, racist as well as gynophobic, to split women characters into the sexual and the chaste, the dark and light. Critics long have recognized this splitting as a commonplace of "classic" American literature. In *The Last of the Mohicans,* which Jane Tompkins has shown to be obsessed with maintaining the purity of cultural, racial, and sexual boundaries (94–121), Cooper attributes Negro blood to the dark, decisive, and sexually vital Cora Munro and ultimately kills her off, making her fair, angelic, and nearly imbecilic half-sister Alice, who survives, the incarnation of civilized femininity. Sedgwick, in contrast, suggests continuing connection between white and Native American women in the form of a deep and abiding kinship. She doubles her white and Indian heroines, imagining the possibility of a sisterhood that crosses racial boundaries. Evading the staple "dark/fair" dichotomy, she makes Hope dark-haired (though some readers have thought her blonde) and downplays Magawisca's darkness; and she makes the two metaphorical sisters.[18] Their first meeting takes place in the Boston cemetery in which their mothers are buried; Hope thinks: "Mysteriously have our destinies been interwoven. Our mothers brought from a far distance to rest together here—their children connected in indissoluble bonds!" (2: 19). In Winthrop, Magawisca and Hope share a symbolic Puritan father, for, in the same letter in which Winthrop passes Magawisca and Oneco on to William Fletcher, he also gives Fletcher guardianship over Hope and her sister Faith. Hope and Magawisca both ambivalently love the same man, Everell Fletcher, and they are literal sisters-in-law, Hope's sister Faith marrying Oneco.

Where historical romance usually concerns itself with individual liberty, this sisterhood opposes a communitarian ethic to the rigid legalism that for Sedgwick undergirds all authoritarian male rule and is summed up in Winthrop's rebuke to Hope's tutor: "Thou art too apt to measure thy orthodoxy by thy charity" (1: 255). After the Fletcher massacre, when a narrow "interpretation of justice" (1: 136) spurs Mononotto to execute Everell Fletcher in retribution for the Puritans' murder of his own son, Magawisca saves Everell by throwing herself between the raised hatchet of the law-bound executioner and his innocent prisoner, losing her arm in the process. In less extreme fashion, Hope enacts this ethic of responsibility within the Puritan state. Commentators have identified her as the embodiment of liberty, equating the liberty she represents with individualism.[19] In the passage usually cited to advance this reading, however, Hope's confidant not only defines liberty ("having our way") as the "privilege we came to this wilderness . . . for" but begins his disquisition by identifying liberty as "what every woman can understand" (2: 68). Presenting women of both races as objects of Puritan imprisonment, *Hope Leslie* defines liberty from a woman's perspective. It is not the capacity for individual development, which canonical literature such as Emerson's "Self-Reliance" would enshrine, but the commitment to principled action on behalf of others who are, like oneself, enchained.

This definition reflects the emphasis on interdependence and altruism characteristic of antebellum women's culture. The identification of individual fulfillment with the achievement of justice for others may overlap with a conservative ethos of feminine self-sacrifice, but in *Hope Leslie,* women's acts in support of liberty, though never committed for the direct gain of the perpetrator, are assertively political: they undermine the Puritans' patriarchal authority. "Liberty" for Hope means subverting the rule of the Puritan fathers in order to aid the Pequods. Promising se-

crecy to Magawisca, she conceals from the Winthrop family her arrangements to meet with her sister Faith, who, captured during Mononotto's
raid on the Fletcher home, has become a Pequod (Hope is the only
white who comes to honor Faith's marriage with Oneco). Aware of the
bigotry that causes the authorities to apprehend Nelema as a witch, she
springs the woman from jail. And she calls all her charm into play, not
for herself, but to cajole and maneuver several men in order to liberate
Magawisca from the Boston jail. Hope's double, Magawisca, underscores
the specifically female slant of such a notion of liberty when, at her trial's
conclusion, she reminds Winthrop of his promise of kindness to her
mother and declares: "In her name, I demand of thee death or liberty"
(2: 174). This echo of Patrick Henry's famous words conflates the law of
the Puritan fathers with the tyranny against which their descendants were
to revolt a century and a half later. It articulates a different concept of
liberty, one rooted in the maternal principle and committed to shared
responsibility among all those who were oppressed in the new nation
the Puritans were founding.

Like Sigourney, Sedgwick can redefine key concepts—liberty, the
founders' politics—but she cannot change what has already occurred.
The Massachusetts Bay Colony is not transformed by the kinship between Hope and Magawisca. But *Hope Leslie* does call attention to the
strategies by which conventional fiction contained and repressed the historical forces Sedgwick took such pains to highlight, for it concludes by
underscoring its own invocation of such strategies. On the surface, it
capitulates almost completely to formulas by which frontier and historical
romance cast historical movement as progress. The remaining Pequods
leave Massachusetts; a seduction plot against Hope, involving a royalist-
Catholic villain, ends with the melodramatic explosion of a pirate ship in
the Boston harbor that rids Massachusetts of all unambiguously repre-
hensible characters; the narrative ends with the marriage between the
white heroine and her young man that, in historical romance, typically
ushers in a more humane order. This proliferation of devices underscores
the heavy fictional artillery needed to bring the forces Sedgwick has un-
leashed under control—and those forces remain stubbornly and openly
unresolved. Most significantly, Faith Leslie resists Puritan civilization and
remains married to Oneco. This, according to Louise Barnett, is one of
only three instances of white-Indian marriage in frontier romance (119)
(the others occur in *Hobomok* and Cooper's *The Wept of Wish-ton-Wish*).
As the only enduring white-Indian union in frontier literature, the marriage of Faith and Oneco renders questionable Cooper's insistence on
keeping Uncas and Cora Munro separate in *The Last of the Mohicans*.
Sedgwick's choice of names for Faith's Indian husband alludes to Cooper's
novel; as Sedgwick knew from the Puritan histories she read, Uncas was

not "the last of the Mohicans," and one of his sons was named Oneco.[20] Sedgwick also strongly implies that Oneco is not the last of the Pequods: Magawisca, Mononotto, Oneco, and Faith migrate farther west, and "[t]hat which remains untold of their story is lost in the deep, voiceless obscurity of those unknown regions" (2: 243). To an antebellum readership this migration might evoke the general American push west and the frontier romances that carried fiction into just such "unknown regions" as those to which the Pequods move. Further, as the example of *Hope Leslie* itself has demonstrated, untold stories and voiceless obscurity await revisionary histories and fictional maneuverings to illustrate them.

Hope's own story concludes in a fashion that is equally double-edged. The narrative flagrantly abjures the responsibility of describing her marriage to Everell Fletcher, "leav[ing] it to that large and most indulgent class of our readers, the misses in their teens, to adjust, according to their own fancy, the ceremonial of their heroine's wedding, which took place in due time, to the joy of her immediate friends" (2: 257). The novel ends, moreover, with the decision of Everell's former fiancee, Esther Downing, to remain single. A dutiful Puritan daughter and spokeswoman for Puritan authority, Esther abruptly moves to center stage, suddenly exemplifying something of the communitarian ethos that Hope herself can no longer embody once marriage absorbs her into Puritan domestic arrangements: "[Esther] illustrated [the] truth . . . that marriage is not *essential* to the contentment, the dignity, or the happiness of woman" and devotes herself to general philanthropy (2: 260; emphasis Sedgwick's). Sedgwick thus remains covertly true to the intent to which she has wittily alluded just after Winthrop describes Hope as a bird in need of jesses: he proposes as Hope's husband the future historian of the Pequod massacre, William Hubbard. Describing William Fletcher's rejection of the suggestion, Sedgwick comments that Hope's repugnance for scholars lost her "the golden opportunity of illustrating herself by a union with the future historian of New-England" (1: 228). Partly through Hope, *Hope Leslie* "illustrates" an untold history that explodes the versions perpetuated by the likes of William Hubbard. It also repudiates the drum-beating patriotism that inspired a commentator in the prestigious *North American Review* to exhort American historical writers to glorify their country's political history by taking up such "great epochs" as "the times just succeeding the first settlement—[and] the aera (*sic*) of the Indian wars" (Gardiner 1: 190).

Together, *Sketch* and *Hope Leslie* suggest two directions nineteenth-century women writers were to take in creating revisionary views of the nation. Sigourney anticipated the later collective and woman-centered visions of Stowe and Jewett, and it is fitting that she reached for a communitarian narrative structure. Sedgwick, maneuvering within bet-ter-known formulas, belongs to a tradition carried on by such writers as Charlotte Brontë, whose novel *Shirley* (1849) explores a past in which masculine leaders subjugate women, workers, and nature in the name of national progress.

Sketch and *Hope Leslie* also cast light on how masculinity has handi-capped the American national character as it was for so long officially de-fined. Two contemporaneous works generically akin to these women's texts, Irving's *Sketchbook* (1819–20) and Cooper's *The Last of the Mohicans,* provide useful comparisons. Both feature what Nina Baym has called "be-set manhood" ("Melodramas of Beset Manhood"). Irving's Rip van Winkle is often seen as a seminal depiction of American masculinity in flight from feminine tyranny and domestic responsibility; Cooper's Deerslayer is viewed as the archetypal hero who can retain his powers as hunter-fighter and his bonds with the wilderness only by evading civilization, generally embodied by women. In fact, as comparison with *Sketch* and *Hope Leslie* suggests, masculinity severely restricted Irving's and Cooper's capacity to imagine America. *Sketchbook* did provide an indispensable impetus for the tradition of women's village sketch literature. Because of its skill and extraordinary popularity, *Sketchbook*'s proto-ethnographic attention to "nooks and corners and by-places" and its use of the sketch form contributed crucially to the elevation of the everyday as a subject of literature (16). Yet Irving could not develop the sketch's potential to focus intently on a single locality, nor could he practice a hermeneutics of the everyday; furthermore, he had to leave his "native land" to write *Sketchbook*. One reason for his restrictive lightness of touch was his pre-occupation with being a gentleman, signified in his choice of name for his persona: Geoffrey Crayon, *Gent. Sketchbook* is confined by a con-ception of authorship as a gentlemanly activity whose subject matter was legitimized by a long-standing literary-cultural canon ("storied and poeti-cal association" [14]). Pervaded by fears concerning plagiarism and liter-ary ancestors, *Sketchbook* nonetheless can feature local culture and types only when they already have been authorized by tradition. The famous tales about America, "Rip Van Winkle" and "The Legend of Sleepy Hol-low," were borrowed from folk tales, and German tales at that. Relying on recorded Germanic traditions for their fantastic quality, they contrast sharply with the focus on a more genuinely American life and the greater ethnographic scrupulousness of a *Sketch of Connecticut.*

On the other hand, *The Last of the Mohicans,* like *Hope Leslie,* spe-cifically asks what the nation's history reveals about the nation's charac-ter. Cooper has rightly been commemorated as an epic writer who el-egized the losses attendant on America's expansion. *The Last of the Mohicans* can be read as an agonized and protracted hunt whose objects, Uncas and Cora, represent all that progress must extinguish. But Cooper unquestioningly accepts the ideology of separate spheres, denigrates the domestic, and defines history as a series of dramatic public events—fragile political alliances, localized conflicts, war. These assumptions help prevent *The Last of the Mohicans* from asking why America's civilization assigned Indians and vital white women to the realm of nature, rather than to that of culture, and why it required their extinction. The narrative cannot pursue connections between the public and private realms, or, indeed, conceive of a complexly organized nation at all. The power, and the limitations, of Cooper's book lie in the conviction with which it mythologizes all the forces it brings into conflict—civilization and expansion as well as Indians and white women.

Works like *Sketch* and *Hope Leslie* thus underscore restrictions imposed by masculinity, not just on writers like Cooper and Irving, but on a nation that still turns to them and to a handful of other men as the crucial exemplars of its early literary self-definition. Sigourney and Sedgwick map the broader contours of the literary, cultural, and political terrain that constitutes our true heritage. These two writers stand as testimony that, near the beginning of this country's conscious commitment to developing a national literature, women were already struggling to expand what America meant.

Notes

1. Works exploring the relationship between antebellum women's fiction and the domestic sphere include Fetterley, Introduction; Kelley, *Private Woman*; and Tompkins; as well as Baym's *Woman's Fiction*.

2. Gossett and Bardes discuss the political implications of Sarah Josepha Hale's *Northwood* and Sedgwick's *Hope Leslie*, including how these works address the question of the nation, while Karcher analyzes how Child's novel reflects on the nation. I am much indebted to both these essays.

3. I thank Lawrence Buell for bringing *Sketch* to my attention.

4. Feminist critical work on Sigourney's prose includes Fetterley's introduction to "The Father"; Douglas, "Mrs. Sigourney"; and Baym, "Reinventing Lydia Sigourney."

5. See Westbrook, esp. ch. 7. Buell identifies the New England village sketch as a relatively abstract genre in which writers maneuver a standard repertoire of traits, among them a homogenous population and a homeostatic situation, in the service of a celebratory evocation of village life, a critical depiction of the village as a backwater, or an interplay between the two modes (ch. 13). That women developed the sketch in their own ways is a premise of Fetterley and Pryse, *American Women Regionalists*, a major

anthology of American women regionalist writers that calls attention to
women's deployment of the sketch; of Pryse's study-in-progress of nineteenth-century American regionalism as a women's form; and of Ammons.
In Zagarell, "The Narrative of Community," I connect women's use of the
sketch with another genre developed primarily by women, the narrative
of community. See also my "'America' as Community in Three Antebellum Village Sketches."

6.   On antebellum women and religion, see Woloch; Douglas, *Feminization*;
     and Welter.

7.   Sigourney was not alone in revising prevalent ideology about Indians or
     seeking to render their viewpoint. Slotkin summarizes a revisionism that
     included Irving and others (354–68); however, like most considerations of
     the literature of the period, this study does not mention Sigourney.

8.   See Slotkin for a discussion (343) of how Barlow's *The Vision of Colum-
     bus* (1787) hints at racial assimilation.

9.   More recently, James D. Hart described Sigourney as a "Connecticut
     poetaster whose sort of pious verse was enormously popular. . . . Her
     lugubrious preoccupation with death caused her to look at every sick child
     as a potential angel, and she so consistently wrote melancholy verses on
     the decease of any prominent person that an elegy from her pen seemed
     as natural a sequence to death as interment" (690).

10. Commentators agree that *Hope Leslie* concerns itself with the nature of the
     national life, but their focus has varied. Bell, *Hawthorne*, sees *Hope Leslie*
     as a typical example of the general historical conflict between repressive
     Puritan forefathers and a younger, liberty-embracing generation emblem-
     atic of America's future; while Gossett and Bardes analyze it as a medita-
     tion on women's exclusion from liberty. Slotkin reads it as a work derived
     from the captivity narrative, expressing the fear of racial contamination,
     and an attempt on the part of white Americans to retain their national-
     cultural purity in the savage New World. Although Gossett and Bardes
     view *Hope Leslie* as a more conservative work than I do, they skillfully
     trace examples of how the book links the condition of white women with
     that of Native Americans.

11. For general information about the Puritan histories, I rely primarily on
     Slotkin and Drinnon; for the historical romance, on Bell, *Hawthorne*; for
     the frontier romance, on Barnett.

12. A keen sense of the character, limitations, and potential of narrative forms
     often shaped Sedgwick's writing. Her first work, *A New-England Tale*, for
     example, stretched the conventions of the religious tract and became the
     first instance of what Baym calls "woman's fiction." Thus far, however,
     her innovation has received little recognition. Bell maintains that *Hope
     Leslie* is "an extraordinarily conventional book" whose interest for twenti-
     eth-century readers lies precisely in the clarity with which it reproduces

the conventions of historical romance in the interest of advancing its—again, conventional—attitude that history and progress are one ("History" 213–14).

13. Sedgwick kept abreast of the literature of her day and knew James Fenimore Cooper, who was a friend of her brother Robert. Her brothers and contemporary reviewers compared her work to Cooper's. See *Life and Letters of Catharine M. Sedgwick,* ed. Dewey, 169–70. Edward Foster summarizes reviewers' comparisons of the two (68–69). When Sedgwick learned that her second novel, *Redwood,* was attributed to Cooper in France, she remarked, "It is to be hoped that Mr. C's self-complacency will not be wounded by this mortifying news" (*Life and Letters,* ed. Dewey, 172). Foster suggests that *Hope Leslie* in part constituted a response to *The Last of the Mohicans* (91–92).

14. Though they have not been fully aware of the ends to which she put them, Slotkin and Foster have remarked on how carefully Sedgwick read the Puritan historical narratives. Kelley, Introduction, also discusses Sedgwick's use of the Puritan sources.

15. For a good discussion of Hubbard's ideology, see Slotkin 88, 207. The summary of the massacre in another of Sedgwick's sources, Trumbell 1: 85, though expressing no remorse, does sound a muted note of awe at the magnitude of destruction.

16. This is a premise of Bell, *Hawthorne.*

17. It is beyond the scope of this study to trace in full *Hope Leslie's* extensive concentration on the semiotics of clothing. The subtlety of Sedgwick's examination of the cultural-personal meanings of clothing helps to make a mode of significant political analysis out of what, according to literary historian Benjamin Spencer, was demeaningly termed "milliner's literature." It also renders questionable the 1846 comment of *Literary World* editor, Everett Duyckinck, that "what are called lady's magazines, with plates of fashions, do not generally enter into an estimate of national literature." See Spencer 216.

18. Some modern readers may find problematical Sedgwick's strategies to respect the Pequods' culture while minimizing differences between white women and Indians. I have tried to suggest that the tendency of her representation is pointedly political as well as broadly humanitarian. President Monroe's 1825 statement that the "tribes could never be incorporated into our system in any form whatsoever" as justification for their removal is a forceful reminder that in the 1820s acknowledging difference without seeing similarity was generally done in the context of annihilating the other (Drinnon, 116).

19. Bell sees in her the spirit of progress and democracy that nineteenth-century America claimed as *its* identifying feature and wished to detect beneath the surface of seventeenth-century repressiveness (*Hawthorne*

164–71). Gossett and Bardes see her as exemplifying the Puritans' denial of liberty to women (20).

20. Trumbell is one source for the information about Oneco, though it clearly was well known; Sigourney also writes about Uncas's son Oneco. Foster as well as Gossett and Bardes point out that this marriage alludes to Cooper's separation of Uncas and Cora.

Works Cited

Ammons, Elizabeth. Introduction. *How Celia Changed Her Mind and Selected Stories*. By Rose Terry Cooke. American Women Writers Series. New Brunswick: Rutgers UP, 1986.

Barnett, Louise. *The Ignoble Savage: American Literary Racism, 1790–1890*. Westport: Greenwood P, 1977.

Baym, Nina. "Melodramas of Beset Manhood: How Theories of American Fiction Exclude Women Authors." *The New Feminist Criticism*. Ed. Elaine Showalter. New York: Pantheon, 1985. 63–80.

———. "Reinventing Lydia Sigourney." *The (Other) American Traditions*. Ed. Joyce W. Warren. New Brunswick, NJ: Rutgers UP, 1993. 54–72.

———. *Woman's Fiction: A Guide to Novels by and about Women in America, 1820–1870*. Ithaca, N.Y.: Cornell UP, 1978.

Bell, Michael. *Hawthorne and the Historical Romance of New England*. Princeton: Princeton UP, 1976.

———. "History and Romance Convention in Catharine Sedgwick's *Hope Leslie*." *American Quarterly* 22 (Summer 1970): 213–21.

Brontë, Charlotte. *Shirley*. London: Smith, Elder and Co., 1849.

Buell, Lawrence. *New England Literary Culture*. Cambridge, England: Cambridge UP, 1986.

Cooper, James Fenimore. *The Last of the Mohicans; a Narrative of the Seventeenth Century*. New York: Stringen and Townsend, 1865.

Douglas [Wood], Ann. "Mrs. Sigourney and the Sensibility of Inner Space." *New England Quarterly* 45 (1972): 163–81.

———. *The Feminization of American Culture*. New York: Knopf, 1978.

Drinnon, Richard. *Facing West: The Metaphysics of Indian-Hating and Empire-Building*. New York: New American Library, 1980.

Fetterley, Judith. Introduction. *Provisions: A Reader from Nineteenth-Century American Women*. Ed. Judith Fetterley. Bloomington: Indiana UP, 1985. 1–38.

———. Introduction to "The Father" in *Provisions*. Ed. Fetterley. 105–10.

Fetterley, Judith, and Marjorie Pryse, eds. *American Women Regionalists, 1850–1910: A Norton Anthology*. New York: Norton, 1992.

Foster, Edward Halsey. *Catharine Maria Sedgwick*. New York: Twayne, 1974.

Gardiner, W. H. Rev. of *The Spy,* by James Fenimore Cooper. *North American Review.* 1822. Rpt. in *The Native Muse: Theories of American Literature from Bradford to Whitman.* Ed. Richard Ruland. New York: Dutton, 1976. 190–91.

Gossett, Suzanne, and Barbara Ann Bardes. "Women and Political Power in the Republic: Two Early American Novels." *Legacy: A Journal of Nineteenth-Century American Women Writers* 2, no. 2 (Fall 1985): 13–30.

Hart, James D. "Lydia H. Sigourney." *Oxford Companion to American Literature.* 5th ed. New York: Oxford UP, 1983. 690.

Hubbard, William. *The History of the Indian Wars in New England from the First Settlement to the Termination of the War with King Philip, in 1677.* Ed. Samuel G. Drake. New York: Kraus, 1969.

Irving, Washington. *The Sketch-Book of Geoffrey Crayon, Gent.* Author's revised ed. New York: Putnam, 1861.

Karcher, Carolyn. Introduction. *Hobomok and Other Writings on Indians.* By Lydia Maria Child. American Women Writers Series. New Brunswick: Rutgers UP, 1986. ix–xxxviii.

Kelley, Mary. Introduction. *Hope Leslie.* By Catharine Maria Sedgwick. American Women Writers Series. New Brunswick: Rutgers UP, 1987. ix–xxxvii.

———. *Private Woman, Public Stage: Literary Domesticity in Nineteenth-Century America.* New York: Oxford UP, 1984.

McDowell, Tremaine. "In New England." *The Literary History of the United States.* Ed. Robert E. Spiller, et al. 3rd rev. ed. New York: Macmillan, 1963. 284–305.

Sedgwick, Catharine Maria. *Hope Leslie; or, Early Times in the Massachusetts.* New York: Harper & Bros., 1842.

———. *Life and Letters of Catharine M. Sedgwick.* Ed. Mary E. Dewey. New York: Harper & Bros., 1871.

Sigourney, Lydia Howard Huntley. *Letters of Life.* New York: D. Appleton, 1867.

[———]. *Sketch of Connecticut, Forty Years Since.* Hartford: Oliver D. Cooke & Sons, 1824.

Slotkin, Richard. *Regeneration through Violence: The Mythology of the American Frontier, 1600–1800.* Middletown: Wesleyan UP, 1973.

Spencer, Benjamin. *The Quest for Nationality: An American Literary Campaign.* Syracuse: Syracuse UP, 1957.

Tompkins, Jane. *Sensational Designs: The Cultural Work of American Fiction, 1790–1860.* New York: Oxford UP, 1985.

Trumbell, Benjamin. *A Complete History of Connecticut.* New Haven: Maltby, Goldsmith, and Co. and Samuel Wadsworth, 1818.

Welter, Barbara. "The Feminization of American Religion, 1800–1860." In *Dimity Convictions: The American Woman in the Nineteenth Century.* Athens: Ohio State UP, 1976. 83–102.

Westbrook, Perry. *The New England Town in Fact and Fiction*. Rutherford, NJ: Fairleigh Dickinson UP, 1982.

Woloch, Nancy. *Women and the American Experience*. New York: Knopf, 1984.

Zagarell, Sandra A. "'America' as Community in Three Antebellum Village Sketches." *The (Other) American Traditions*. Ed. Joyce W. Warren. New Brunswick, NJ: Rutgers UP, 1993. 143–63.

———. "The Narrative of Community: The Identification of a Genre." *Signs: Journal of Women in Culture and Society* 13, no. 3 (Spring 1988): 498–527.

CHAPTER 4

Reinventing Lydia Sigourney

Nina Baym

If Lydia Howard Huntley Sigourney (1791–1865) had not existed, it would have been necessary to invent her. In fact, she *was* invented. As American women writers published in ever larger numbers before the Civil War, one of them was bound to be construed as an epitome of the specifically *female* author in her range of allowed achievements and required inadequacies. From the late 1830s on, the prolific Sigourney was so well known that she naturally became a candidate for this role. And much in her accomplishments and life history fitted her for it.

She was, as it happened, a poor, virtuous, essentially self-educated woman whose writing originally had been sponsored by one of the leading families in Hartford, Connecticut, and patronized by many other New England aristocrats.[1] She published pious poetry on domestic subjects in the major magazines and wrote for the Sunday School League. Having made a good marriage (from the social point of view), she faithfully performed her duties as wife, mother, and hostess; and she began to write for money only after financial reverses put the family under economic duress. She was, in short, a woman whose life could be used to show would-be literary women what they could do, what they should do, and also what they had better not do. Hers also was a life in which a modern success story of upward mobility through hard work and self-sacrifice led to an affirmation of the traditional class structure.

The social construction of Lydia Sigourney began, then, in her own lifetime. And, with Sigourney's canny participation, it continued throughout her lifetime as well. For example, the prefatory "advertisement" by Daniel Wadsworth to her 1815 *Moral Pieces, in Prose and Verse* stresses the necessary haste with which she wrote: for the most part, her compositions "arose from the impulse of the moment, at intervals of relaxation from such domestic employments, as the circumstances of the writer, and her parents, rendered indispensable." Thirty-two years later, Sigourney's preface to the fifth (1847) edition of her *Select Poems* iterates the implications of that early notice; most of the poems in the book "were suggested by

passing occasions, and partake of the nature of extemporaneous productions; all reveal by their brevity, the short periods of time allotted to their
construction" (vii). The poet encourages readers to think that she wrote
only short poems, and wrote them quickly; one would never guess from
this preface that by 1847 she had also written (among other things) a
four-thousand-line historical epic in five cantos and two other historical
poems, each over five hundred lines long.[2] Haste, perhaps; extemporaneous brevity, no.

But *Select Poems* collects mainly "the more popular poems which
had appeared during several years in various periodicals" (*Letters* 337).
That is, this book, designed to recirculate such work as had already
proved itself in the public arena, was geared to the preferences of audience rather than author (or, the author preferences to which it was
geared were reputation building and money making). The incremental
popularity of collections of the already popular works (*Select Poems*—
called simply *Poems* in its first edition of 1834—went through more than
twenty-five editions during Sigourney's life) further consolidated a representation of the author based on her best-loved, or most widely known,
poetry. The reappearance of these poems in anthologies such as Rufus
Griswold's or Caroline May's added to the effect. In sum, the Lydia
Sigourney who was so often—albeit so ambiguously and ambivalently—
praised in her own lifetime, and has been so heartily calumniated subsequently, is a representation based on only some fraction of what she wrote
and published. The Sigourney of the consolation elegy, the funerary poem,
the Sigourney obsessed with dead children and dead mothers, has been
constituted by a succession of critical audiences, each basing its commentary and opinion on an ever smaller segment of the author's published writings. Accordingly, even now, when writing by antebellum
American women is more highly valued than it has been for a long time,
the mention of Sigourney's name invokes a caricature: a mildly comical
figure exemplifying the worst aspects of domestic sentimentalism.[3]

There is no Sigourney bibliography; many of her published books
are difficult to find, and much, if not most, of the uncollected periodical
material now probably is unrecoverable. But the surviving work does
not show Sigourney to be primarily a poet of mortuary verse. This is not
to say that Sigourney did *not* write many poems about death, among
them poems about dead mothers and children. But such poems do not
dominate even her poetic practice, and she also wrote significant quantities of prose. I count 16 elegies out of 114 pieces in her 1827 *Poems*; 50
out of 172 in the 1835 *Zinzendorff, and Other Poems*; 15 out of 115 in
the 1841 *Pocahontas and Other Poems*; and 32 out of 126 in the *Select
Poems* already mentioned; overall, this works out to 32 percent. Perhaps

in recognition of the popularity of this segment of her writing, Sigourney herself frequently called attention to it, as, for example, in her preface to *Zinzendorff*:

> Should it be objected that too great a proportion of [the poems] are elegiac, the required apology would fain clothe itself in the language of the gifted Lord Bacon:—If we listen to David's harp, we shall find as many hearse-like harmonies, as carols; and the pencil of Inspiration hath more labored to describe the afflictions of Job, than the felicities of Solomon. (6)

The category of elegy, or consolation poetry, or funerary verse, moreover, is a broad one; and one may discern within the Sigourney elegiac corpus three poetic subtypes. There are reflective *memento mori* poems deriving from some general observation in nature or the world; there are what I would call generic or situational elegies, whose subject is denoted as a member of a class rather than as an individual; and there are elegies for named persons—memorial or obituary poems. One need go no further afield than the table of contents of *Zinzendorff* for examples of each type. "Death among the Trees" is a general reflection on the inevitability of death, as is "Thoughts for Mourners." "Death of the Wife of a Clergyman, during the Sickness of Her Husband," "Death of a Young Wife," "Burial of Two Young Sisters," "Death of a Young Lady at the Retreat for the Insane," "Farewell of a Missionary to Africa, at the Grave of his Wife and Child," and "Death of a Young Musician" are situational elegies. "Funeral of Dr. Mason F. Cogswell," "Death of the Rev. Gordon Hall," "Death of Mrs. Harriet W. L. Winslow," "Death of a Son of the Late Honorable Fisher Ames," "Death of the Rev. Alfred Mitchell," and "Death of the Rev. W. C. Walton" are some of the specific memorials.

My distinctions here are not merely formal, or rather they are formal in Aristotle's sense of being configured with regard to an audience response. Each of the three kinds invokes a different type of occasion. (And, as the titles above show, the subjects are by no means exclusively women and/or children.) The *memento mori* poem, which Sigourney practices least among the three types, is an internal dialogue that dramatizes the persona's efforts to come to terms with death in general, with the death of a loved one, or with one's own inevitable death. Because the poem is reflective, it is distanced from the immediacy of death. Thus, it bespeaks an interval of leisure, privacy, and solitude for the persona as well as any reader whose mental processes it may seek to guide and mime.

The generic and specific consolation poetry that Sigourney most often wrote is designed, in contrast, for immediate intervention at the moment of death or funeral. A generic elegy, like a greeting card, is available to the large number of people whose circumstances it suits at the moment; while the memorial for a named person is intended to palliate the grief of a unique set of mourners. This set extends beyond close family to encompass friends, acquaintances, or those who knew the dead person by name only. Newspaper obituaries serve this function today. Thus, both the situational elegy and the obituary poem bespeak a public arena and a practical goal. They do not have time to expatiate on religious uncertainty, to exhibit the depth and extent of one's own grief, or to manage a personal catharsis; they aim to make suffering people feel better—and make them feel better fast. "Her muse has been a comforter to the mourner," Sarah Hale observes, and one necessary aspect of this comforting function is that the elegies are never about the speaker, always about others (783).

Invariably, these useful poems, designed specifically for Christians, incorporate a strong affirmation of the life to come. From the converging perspectives of High Victorianism and High Modernism, Sigourney's unsympathetic biographer Gordon Haight derides the intellectual simplicity of her religiosity; but *In Memoriam,* to which he invidiously compares Sigourney's elegiac corpus, certainly was not supposed to comfort any mourner besides its author.[4] Perhaps this other-directedness of Sigourney's elegiac voice also explains her low ranking in the "narcissistic" woman's poetic tradition outlined by Cheryl Walker in *Nightingale's Burden,* a tradition that focuses on the topic of how hard it is to be a woman poet.[5] The activist and interventionist element in Sigourney's elegiac poetry—an element that by all accounts succeeded in its intentions—also seems to tell against Ann Douglas (Wood)'s construal of Sigourney's death poetry: its "heroine was herself, but emptied of conflict, sublimated, and desexualized . . . a small figure . . . seemingly submissive, submerged, half-hypnotized and half-automaton." Further, that activist element qualifies Richard Broadhead's Foucauldian speculations on the antebellum construction of women readers as isolated and passive consumers of mass-produced literary goods. Without denying that such a reading practice may have existed, I would see it as only one of a range of practices; the memorial poem that forms part of the public occasion of the funeral, and is then used, reused, and adapted by successive groups of mourners who find it pertinent, implies another kind of reading (Douglas, "Mrs. Sigourney" 17–71; Broadhead, "Sparing the Rod" 67–96; Broadhead, "Veiled Ladies" 273–94).[9]

In terms of a self-conscious poetics, Sigourney's elegies might be setting themselves against a male model of romantic egoism or a stereotype of women as withdrawn in narcissism. Thus, even were we to characterize Sigourney with reference to her funerary verse alone, we would need a less homogeneous and implicitly contemptuous representation of her project. But her other poetry and her prose writings provide materials for the construction of a very different Sigourney. This different Sigourney is what I call a "Republican public mother," a phrase applicable of the self-presentation of many literary women active in the early national years. Whereas the type of Republican mother made familiar to us by historians of American women in the post-Revolutionary era (a woman who carries out her civic duties by training her children in patriotism and republican values) performs her activities in the home space, "Republican public mothers" are public figures. As writers, they aim to enter the public sphere and influence the formation of public opinion. Sigourney's non-elegiac writings often take public positions and make public statements; she is by no means a "sentimental domestic," to use Mary Kelley's phrase.[7]

Even where titles like *Letters to Young Ladies, Letters to Mothers,* and *Whispers to a Bride* might seem to imply the Victorian female world of love and ritual or the Cult of True Womanhood, the content reveals something much more political and much less emotional.[8] In these books, Sigourney's domestic ideology is inseparable from patriotic and republican politics. In the often-reprinted *Letters to Young Ladies,* for example, she writes that "the foundation of the unity and strength of all nations is laid in the discipline of well-ordered families; and the consistency and beauty of a well-balanced character may be resolved into the element of self-control"; that "to a republic, whose welfare depends on the intelligence and virtue of the people, the character and habits of every member of its family are of value"; that "women possess an agency which the ancient republics never discovered"; and, finally, that women, in return for all that America has given them, owe it to their country to give their "hands to every cause of peace and truth, encourage temperance and purity, oppose disorder and vice, be gentle teachers of wisdom and charity" (125–43, 144–45).[9] The motherly persona adopted by Sigourney in her advice books contains a significant Spartan element in her makeup, and her advice authorizes—indeed, urges—women to move outside of the home when the cause is right.

Sigourney herself, in her many historical writings, moved well beyond the halfway literature of domestic instruction (halfway, that is, between the private and public realms) into a clearly public sphere. Like many women educators in the early years of the century, Sigourney—who taught school for several years before her marriage in 1819—saw history as the core of a republican woman's education, so that in some sense the domestic preceptress and the historian are facets of the same female construction. In *Letters to Young Ladies,* she writes—quite conventionally—that fiction should be eschewed and history embraced: "History has ever been warmly commended to the attention of the young. It imparts knowledge of human nature and supplies lofty subjects for contemplation" (65). Her memoirs recall her pleasure in unfolding with students "the broad annals of History. Seated in a circle, like a band of sisters, we traced in the afternoon, by the guidance of Rollin, the progress of ancient times, or the fall of buried empires" (*Letters* 203). But, as a writer rather than a teacher of history to girls, Sigourney is more directly part of the polity, for historical writings construct a view of the public sphere that extends well beyond women, and they aggressively comment on it. It would appear, in fact, that well over half of what she published in both prose *and* poetry was historical in content; and it was also political—in a fairly conventional sense of the term—in implication. Through the learning, teaching, and writing of history, Sigourney, like a number of other literary women between 1790 and the Civil War, enacted womanly behavior that in many ways nullified the distinction between public and private that operated so crucially in other contexts.[10]

The subject matter of Sigourney's historical writing is of four types: ancient and Biblical history; the local history of the region around Hartford, Norwich, and New London, Connecticut, from settlement through Revolution; the American Revolution;[11] and the history of the American Indians after the European arrival on the continent. Although she wrote numerous biographical sketches of exemplary women, she did not attempt to construct a separate history of women; indeed, her progressive Christian view suggested that women only very recently had emerged as a force in history. There is history in Sigourney's short poems and long poems; in sketches of varying lengths; in free-standing and embedded fictional narratives; and in a variety of nonfictional modes, including biography, narrative history, and children's textbooks designed for school or home use.[12]

The only work from this sizable segment of Sigourney's output previously excavated and analyzed is the 1824 *Sketch of Connecticut, Forty Years Since* (Hartford: Oliver D. Cooke). An important essay by Sandra A. Zagarell describes the *Sketch* as "quite directly concerned with the foundations and organization of public life," with a vision that "deliberately extended official definitions of the nation to imagine an America grounded in inclusiveness and communitarianism."[13] Since the sketch features real events from the past, I take it to be a work of history which indeed has public intentions. But rather than psychologize those intentions, as Zagarell does, I prefer to historicize them. Then, Sigourney's politics emerge as a self-conscious advocacy of the tenets of "classical" (i.e., conservative) republicanism in an age of increasing liberalism; as an urging of the merits of nonsectarian evangelical Christianity on an increasingly disputatious and fragmented religious scene; and as an effort to reconcile the civic with the spiritual realms in an amalgam of Protestant Christianity and republicanism.[14]

The *Sketch* is designed to celebrate the benevolent aristocratic widow Madam L——, a woman whose charities and liberalities sustain a hierarchical republican community in productive harmony. Almost certainly it would have been recognized as a political counterstatement to the Scotswoman Anne Grant's intensely Tory and anti–New England *Memoirs of an American Lady: with Sketches of Manners and Scenery in America, as they existed previous to the Revolution,* a work similarly configured around a benefactress recalled from childhood; that book had its American publication in Boston in 1809. The real-life model for Sigourney's *Sketch* was Jerusha Talcot Lathrop, widow of Daniel Lathrop, a prosperous druggist of Norwich. Until Madam Lathrop died in 1806, Sigourney's father, Ezekial Huntley, was gardener and general handyman on her estate. After her death, the family of a nephew, Daniel Wadsworth, took an interest in the Huntleys and in Lydia in particular (see n1). Sigourney's own life history, then, would have confirmed to her the efficacy of a moral republicanism wherein the fortunate supported the virtuous poor by giving them opportunities to support themselves.

This conservative republican theme is sounded at the very start of the sketch, with its evocation of the town of N—— [Norwich] as site of "the singular example of an aristocracy, less intent upon family aggrandizement, than upon becoming illustrious in virtue" (4). Unlike other sections of the country in the years immediately following the Revolution, Connecticut experienced no "agitation" because "the body of the people trusted in the wisdom of those heroes and sages of whom they had furnished their proportion. They believed that the hands, which had been strengthened to lay the foundation of their liberty, amid the tempests of war, would be enabled to complete the fabric, beneath the smiles of peace" (16). Madam L——'s contribution to the fabric, as a woman of social prominence and fortune, is to disburse appropriate charity and thereby maintain harmonious relations among the social classes. She gives out money, food, clothing, jobs, and advice to the deserving poor around her, in return for their loyalty and subordination.

Madam L——'s beneficence usually succeeds in producing a peaceful and cohesive community, and is especially effective with marginalized women. As one impoverished woman is made to say, "What a blessed thing it is, when the hearts of the rich are turned to give work to the poor, and assist them to get the necessaries of life, for themselves and families" (73). But with the Indians, the story is different. And nine of the eighteen chapters of the *Sketch*—fully half of the book—are about the remnant of the Mohegan tribe. In chapters 12 and 13, two tribal leaders—its chief and its Christian minister—inform Madam L—— that most members of the tribe have decided to leave N—— and move to the interior, where they will unite with another tribe. This decision shows that Madam L——'s charities are insufficient and beside the point where Indians are concerned. Individualistic Indians cannot accept a position at the bottom of a class hierarchy, which is where the community of N—— places them. Their distaste for settled agriculture makes it impossible for them to survive on their reservation, which "would have been more than adequate to their wants, had they been assiduous in its cultivation" (31). Most of all, they believe—they know—that the whites are determined to exterminate them (always excepting Madam L—— herself), and after experiencing a century and a half of violence, they have given up all thought of resisting. Their move is only a stopgap. "Ere long, white men will cease to crush us, for we will cease to be" (160). Occum, the minister, insists that Christianity holds promise for Indians, but Robert Ashbow, the chief, counters that "Christianity is for white men" (161). As they depart, one young warrior asks despairingly, "Whither shall we go, and not hear the speech of the white man?" (173).

In fact, of the four historical subjects that most concerned Sigourney, the American Indians ranked foremost. The history of her own region and Indian history were in some sense identical: the Pequod War had been waged there, the Mohegans had fought with English settlers first against the Pequods and then against the Narragansetts, and the Mohegan chief Uncas was supposed to have given the land around Norwich to the English in exchange for protection from King Philip and other enemies. This history meant that the establishment of the Christian American community, which Sigourney extolled in the *Sketch of Connecticut* and elsewhere, depended directly on white access to Indian land.

Sigourney drew from this history the moral conclusion that the Anglo-American national character was defined by how whites acquired the land they needed and what happened to the Indians afterwards. In writing about the Indians, she confronted an insoluble narrative problem: while three of her subjects were representable as comedies (the pagan world gave way to the Christian; the American Revolution was won by the right side; the Connecticut Valley fostered the most moral society ever known on earth), the fourth was an unmitigated tragedy. Sigourney also faced the insoluble *political* and *moral* problem that the triumphs of Christianity and republicanism in America were achieved at the cost of betraying their own basic tenets. In destroying the Indians rather than domesticating them, republicanism ignored its commitments to civic virtue and to the amelioration of the lot of the needy by the fortunate; Christianity neglected its imperatives of charity and of taking all souls as equals before God. Sigourney's historical writings are internally fractured because their attempt to affirm the progress of history is continually frustrated by the evident failure of Christian-Republican ethics to meet the single most important test of the moral caliber of the American nation—

the obligation to preserve the continent's "aborigines" by Christianizing them and integrating them into American society.

The *Sketch of Connecticut* concludes, for example, with three fantasy chapters given over to the story of Oriana, a beautiful white woman whose life has been saved in war by a Mohegan warrior who adopts her to replace his own dead daughter. In this allegory, the historically documented Indian behavior of welcoming, feeding, and protecting the original white colonists, wherever they set foot on American soil, is reciprocated by Oriana's willingness to become a daughter of the Indians and to help Christianize them. At the same time, the story neutralizes a fear widespread in society: that white people—especially women—who were adopted into Indian tribes became hopelessly Indianized. Oriana stays white, buoyed by a radical Christianity that leaves republican ideology, even as practiced by the exemplary Madam L——, completely out of the picture. Sigourney's fondness for this segment of the *Sketch* may be seen in the fact that she republished it as "Oriana" in her twice-reprinted *Sketches*.

In contrast to the imaginary Oriana's example, the core story of American Indian history after the European arrival, as presented in Sigourney's writings, is one in which Indian generosity is answered by European brutality. A paradigm of this narrative occurs in a short poem called "The Indian's Welcome to the Pilgrim Fathers," which appeared in *Zinzendorff* and reads in part:

When sudden from the forest wide,
    A red-brow'd chieftain came,
With towering form, and haughty stride,
    And eye like kindling flame:

No wrath he breath'd, no conflict sought,
    To no dark ambush drew,
But simply *to the Old World brought,*
    The welcome of the New.

That *welcome* was a blast and ban
    Upon thy race unborn.
Was there no seer, thou fated Man!
    Thy lavish zeal to warn?

Thou in thy fearless faith didst hail
    A weak, invading band,
But who shall heed thy children's wail,
    Swept from their native land? (47–48)

Sigourney's narratives of the Indian disaster lead to the culminating plea that her countrymen should return to the essence of republican and Christian doctrine and stop destroying the Indians by murder and relocation. But this plea undermines the affirmative dynamic of her other historical representations by substituting an implicit declension model of American and Christian history; and it does this without mitigating in the least the unrepublican and un-Christian carnage that has already taken place. From her historical perspective, the cessation of Indian destruction in the future—though it is much to be hoped for and though her writings are in part designed to further that goal—could not justify or erase past massacre. Whatever happened in future, that is, it was necessary to remember what had happened in the past. Unwilling to adopt a tragic or ironic stance toward history (though she could not always avoid doing so), Sigourney could not accept the palliating conviction found in so many writings of the time that the destruction of the Indians was merely inevitable. Convinced that a Christian must see the Indians as human kin, however "other" they may be, she could not write a history in which their obliteration could be presented frankly as a sign of historical progress.

There is no honest way to resolve her dilemma, so Sigourney's Indian narratives typically end with a forthright contradiction. "We are struck with the prominence and discordance of some of the features in the character of our ancestors," she writes in a prose sketch called "The Fall of the Pequod." Boldness, cruelty, and "the piety to which they turned for sanction, even when the deed and motive seemed at variance," make a strange combination:

> The unresting vigilance with which they blotted out the very name of Pequod . . . was not less arbitrary than the dismemberment of Poland, and savored more of the policy of heathen Rome than of Christ. Mason, in common with the historians of that age, bitterly blamed the Indians for stratagems in war, but chose to adopt the creed he had denounced, and to prove himself an adept in the theory that he condemned. . . . The once-powerful aboriginal tribe . . . perished without a hand to write its epitaph: an emblem of the fate of that vanishing race to whom the brotherhood of the white man hath hitherto been as the kiss of Judas. (*Myrtis* 137–38)

No doubt, some might see prose like this as intellectually confused. But it equally well could be described as intellectually forthcoming, in a political setting where crude hypocrisy and debonair obfuscation were the order of the day.

"Traits of the Aborigines of America," which preceded the *Sketch of*

Connecticut by two years, was Sigourney's first work about American Indians. Despite its bland title and its anonymous publication, this five-canto work of four thousand blank-verse lines, with extensive scholarly annotation, is her longest and most ambitious poem, packed with classical references and historical allusions, and dense with information about Indian tribes.[15] This poem ought to be considered a belated entry in the competition for "the" American epic. It is uniquely structured from the Indian point of view, and its narrative extends beyond the territorial United States to include the story of the North American continent, from the Arctic Circle to South America. This story, regardless of where it transpires, is always the same: the Indians welcome the newcomers and are exterminated.

Canto I begins with the Indians in undisturbed possession of the continent and then introduces a chronicle of incursion: "First, to their northern coast / Wander'd the Scandinavian" (I, 253–54). After a while Columbus comes—the Indians thought he and his men were Gods, "nor dream'd their secret aim / Was theft and cruelty, to snatch the gold / That sparkled in their streams, and bid their blood / Stain those pure waters" (I, 44–47). Portuguese, French, Irish, English—everybody comes. Christians come, too, bringing the potential benefit of their religion to the Indians. But that benefit does not develop, because the Christians do not behave like Christians.

In Canto II, incursions become more extensive and frequent: "Almost it seemed / As if old Europe, weary of her load, / Pour'd on a younger world her thousand sons / In ceaseless deluge" (II, 8–11). The bulk of the canto narrates the life of John Smith, allowing the poet to provide, through a chronicle of his travels, a geography and history of most of the world. Pocahontas's rescue of Smith is compared to the rescue of Moses by Pharaoh's daughter—with the same ultimately disastrous effect on her people: "little thought / The Indian Monarch, that his child's weak arm / Fostered that colony, whose rising light / Should quench his own forever" (II, 1093–96). Sigourney vacillates between comic and tragic interpretations of the narrative, and simultaneously avoids and intensifies both readings by focusing on the conversion and early death of Pocahontas herself. There is some unspecified and contradictory connection between the conversion and the death—on the one hand, it seems that Christianity itself is what kills Pocahontas; on the other, that, thanks to her conversion, she dies regenerate. The canto ends with brief attention to the founding of Pennsylvania, Delaware, and Florida, always from the vantage point of those who are forced out by European settlement: "Pressing west / O'er the vain barrier, and retreating tide / Of Mississippi, spread our ancestors, / Taking a goodly portion, with the sword, / And with their bow" (II, 1186–90).

Canto III positions itself with the Indians, now outcast and under-standably hostile, in their various forest refuges. It describes many in-stances of savage warfare and contains a ringing attack on whites for their instigatory barbarism as well as their hypocrisy in faulting the Indi-ans: "Who are these, / Red from the bloody wine-press, with its stains / Dark'ning their raiment? Yet I dare not ask / Their clime and lineage, lest the accusing blasts, / Waking the angry echoes, should reply / 'Thy Countrymen!'" (III, 905–10). Sigourney's target here is the truism that In-dians were naturally vengeful. She shows that they are naturally gener-ous and reveals the truism as a white construction, part material (the Indians are responding self-defensively to white brutality) and part rhe-torical (the Indians often are misrepresented as vengeful when their be-havior is anything but that).

Canto IV, the shortest in the poem, begins by praising the few mis-sionaries—Eliot, Heckewelder—who went among the Indians to preach Christianity, but gives most of its lines to Tuscarora, who mocks those of his tribe who want to convert:

Behold! what glorious gifts
Ye owe to white men. What good-will and peace
They shed upon you! Exile and the sword!
Poisons and rifled sepulchers! and see!
They fain would fill the measure of their guilt
With the dark cheat of that accursed faith
Whose precepts justify *their* nameless crimes,
Your countless woes. (IV, 348–54)

The point that Sigourney is after here is that the whites have created not only justifiable Indian hostility toward them as a group, but hostility as well to the Christianity that they claim to represent. The necessary task of joining with the Indians in brotherly love has been made infinitely more difficult by the white people's betrayal of their own religion.

Canto V then departs from the historical record to urge on Christian Americans the true obligations of their Christianity: "Make these foes your friends" (V, 546–47). The narrator acknowledges that most living Indians already are demoralized and degraded, and sees the possibility—albeit at some horrendously bloody cost to themselves—of the whites com-pletely exterminating the Indians. But she argues vehemently that "our God hath made / All of one blood, who dwell upon the earth" (V, 406–7); the only important difference between red and white people is that whites are (supposedly) Christian. Their very religion requires whites to Christianize the Indians. And when the Indians also become Christians, their justified desire for revenge will be set aside; they will then become an integral part of the American republic, and that republic, though no longer purely white, will be purely Christian.

Not the least interesting aspect of "Traits" is its continual recourse to references from what the era called "Universal History," simultaneously to heroicize the Indians and deheroicize the Europeans. At various points in the poem, the Indians are likened to, e.g., "stern Regulus" (I, 60); "the warlike Earl, stern Steward" (I, 208); "the Scythian tribes" (I, 224–25); "sublime Demosthenes" (II, 143); "the impetuous Hannibal" (III, 535); and "the stern, Spartan lords" (III, 656). Sometimes Sigourney accompanies these comparisons with the lament that the Indians—as valiant, noble, and eloquent as these historical figures—are doomed to extinction *without a history*, and hence are to be consigned to oblivion rather than remembrance. Sometimes she interrupts the Indian narrative for long accounts of historical carnage that far exceed anything that the Indians have perpetrated: "O'er the tow'rs / Of lofty Ilion, wreck'd by Grecian wiles, / Why does the dazzled eye prolong its gaze / In breathless interest, yet averts its glance / Disgusted, and indignant, at the scenes of Indian stratagem?" (III, 721–26).

Sigourney's missionary perspective is, of course, culturally chauvinistic. It depends on an idea of the Indians' likeness to whites, rather than of their dignity in difference; it also assumes that Indian culture is inferior to that of whites because it is not Christian. But, as we have seen, Sigourney is much more critical of white culture for failing to live up to its Christian ideals than it is of Indian culture with no such ideals to guide it. Overall, indeed, "Traits of the Aborigines" makes public demands on white American society that, at the time, were thoroughly Utopian. In the memoir written some forty years later, Sigourney dryly observes that the poem "was singularly unpopular, there existing in the community no reciprocity with the subject." But her own views had not changed in the intervening years: "Our injustice and hard-hearted policy with regard to the original owners of the soil has ever seemed to me one of our greatest national sins" (*Letters* 327).

The poem that gives the *Zinzendorff* (1835) volume its title is another work about Indians. The 584-line annotated poem in blank verse centers on the mission of Count Zinzendorff, founder of the radical Christian Moravian sect, to the Indians of the Wyoming Valley in 1742. It praises Zinzendorff for going among Indians whose experience with whites makes them deeply suspicious of him. "Sought he to grasp their lands? / To search for gold? to found a mystic throne / Of dangerous power?" (lines 100–102). Zinzendorff's peaceful persistence and his appeal to the women, children, and old people of the tribe, as well as the evidence of his remarkable escapes from plots against his life, persuade the Indian rulers to take his message seriously.

Sigourney begins this poem with a brief mention of a much-written-about incident of the Revolution, the Wyoming Valley massacre of 1778, in which allied Tory Pennsylvanians and Indians slaughtered emigrant patriot settlers from Connecticut. She explains that white appropriation of Indian land in the decades before the massacre had aroused Indian hostility and thus actually was the cause of the massacre. Zinzendorff, in contrast, had gone among the Indians with only Christian motives. When, toward the end of the poem, the Indians are made to lament Zinzendorff's return to Europe, their grief is interpreted by the poet as prophetic of their future at the hands of people who will settle with self-aggrandizing rather than self-effacing intentions (lines 495–505). In brief, Zinzendorff's was the road not taken. The poem closes with an appeal to Christians to desist from sectarian controversy and unite in peaceful missionary activities among the Indians. There may still be time, the poem says, to reverse history's direction and bring Indians into the nation.

Sigourney wrote another piece about the Wyoming massacre, the "Legend of Pennsylvania," collected in *Myrtis*. She begins with the history that led to carnage: "The Connecticut colonists evinced their national courage and tenacity in defense of their homes, and what they deemed their legal possessions. The Pennsylvanians were equally inflexible in what they considered their antecedent rights. The Aborigines contended for their favorite dominion with a lion-like despair" (179). One disaster after another is represented in the destruction of families and registered in the responses of surviving women. At the story's end, the last member of a once-thriving family of Connecticut pioneers in the valley joins the community at Nazareth, living out the rest of her life as a teacher in the girls' school there. The Moravians had an interest in women's education and founded some of the earliest boarding schools for young women in the country, facts that endeared them to Sigourney, who in later life looked back at her teaching years as the happiest she had known. In the poem, Sigourney typically invokes the pacific and womanly alternative to carnage.

The mood of "Pocahontas," published in *Pocahontas, and Other Poems* (1841), is not hopeful. The 504-line poem, in fifty-six modified Spenserian stanzas, recounts the life of Pocahontas as a memorial to the Indian princess. Although American literature by 1841 was full of tributes to her, Sigourney puts a recognizable stamp on the story material. She begins as she had begun "Traits of the Aborigines," in the New World before the Europeans arrive, taking an assumed Indian perspective. Apostrophizing the "clime of the West," she asks whether it was not "sweet, in cradled rest to lie, / And 'scape the ills that older regions know?" An entrance into history, long deferred, begins when the "roving hordes of savage men" look up to "behold a sail! another, and another!"

She sounds her motif of Christian brotherhood: "What were thy secret thoughts, oh red-brow'd brother, / As toward the shore those white-wing'd wanderers press'd?" And when Powhatan, moved by his daughter's intercession, spares John Smith's life, Sigourney notes the ironic outcome of that event, using the same comparison to Pharaoh's daughter that she had made in "Traits" (stanza 20).

"Thou wert the saviour of the Saxon vine, / And for this deed alone our praise and love are thine" (stanza 21), Sigourney says, once again stressing the self-destructive, ironically Christian tendency of the Indians to nurture and protect white intruders. Then, moving forward in time to the era of Indian surprise attacks on white settlements, she challenges the historians' accounts: "Ye, who hold of history's scroll the pen, / Blame not too much those erring, red-brow'd men, / Though nursed in wiles. Fear is the white-lipp'd sire / Of subterfuge and treachery. 'Twere in vain / To bid the soul be true, that writhes beneath his chain" (stanza 24). The whites, answering Indian generosity with oppression and dislocation, created the vengeful Indians whose behavior they now slander and use as a pretext for further incursions against them.

The poem then chronicles Pocahontas's capture, conversion, marriage, journey to England, and early death; but it refers beyond this personal narrative to another, larger narrative—especially when it returns at the end to the long view with which it began, and addresses the Indians en masse:

> I would ye were not, from your fathers' soil
> Track'd like the dun wolf, ever in your breast
> The coal of vengeance and the curse of toil;
> I would we had not to your mad lip prest
> The fiery poison-cup, nor on ye turn'd
> The blood-tooth'd ban-dog, foaming, as he burn'd
> To tear your flesh; but thrown in kindness bless'd
> The brother's arm around ye, as ye trod,
> And led ye, sad of heart, to the bless'd Lamb of God. (Stanza 54)

I wish we hadn't, but we have—this is undoubtedly a weak, sentimental acknowledgment of national crime; but at least it is an acknowledgment. Sigourney's conventional memorializing of Pocahontas, savior and servant of the whites, leads to an invocation of those nameless Indian dead who heroically *resisted* white incursion—"King, stately chief, and warrior-host are dead, / Nor remnant nor memorial left behind" (stanza 56). Sigourney's poem memorializes them as well as Pocahontas.

All history writing, in Sigourney's literary approach to it, is a memorial to the past—not the past made to live again, not even a representation of the past, but a memorial of it. (And this point allows us to think of her elegiac verse as another, individualized, form of history writing.) Her writing about Indians can be seen as an attempt to influence the present moment in three ways. First, it argues for a sense of white responsibility toward the surviving remnants of Indian tribes. Second, it tries to ensure that the Indian story becomes a part of American history, no matter how badly the story reflects on the white conquerors. Third, it insists that the Indians are Americans. Here, her schooling in ancient history, with its chronicle of aggressor empires, culminating in the mighty yet decadent Rome, served as a storehouse of parallels for interpreting and representing more recent history. The conventional classical references through which the Founders historicized their vision of a nation became, when Sigourney treated the Indians, references rather to empire than to republic.

In the 1850s, Sigourney turned her attention to the West and the New England pioneers who were settling it. A long poem from this decade, "The Western Home," about a pioneer family from Connecticut settling in Ohio, features a stalwart Indian woman whose medicinal skills save the life of one of the settler children. Another work, the quasi-fictional, quasi-autobiographical *Lucy Howard's Journal* conjoins Lucy Howard, the New England heroine, with both a black and an Indian woman in an image of triracial (although inegalitarian) harmony. The historical strain in her writing continues to the end of her life, when *Letters of Life* returns to the Norwich of her girlhood, the beloved Madam L——, and the memories of early republican Connecticut that had animated the *Sketch* of 1822. Whether Sigourney was a "good" writer or not, she obviously was an important one in her own time; we will understand that time much better if we abandon a social construction of her based on extremely limited awareness of her work. In particular, that a writer with so obviously public a program should come down to us as the most private and domestic of antebellum women authors suggests the need to look again at the scope of antebellum women's writing.

Notes

1. Sigourney's first book was *Moral Pieces, in Prose and Verse* (1815). Daniel Wadsworth of Hartford arranged publication. The 721 subscribers (listed at the back) constitute a virtual roll-call of conservative leading families from Hartford, Fairfield, Farmington, Litchfield, Middletown, New Haven, New London, Norwich, Boston, Cambridge, Charlestown, Marblehead, Salem, and other Connecticut and Massachusetts towns.

2. Sigourney's memoir, *Letters of Life,* lists 56 books published in her lifetime, a few of these edited; *Letters of Life* makes the total 57. She says that

uncollected material from almost 300 different periods could produce several additional volumes (366). See also the only biography: Haight, *Mrs. Sigourney* 173.

3.   E.g., Tompkins alludes to "Mrs. Sigourney—who epitomizes the sentimental tradition for modern critics" (160). In *Notable American Women*—whose purpose, one thought, was to dismantle stereotypes—Gordon Haight says that "death was always her favorite theme—the death of infants, of consumptive children, of missionaries in Burma and Liberia, of poets and lunatics, of artists and sailors, of college students and deaf-dumb-and-blind girls. Her rhyming of pious truisms made a wide appeal and established a trade that newspaper poets have carried on prosperously" (*NAW* 3: 289). Students of American literature think that what Griswold did to Poe is a national calamity; for many, still, what biographers have done to women passes for urbanity and even (heaven help us) gallantry.

4.   "There were plenty of strong souls in the Victorian age whose 'piping took a troubled sound' when they chose to struggle with their doubts rather than drown them out with the cymbals of conformity" (Haight, *Mrs. Sigourney* 160).

5.   Walker briefly cites three Sigourney poems—two elegies and a poem praising Felicia Hemans—but centers the antebellum women's poetic tradition on Frances Osgood and Elizabeth Oakes Smith.

6.   For Watts, Sigourney's obituary verse registers but laments women's isolation from public life in antebellum culture (83–97).

7.   The elegies too are public poetry. On republican motherhood, see Kerber, *Women of the Republic,* and Norton. See also Kelley. On the literary figure of the "Republican public mother," see Baym, "Mercy Otis Warren's Gendered Melodrama"; and Baym, *Feminism.*

8.   I allude to two well-known essays: Smith-Rosenberg and Welter.

9.   My discussion draws on a reading of 18 of Sigourney's books and her comprehensive descriptive list of all of them in *Letters of Life* 324–65.

10.   Kerber, "Separate Spheres," treats the "separate spheres" as a discursive construct rather than an empirical fact and discusses its uses and limitations as a tool of cultural analysis.

11.   One of Sigourney's first pupils and a lifelong friend, Frances Manwaring Caulkins (whose name has disappeared completely from literary history) wrote two massive local histories of Norwich and New London and became the first (and for a long time the only) female member of the Massachusetts Historical Society; her work was in part inspired by Sigourney's teaching.

12.   For Sigourney's lesson books, see Sigourney, *Evening Readings in History,* "written with a desire of aiding a laudable custom, established by some of my particular friends, of devoting an hour in the evening to a course of reading with the younger members of their families, and examinations into their proficiency on the general departments of Education"

(v); and Sigourney, *History of Marcus Aurelius:* "This book was commenced as an assistant to parents in domestic education. Its highest ambition is to be in the hand of the mother, who seeks to aid in that most delightful of all departments, the instruction of her little ones" (iii). The bibliography in Haight, *Mrs. Sigourney,* misattributes Lydia Child's *History of the Condition of Women* (1837) to Sigourney.

13. Zagarell, "Expanding 'America'"; see ch. 3 of this volume. Zagarell, "Narrative of Community" 498–527, places Sigourney's *Sketch of Connecticut* in a female genre conformable to the paradigm offered in Gilligan.

14. For succinct descriptions of republican ideologies, see Kerber, "Republican Ideology"; and Appleby. On the religiocentric strain in antebellum New England writing, see Buell.

15. Sigourney says in *Letters of Life* that the poem "Traits of the Aborigines of America" was written two years before her marriage in 1819 (i.e., in 1817) but that its publication was delayed. Even the 1822 dates make this one of the earlier non-captivity publications on the Indian topic. Haight declares that it was Charles Sigourney's idea to annotate the poem and that he wrote the notes as well (*Mrs. Sigourney* 25; *NAW* 3: 289); Sigourney says only that her husband helped her revise the notes (*Letters of Life* 327).

Works Cited

Appleby, Joyce. "Republicanism in Old and New Contexts." *William and Mary Quarterly* 43 (1986): 20–43.

Baym, Nina. *Feminism and American Literary History: Essays.* New Brunswick: Rutgers UP, 1992.

———. "Mercy Otis Warren's Gendered Melodrama of Revolution." *South Atlantic Quarterly* 90 (1991): 531–54.

Broadhead, Richard. "Sparing the Rod: Discipline and Fiction in Antebellum America." *Representations* 21 (1988): 67–96.

———. "Veiled Ladies: Toward a History of Antebellum Entertainment." *American Literary History* 1 (1989): 273–94.

Buell, Lawrence. *New England Literary Culture: From Revolution Through Renaissance.* New York: Cambridge UP, 1986.

Douglas [Wood], Ann. "Mrs. Sigourney and the Sensibility of the Inner Space." *New England Quarterly* 45 (1972): 163–87.

Gilligan, Carol. *In a Different Voice: Psychological Theory and Women's Development.* Cambridge: Harvard UP, 1982.

Haight, Gordon. In *Notable American Women.* Cambridge: Harvard UP, 1971. 3: 289.

———. *Mrs. Sigourney: The Sweet Singer of Hartford.* New Haven: Yale UP, 1930.

Hale, Sarah. *Woman's Record*. 2nd ed. New York: Harper, 1855.

Kelley, Mary. *Private Woman, Public Stage: Literary Domesticity in Nineteenth-Century America*. New York: Oxford UP, 1984.

Kerber, Linda. "Separate Spheres, Female Worlds, Woman's Place: The Rhetoric of Women's History." *Journal of American History* 75 (1988): 9–39.

———. "The Republican Ideology of the Revolutionary Generation." *American Quarterly* 37 (1985): 474–95.

———. *Women of the Republic: Intellect and Ideology in Revolutionary America*. Chapel Hill: U of North Carolina P, 1980.

Norton, Mary Beth. *Liberty's Daughters: The Revolutionary Experience of American Women*. Boston: Little, Brown, 1980.

Sigourney, Lydia Howard Huntley. *Evening Readings in History: Comprising Portions of the History of Assyria, Egypt, Tyre, Syria, Persia, and the Sacred Scriptures; with Questions, Arranged for the Use of the Young, and of Family Circles*. Springfield: G. & C. Merriam, 1833.

———. *History of Marcus Aurelius, Emperor of Rome*. Hartford, Conn.: Belknap & Hamersley, 1835.

———. *Letters of Life*. New York: D. Appleton, 1866.

———. *Letters to Young Ladies*. Hartford, Conn.: P. Canfield, 1833.

———. *Lucy Howard's Journal*. New York: Harper, 1858.

———. *Moral Pieces, in Prose and Verse*. Hartford, Conn.: Sheldon & Goodwin, 1815.

———. *Myrtis, with Other Etchings and Sketchings*. New York: Harper, 1846.

———. *Pocahontas, and Other Poems*. New York: Harper, 1841.

———. *Poems*. Boston: S. G. Goodrich, 1827.

———. *Select Poems*. Philadelphia: E. B. & J. Biddle, 1847.

———. *Sketch of Connecticut, Forty Years Since*. Hartford: Oliver D. Cooke & Sons, 1824.

———. *Sketches*. Philadelphia: Key & Biddle, 1834.

———. "The Western Home." In *The Western Home, and Other Poems*. By Sigourney. Philadelphia: Parry & McMillan, 1854.

———. "Traits of the Aborigines of America. A Poem." Cambridge, Mass.: "from the University Press," 1822.

———. *Zinzendorff, and Other Poems*. New York: Leavitt, Lord, 1835.

Smith-Rosenberg, Carroll. "The Female World of Love and Ritual: Relations between Women in Nineteenth-Century America." *Signs* 1 (1975): 1–29.

Tompkins, Jane. "The Other American Renaissance." *Sensational Designs: The Cultural Work of American Fiction, 1790–1860*. New York: Oxford UP, 1985. 144–85.

Walker, Cheryl. *The Nightingale's Burden: Women Poets and American Culture Before 1900*. Bloomington: Indiana UP, 1982.

Watts, Emily Stipes. *The Poetry of American Women from 1632 to 1945*. Austin: U of Texas P, 1977.

Welter, Barbara. "The Cult of True Womanhood: 1820–1860." *American Quarterly* 18 (1966): 151–74. Rpt. in *Dimity Convictions: The American Woman in the Nineteenth Century*. Athens: Ohio UP, 1976. 21–41.

Zagarell, Sandra A. "Expanding 'America': Lydia Sigourney's *Sketch of Connecticut*, Catharine Sedgwick's *Hope Leslie*." *Tulsa Studies in Women's Literature* 6 (1987): 225–46. Adapted as ch. 3 of this volume.

———. "Narrative of Community: The Identification of a Genre." *Signs* 13 (1988): 498–527.

CHAPTER 5

The Politics of Survival:

Sara Parton's *Ruth Hall*

and the Literature of Labor

Kristie Hamilton

In an 1868 sketch, "The Working-Girls of New York," Sara Payson Willis Parton (Fanny Fern) writes in explicit opposition to "wax-doll theories" of women, asserting that "conservatism and indifference gaze through their spectacles at the seething elements of to-day, and wonder 'what ails all our women'" (*Ruth Hall and Other Writings* 347). Parton thus defines popular, reductive representations of womanhood as the products of political regressiveness, self-protective male privilege, and a recalcitrance among women, variously motivated, toward making public the conditions of women's experience: "Authors and authoresses of little, and big repute, have expressed themselves on this subject, and none of them as yet have begun to grasp it. . . . women—because they dare not, or will not tell us that which most interests us to know" (347). "Fanny Fern" will, she implies, exchange flesh for wax and progressivism for conservatism in this sketch, establishing an overt alliance with the working-class women of the 1860s who had begun a third wave of collective agitation for higher wages and improved working conditions (Kessler-Harris 75–85).

The first stage of Parton's revision of "wax-doll theories" is to distinguish along class lines the problems facing "our women." Having described the emotional neglect suffered by economically "fortunate" women, Parton turns to "what ails the working-girls," who begin the day in unventilated rooms in tenements:

> Now follow them to the large, black-looking building, where several
> hundred of them are manufacturing hoop-skirts. If you are a woman you
> have worn plenty; but you little thought what passed in the heads of these
> girls as their busy fingers glazed the wires or prepared the spools for
> covering them, or secured the tapes which held them in their places. *You*
> could not stay five minutes in that room, where the noise of the ma-
> chinery used is so deafening. . . . Five minutes! Why, these young crea-

tures bear it, from seven in the morning till six in the evening; week
after week, month after month, with only half an hour at midday to eat
their dinner of a slice of bread and butter or an apple, which they usually eat in the building. . . . (348)

This passage suggests that Sara Parton shared the aim expressed by one
working woman quoted in the *New York Sun* in 1863: "I do not see how
these grinding evils of small pay and unjust treatment from employers
can be remedied except by holding up to the public gaze and reflection
the names and places of business of those who are living on the tears,
pain and toil of the daughters of Free America" (qtd. in Kessler-Harris
79). Along with employers' exploitation of women laborers, Parton exposes the complicity of the middle-class woman, whose "indifferen[t]
gaze" is discovered to be shaded by her own interests as a consumer in
the materials labored over by the young women she ignores. While Sara
Parton never participated in organized political movements (Warren, Introduction, *Ruth Hall* xxxi), she here lends the authority and reach of
Fanny Fern's voice to working-class women's collective action.

"The Working-Girls of New York" reveals Parton's familiarity as well
with the specific arguments and rhetorical figures introduced to mainstream antebellum culture by labor activists. In fact, her representation
of factory women draws upon a revision of fictional techniques for writing American women's lives that had been initiated by factory women in
the 1840s, arising out of a movement to effect legislative change in the
face of increasingly exploitative practices by the owners of textile facto-
ries in New England. While Parton's "Working-Girls" may be her most
explicit intervention in labor debates, this sketch is not the first of her
works to show traces of a discourse of reform produced by members of
the working class. Yet, though the 1868 sketch could be termed a "political sketch," given its public articulation of a discourse being utilized
to effect socioeconomic and legal change, Parton's most important novel,
Ruth Hall (1855), which shares a number of the progressive strategies
and fictional formulations used by labor activists, was not received as a
"political novel." In this essay, I shall explore the politics of Parton's
novel as these shed light on the evolution of bourgeois formulations of
literature at mid-century in the United States.

Nina Baym has described the recurrent plot of "woman's fiction" as
a lesson in survival. The heroine "must learn to strike a balance between
total submission, which means self-denial to the point of death, and an
equally suicidal defiance. She has to learn how to comply as a practical
necessity, without being violated" (*Woman's Fiction* 37). In *Ruth Hall*,
Sara Parton reformulates the conditions of survival that Baym rightly
places at the thematic center of nineteenth-century women's texts. Her

novel stands as evidence that, by the 1850s, supernaturally authorized compliance[1] could be challenged as an inadequate model for women's subjectivity and agency. My essay intervenes in the feminist historical enterprise, inaugurated by Jane Tompkins's study of the politics of nineteenth-century American women's fiction, by further historicizing the terms of the analysis and by complicating the chronology it traces.[2] In *Declarations of Independence,* Bardes and Gossett observe that labor activism in the 1840s had little effect on antebellum bourgeois women's representations of factory labor. Therefore, following Baym's assessment (*Woman's Fiction* 46–47), they locate the emergence of class consciousness in the works of middle-class writers after the Civil War (10–11, 108–9). As a description of the majority of literary texts written by antebellum white, middle-class women, their view is accurate. However, by focusing on Parton, a middle-class writer who exhibits class consciousness and responsiveness to the issues placed in the cultural arena by labor activism before the Civil War, I wish to show that it had become possible for an urban writer at mid-century to *rethink* class difference. In fact, Parton's novel shows early signs of an emergent aesthetic reformulation of women's experience that originates in antebellum labor literature. *Ruth Hall,* with its incorporation of elements from texts shaped by conditions outside the middle class, suggests that discourses of power are interactive between classes. The novel thus challenges the assumption that literary conventions pass in only one direction—from white bourgeois writers to others.

By incorporating a "reconstruction of womanhood"[3] already deployed by activist factory women since the 1840s, Sara Parton made of *Ruth Hall* a text that transcended the boundaries that separated dominant antebellum constructions of "political" and "literary" discourse. Parton's novel, therefore, represents a shift in the politics of mid-nineteenth-century, middle-class "woman's fiction" as these have been delineated by late-twentieth-century feminist literary historians. At the time Parton wrote her first novel, the Cult of True Womanhood defined the standards against which antebellum women were measured (Welter), so that, even when middle-class women writers incorporated resistances to that role in their fiction, their narratives still were delimited by dominant cultural assumptions concerning woman's sphere and duties. By 1854, the year *Ruth Hall* was published, however, working-class women (seamstresses and factory workers) had gained the attention of the public by organizing, speaking, and writing in opposition to the abuse and exploitation of women facilitated by studiedly pleasant and increasingly narrow social and literary paradigms of women's experience. When working-class women wrote sketches about the hardships they endured, without the compensation of happy endings, their works were identified as "political" rather than "literary"—in part because these sketches were meant to encourage actual legislative change in the conditions of labor, and in part because they told stories that diverged from bourgeois domestic literary conventions. And while it had become more acceptable for women to produce "literature" by mid-century, it was considered "unlady-like," as one Lowell mill worker put it, for a woman to contribute publicly to a "political" debate (Foner 62). When read in the context of working-class women's writing, Parton's novel, often identified by twentieth-century critics as anomalous and progressive, may be seen to incorporate issues and narrative strategies that were perceived as political when discussed by antebellum women. Yet, Parton escaped the contemporary censure of being classed a "political writer" by creating a character, Ruth Hall, who embodied at once middle-class, "feminine" respectability and American individualism, even as Ruth's consciousness and values were transformed by a growing recognition of the collective vulnerability and subjection of women. Thus, an assessment of the politics of Parton's *Ruth Hall* must be an examination of the cultural-political interests in the mid-nineteenth century that directed the novel's evasion of the overtly political. It must also be an analysis of the fictive qualities in *Ruth Hall,* and of their origins in the "seething [social] elements of today." These qualities threatened to dissolve the antebellum literary/political binarism but also created the book's productive tensions, which made it controversially salable in the literary market of the 1850s.

The Voices of Industry and the
Politics of Literature

In the 1840s, an exploited population of working-class women in the textile mills of Massachusetts was confronted with the problem of how to engender communal identity and solidarity, not only among themselves but also across class lines. Mill workers could fight the dominant middle class's prejudice against working-class women by asserting their adherence to the domestic ideal—an attempt to prove that the conditions of factory work did not compromise their "womanly" dignity. This struggle for status would occur within the discursive field of domestic ideology. Alternatively, factory "operatives" could emphasize the material differences in the conditions of labor and those of middle-class leisure in order to expose corporate exploitation and to argue for improvements in such areas as the length of the work day, wages, and financial support during illness. The dilemma facing factory women was precisely how to measure and utilize the power of the "discursive" and the force of the "material" in order to dismantle the economic and ideological partitions between laboring and middle-class women.

The division within communities of factory workers about how best to portray life at the mills was made public in the mid-1840s. In Lowell, Massachusetts, the dispute became a self-conscious debate about whose interests were served by the representations of conditions at the factory appearing in the *Lowell Offering*. The *Offering*, published between 1840 and 1845, was a magazine, edited and eventually owned by factory women, that contained sketches, editorials, and poetry written by "operatives." Widely read and respected in Europe and the United States (Eisler 35, 41), it nevertheless was attacked by many factory women in the last year of its existence as an instrument of the corporation that owned the mills, because it deflected attention from problems in the factory system. The significance of the argument lies in the terms chosen to define the grounds of disagreement; charges of complicity with the corporation or, conversely, of excessive discontent are identified, respectively, with "literary" or "political" discourse. The writings of women in Massachusetts textile mills make it possible to examine these contested terms, not only in relation to what some might describe as a "theoretical" or abstract construct, but also within a specific set of historical circumstances.

On July 4, 1845, Sarah G. Bagley, who, as president of the Lowell Female Labor Reform Association, became the first woman labor leader in the United States, opened the debate by criticizing the *Offering* for giving "a false representation to the truth."[4] A dialogue ensued on the editorial pages of local newspapers between Bagley, along with other labor activists, and the editor of the *Lowell Offering*, Harriet Farley.[5] In her first letter to the *Voice of Industry*, Bagley and the *Voice* editors explained their position: "We hold the literary merits of the *Offering* in high esteem—it reflects much honor upon its talented conductors," but they went on to identify the periodical's "true character and standing":

> It is, and always has been under the fostering care of the Lowell Corporations, as a literary repository for the mental gems of those operatives who have ability, time and inclination to write—and the tendency of it ever has been to varnish over the evils, wrongs, and privations of factory life. (Foner 61)

This is the first example of a consistent identification by Bagley and her allies of the "literary" with the interests of capital and thus with the middle class. The metaphors in this passage are pointed; sketches in the *Offering* are "gems" in a "repository," or, to put it crudely, money in the bank for the Lowell Corporations. Inasmuch as they are characterized as "gems" instead of dollars, the sketches are represented as the tribute offered to a patron. Bagley provides an example of concrete ways in which the *Offering* contributed to the continued profits of the mill owners by citing one "Mr. Mellen, of Boston, [who] made an attack upon the operatives of our city, and as an argument in favor of our *excellent* rules, stated that we had the Offering under our control, and had never made one word of complaint through its columns" (Foner 62). In Bagley's view, then, these literary gems denied the need for change and excused the public from scrutinizing the factory system. The literary activity of writers for this corporate repository is cast as contingent upon the "ability" and "inclination" of the contributors, but, in the context of the ordinary factory worker's thirteen-hour work day, the weighted term here is "time."[6] That these writers have "time" to write under the "fostering care" of mill owners suggests their privileged status among workers and implies that the seemingly aesthetic choice to "varnish over evils, wrongs and privations" actually is conditioned by their privilege and its source.

Bagley posits an alternative to such practices in response to a published letter from Farley: "I have not the least objection to a controversy with Miss Farley on the *Offering*, although *she* has literary talents to which I lay no claim: but I have facts, and that is better" (Foner 67). In an anonymous piece written for the *Voice of Industry* (December 1847), an author recapitulates Bagley's analysis that the representation of factory life to the public is drawn more from dominant literary paradigms than from the actual conditions of factory work. Moreover, she points to the effect literary productions have on what can be seen by the audience whose interests factory work serves:

> Aristocratic strangers, in broad cloths and silks, with their imaginations excited by the wonderful stories—romances of Factory Life—which they have heard, have paid hasty visits to Lowell, or Manchester, and have gone away to praise, in prose and verse, the beauty of our "Factory Queens," and the comfort, elegance and almost perfection, of the arrangements by which the very fatherly care of Agents, Superintendents, Overseers, &c., has surrounded them. . . . They see the bright side of the picture, and that alone. (Foner 92)

The author suggests, then, that the literary mode of "romance" structures descriptions of the factory, so that narrative conventions override material evidence. The "romance of factory life" benefits the already privileged, providing a role and an angle of vision for "aristocratic strangers" that allows them to see the factory as a quaint setting for the heroines who populate their imaginations. The residual ideology of agrarian paternalism is translated through "wonderful stories" into a rationale for the hierarchy of the factory system.

The anonymous author of the passage above moves from "romance" to "reality" in the paragraph that follows:

> These lovers of the Romance of Labor—they don't like the *reality* very well—see not the pale and emaciated ones. They see not those who wear Consumption's hectic flush. They think little of the weariness and pain of those fair forms, as they stand there, at the loom and spindle, thirteen long hours, each! They know not *how* long these hours of toil seem to them, as they look out upon the fields, and hills, and woods. (Foner 92)

As the contrast between literature and facts, romance and reality, continues to provide internal structure for the author's argument, what is significant is the way she translates the real into discourse. The unspeakable in literary representations of labor is identified first as the physical effects of factory work and second as the psychic disturbance caused by the inability of factory workers to realize the promise of picturesque landscapes held out by romance. Literature is, in effect, called to task by this working-class woman for failing to acknowledge her condition and for failing to deliver the opportunity of which it claims to be a record and a pledge.[7]

Harriet Farley, who worked in the clothing trades and ultimately in the mills from the age of fourteen until she gained full-time editorship of the *Lowell Offering* (Foner 28), could not have been unaware of the differences and difficulties of a woman laborer's life, compared to that of a middle-class woman. However, her own successful socioeconomic ascent had been accomplished by minimizing those differences, building an ideological bridge between factory and parlor which would support the passage of a few to relative prosperity. With conviction, then, she rejects Bagley's point of view: "It is impossible for the *Offering* to benefit the corporations only, as it elevates the *character* of the operatives, and removes the unjust prejudices against them" (Foner 64, my emphasis). Placing the issue of factory women's "character" at the center of her argument, Farley accepts and advocates as the standards by which human worth is evaluated the abstract categories of morality and manners that empower the new middle class. Her words exemplify the power of bourgeois hegemony to shape the desires and goals of those among the poor and working classes who seldom reaped its benefits.[8]

From the tenuous subject position of a laborer aspiring to middle-class acceptance, Farley contains Bagley's differing representation of factory experience by distinguishing herself from the other woman along the dividing line between privacy and publicity—a boundary her antagonist was calling into question. Upon learning of Bagley's assessment of her editorial policies, Farley states her "disapprobation of any thing tending to bring the *Offering* into a *political* controversy. And this I dislike because I know, and can know but very little about party politics, and could not do myself or my cause justice in a discussion of this kind" (Foner 63, my emphasis).[9] Farley then goes on to clarify the difference between herself and "Miss B.": "I cannot make a speech, or talk politics, or speak of the factory system as she represents it, for it never seemed to me a 'durance vile.' . . . I never felt disposed to croak or whine about my factory life, and have endeavored to impose a cheerful spirit into the little magazine I edit" (Foner 65). Inscribed in the cultural perspective Farley articulates is the assumption that to criticize the factory system, "to croak or whine," is a political act, whereas to "impose a cheerful spirit" is not—because a "cheerful spirit" is the new literary "disposition" informing the early-nineteenth-century bourgeois aesthetic.[10] In dominant antebellum divisions of discourse, the "literary" was understood to occupy an innocent, neutral territory outside the "political" arena, because the former was made to be enjoyed privately, not to be used for a group's or "party's" interests. Farley's editorial policy established one way of preserving the *Offering*'s "literary" quality: "With wages, boards, etc., we have nothing to do—these depend on circumstances over which we have no control" (Foner 99, Eisler 36).

Sarah Bagley and her colleagues did not refute the claim that their writing was of a political nature; what they did deny, however, was Farley's assertion that hers was not. In a response to Farley, Amelia Sargent writes of the *Offering*: "[I]ts political character is such, as utterly to sink it in the estimation of every honorable mind, if once fairly displayed" (Foner 70). Bagley would later explain: "Led on by the fatal error of neutrality, it has neglected the operative as a working being. . . . [T]he very position of the *Offering* as a factory girls' magazine, precludes the possibilities of neutrality" (Eisler 40). That quality of the *Offering* which associated it in the minds of dissenting writers with the "literary" also was the magazine's claim to neutrality—its neglect of the operative "as a working being." To correct this "fatal error," women writers in activist periodicals began to fashion new stories of factory life, revising, as they did so, the literary conventions that misrepresented their experience and that omitted the "facts" they wished to publicize. The author who had placed in opposition the "Romance of Labor" and "*reality*" went on to trace, for instance, a paradigmatic history of "the pale and emaciated ones," who leave "their country homes" for the factory in order to support their aging parents or to put a brother through college. Preventable death, cast as waste and victimization, is the denouement of this story, as young women's "overtasked systems give way" from excessive

toil (Foner 92–94). In another sketch, the spatial and experiential boundaries of women's lives are redrawn when a young woman who arrives at
the "city of spindles" must bypass the conventional parlor welcome (e.g.,
Eisler 83) and go straight to the counting-room where "Regulation paper[s]"
are distributed. In the counting-room, the romanticized "fatherly care of
Agents, Superintendents and Overseers" (Foner 92) is revealed to consist
in their enforcement of "the tyrannous and oppressive rules" of the textile business (Foner 135). With such revisions of working-class narratives, labor reform writers re-presented living and working conditions in
Massachusetts textile mills.

At issue in the works of both reform writers and contributors to the
Offering was an imagined dichotomy, gaining currency in antebellum
culture, between manual and mental labor, a distinction that was being
naturalized, as Nicholas K. Bromell recently has explained, to justify "the
social distinction between the laboring and learned (or professional)
classes" (546). Thus, Farley's editorial and authorial adherence to the dictates of bourgeois literary convention may be seen as a strategy for prov-
ing that factory workers had the "deeper" capacity and inclination to
perform mental labor—hence her desire to avoid dwelling on the physical toil of factory work. Placing the condition of the body at the center of
discussion, Bagley and her colleagues directly challenged what Bromell
identifies as the "metaphysics" of the manual/mental split by offering evidence that this ideological division of labor depended upon the material
imposition of prohibitive physical requirements on manual laborers; readers were reminded that the mind and body were inseparable. The demise of the *Lowell Offering* for lack of local subscribers may indicate the
recognition on the part of most workers in the Lowell Mills that a literature which approved the status quo, emphasized internal improvement,
and idealized passivity actually worked against the betterment of conditions at the factory and thus was, after all, political.

Ruth Hall and the Publicity of Labor

When antebellum labor activists wrote, they placed at issue not only what
women could do, but also what the "literary" could do. Their writing
challenged dominant assumptions about the definition and function of
literature, which identified certain topics, spaces, and aims as off-limits
for women and, hence, for literature written by women. Nina Baym's
Novels, Readers, and Reviewers further illuminates antebellum critical assumptions about what constituted literature in its most recognizable form:

The kind of novel that reviewers thought the best . . . was one in which the world was detachedly contemplated and hence presented to the reader as an object from which detachment was possible. (213)

[R]eviewers distinguished sharply between ethicomoral content, which they thought to be transcendent, and sociopolitical content [identified as "advocacy"]. . . . The former represented the perfection of the genre, the latter a troubling and troublesome hybrid. (223)

The literary compositions by labor activists, therefore, would have been identified as "hybrid" advocacy literature; *The Offering* was fashioned by its editors to be recognized as more "perfectly" literary.

The majority of reviewers of Sara Parton's *Ruth Hall* did not read the book as an advocacy novel, even though the focus of negative criticism by male and female critics was defined by assumptions about what a woman's novel should and should not do (Warren, *Fanny Fern* 124–30). Parton had published *Ruth Hall* under the pseudonym "Fanny Fern"; yet, because her identity was exposed by an unfriendly former editor in the same month the novel was published (December 1854),[11] it was immediately read as autobiography and indicted for being "unfeminine" both in its satire of her family members and in its indulgence in unseemly "self-praise" (Warren, *Fanny Fern* 125). The transfer of critical attention from Parton's novel to her life, and more specifically to the question of her womanliness, blinded antebellum reviewers to the larger revisionary elements in the novel. As Joyce Warren points out, antebellum critics "found it almost impossible to envision the female protagonist as the same self-reliant hero" they could recognize in James Parton's *The Life of Horace Greeley* or Horatio Alger's *Ragged Dick* (Warren, *Fanny Fern* 139–42). Elizabeth Cady Stanton was exceptional in her recognition that "the great lesson taught in *Ruth Hall* is that God has given to woman sufficient brain and muscle to work out her own destiny unaided and alone" (*The Una*, Feb. 1855, qtd. in Warren, *Fanny Fern* 140). It was Stanton also who saw in Parton's work a collective political significance for women, when, in the same review, she described *Ruth Hall* as "a slave narrative" (Conrad 173), an analogy that had been deployed in the 1840s by activist factory women to articulate their exploitation by textile corporations.

When read in the context of novels written by middle-class women and men, Parton's appropriation of heroic individualism for women becomes apparent, as does her accommodation of the domestic ideal within this new woman's story.[12] Parton's novel thus clearly remains within the parameters of bourgeois literary conventions. However, when read in relation to working-class women's literature of the 1840s, the author's attempt to grapple with the unstable economic conditions and the ideological strictures and failures facing middle-class women locates *Ruth Hall's* plot on the literary-political borders redrawn by labor activists' texts. Such a comparative reading allows us to see Parton's novel as positioned between middle-class ideologies of domestic individualism and the rhetorics of collective agitation found in factory reform fiction. We may, that is, self-consciously place more weight on Stanton's identification of *Ruth Hall* as a novel of advocacy—a *political* novel, as that term would have been understood by the dominant culture at mid-century.

Parton's revisions of the middle-class domestic tale to make it speak to, as her subtitle suggests, "the Present Time" may be divided into six categories that recall the work of activist writers: (1) she challenges the domestic idyll and "womanly" passivity, (2) she relocates women in the public sphere, (3) she associates the interests of the patriarchy, capital, and middle-class exclusivity with the aestheticization of experience, (4) she thematizes "facts" and "reality," (5) she foregrounds the conditions of women's labor, and (6) she interrogates the collective as a practical and/or potential social model in antebellum culture. In these ways, *Ruth Hall* manifests a reconfiguration of the structures of feeling that had informed conventions of the sentimental novel for at least three decades. That is, read alongside women's labor reform literature, Parton's novel reveals a structure of feeling shared among some antebellum women that crosses class lines and discovers the historical circumstances that mark a discomposing of the counterpolitics of sentimental domesticity.[13]

Parton devotes the first third of *Ruth Hall* to the deconstruction of the middle-class ideal of love and marriage as promised sanctuary for women. By its very structure, then, Parton's novel becomes a critique of antebellum sentimental fiction that conventionally concluded with the marriage or projected marriage of the heroine. The happy ending, placed at the beginning of Parton's novel, is immediately and systematically dismantled. At the outset, Ruth's parents' marriage is shown to have been imperfect, so that Ruth's thoughts the night before her wedding are of gaining from her groom the love and security she had not found in her own home. From the premarital state of wishing only "that she might be loved" (*Ruth Hall* 13), Ruth moves through successive stages, described by Parton as "blissful dream[s]" (18), in which she also imagines for herself "the new freedom . . . [of] being her own mistress" (18, 28). Each "dream," however, is supplied with its own rude awakening: first, a cruel and selfish mother-in-law, then the death of a child, and finally the death of Ruth's husband, accompanied by the impoverishment of his wife and surviving children. Constructing a paradise before the fall, Parton has Ruth relocate from the city, where she had lived with her father and then with her in-laws, to the American pastoral ideal of the country home. Parton allows her character to realize the fullest elaboration of the domestic idyll and then shows this blissful arrangement to be contingent upon the physical and economic well-being of husband and children. The literary convention of the "happy ending" thus is reinstalled in history, and Parton has, in effect, begun her exposure of the middle-class version of "The Romance of Labor," which is to say that she has shown the "Romance of Marriage" to be built upon the insubstantial materials of hope, dream, and nostalgia. This romance carries no more guarantees than does that of the "far famed 'city of spindles'" for the women whom it seduces.

As in the literature of labor, Parton's representation of the contrast between "romance" and "reality" is figured as a removal from the pastoral countryside to the city. For Ruth Hall, this journey is one from the imagined privacy of her country cottage to the publicity of urban dwelling and financial need. Parton foregrounds the cultural inscriptions of class and gender on urban spaces that are figured in this geographical transition by making Ruth immediately subject to the collective male gaze of her fellow boarders:

> "JIM, what do you think of her?" said a low-browed, pigfaced, thick-lipped fellow, with a flashy neck-tie and vest, . . . "prettyish, isn't she?"
> "Deuced nice form," said Jim, lighting a cigar . . . . "I shouldn't mind kissing her." (73)

Despite Ruth's sound moral character—the internal signifier of bourgeois class affiliation that the *Lowell Offering* had sought to exhibit in factory women—the young widow Hall is open to sexual objectification as a "nice form" by virtue of both the kind of residence she occupies and her lack of a husband. The bourgeois dream(/scheme) of inviolable and legitimating privacy, which in urban geography was defined by the parlor (Haltunnen 167), is further debunked when the men who gaze at Ruth are joined by the landlady of the boardinghouse: "[T]his parlor is the only place I have to dress in; can't you do your talking and smoking in your own rooms?" (74). Parton's middle-class readers would have seen this redefinition of the parlor as the space where men smoke and women dress as a perversion of architectural decorum; they would understand that Ruth had been thrust into territory alien to True Womanhood. Directing her readers' response to Ruth's dilemma, however, Parton subordinates condemnatory characterization of some boardinghouse occupants to a more vituperative satire of the complicity of Ruth's privileged female "summer friends," who abandon her for fear of a loss of "caste" if they are "seen in such a quarter of the city" (82). Thus the problem presented by the boardinghouse is made as much the responsibility of the class that denies connection with it as of the class whose values are defined, in advance, by the building's disrepute.

Parton does not limit Ruth's public exposure to her new home, however; rather, she takes Ruth, her daughter, and women readers to the streets, to City Hall, and to a number of "counting rooms," all places which, according to the early-nineteenth-century division of space, were "beyond the pale of [middle-class] female jurisdiction" (74). Driven by the necessity of feeding her children, Ruth seeks employment as a seamstress, as a teacher, and finally as a writer, in each case experiencing "that feeling of utter desolation [that] came over her, which was always so overwhelming whenever she presented herself as a suppliant for public favor" (100–101). The extremity of Ruth's discomfort arises, of course, as much from being a woman in a masculine "sphere" as from being a "suppliant" (e.g., 122). Thus, for Parton as for activist working-class women, the first step to challenging the dominant narrativization of women's roles and limited powers was to invoke the predisposed outrage of a bourgeois audience at the prospect of women being forced into public spaces, especially counting rooms and offices, where they were understood to be subject to a transgression of the boundaries of their very womanhood. Whether, as is likely, Parton, Bagley, and others like them experienced this publicity as violation, the middle-class author, with her working-class sisters, reappropriates the public space into which she inserts Ruth as a place where women's subjectivity (not subjection), insight, and self-protection may be secured.

Throughout the novel, Parton places Ruth Hall in situations that point to the systematic exploitation and abuse of women by the social elite, the legal system, mental health institutions, boards of education, factory owners, men seeking prostitutes, and finally the literary establishment. In the process, she incorporates a recurrent association of oppressive corporate, patriarchal, and class interests with the aestheticization of experience that served to distract the public from grappling with women's hardship. Thematizing "facts" and "reality" in contrast to "romance," Parton makes her most powerful indictment of the institutional employment of aesthetic practices to mask harsh social discipline when Ruth and Katy happen upon the insane asylum where Mary Leon has been confined:

> "What is it on the gate? Spell it, mother," said Katy, looking wistfully
> through the iron fence at the terraced banks, smoothly-rolled gravel
> walks, plats of flowers, and grape-trellised arbors. . . . Fair rose the build-
> ing in its architectural proportions; the well-kept lawn was beautiful to
> the eye; but, alas! there was helpless age, whose only disease was too
> long a lease of life for greedy heirs. There, too, was the fragile wife, to

whom *love* was breath—being!—forgotten by the world and him in whose service her bloom had withered, insane—only in that her love had outlived his patience. (109)

Underscored by melodrama, this passage and the rest of the chapter make clear that the artfulness with which the asylum was made to evoke an inviting pastoral domesticity actually served the interests of a male-dominated, capitalist culture; the conditions of the people within its walls are subordinated to the pretty picture presented from without. Just as the anonymous Lowell activist had drawn her readers inside the factory to dispel the blindness created by the Romance of Labor, so Parton takes Ruth inside the asylum to reveal a woman chained and screaming for the child taken by her husband, with consent of the courts, because "the law is generally on the man's side" (111). Also inside, of course, is the corpse of Ruth's friend Mary Leon, whose husband had arranged for her confinement with his "intimate friend," the superintendent of the asylum (110).

The sight of the formerly beautiful Mary Leon's "emaciated form, . . . sunken eyes and hollow cheeks" (111) represents not only a turning point in the novel but a revision of literary convention as well. That Mary's note, read over a body so recently and evidently in pain, pleads for her rescue, makes the loss of her not that of a martyr who empowers those around her to sacrifice themselves for heavenly rewards, but that of a brutalized victim whose death could have been prevented were worldly power distributed differently. Parton's direction of reader attention toward the body, not the "character," of Mary Leon is evidence of the author's break with the dominant bourgeois constructions of women as either ornamental objects or receptacles of abstract virtues.

It is after Mary's funeral that Ruth makes her decision to write the newspaper pieces she eventually will collect in a book entitled *Life Sketches* (202). Parton's own revisionary aims are transferred to her fictional author when she sets Ruth's book in comparison with those published by her female contemporaries. As their titles imply, *Shadows, Sunbeams,* and *Fairyland* may reproduce the dreamscapes of romance (206) or, as Parton later articulates the effect in "Working-Girls of New York," they may promote "waxdoll theories" about women. *Life Sketches,* on the other hand, "have got the *real* stuff in 'em" and "call things by their right names" (135, my emphasis; 133).

Sara Parton's novel is not the first or only work of middle-class fiction to make reality claims. In 1797, Hannah Webster Foster had published *The Coquette* as "A Novel; Founded on FACT." Caroline Kirkland had sought to dispel romantic notions of the frontier experience by vividly depicting "Michigan mud-holes" in *A New Home—Who'll Follow?*

Alice Cary wrote her Clovernook sketches (1851, 1853) in direct opposition to "writers of romance," claiming that her representations of the "farming class" in Ohio were composed with the "simplest fidelity" (8). Harriet Beecher Stowe's *Uncle Tom's Cabin* was presented as "sketches drawn from life" ("Concluding Remarks," 618). However, despite their shared aim to make fiction a suitable vehicle for describing the conditions of "lived experience," these authors did not always share assumptions about what constituted the "real" or about how to integrate actuality into the sets of literary conventions made available to them by their culture. One of Sara Parton's most significant contributions to the development of middle-class white women's fiction lay in her explicit illustration, in Ruth Hall, that "wages, board, etc." (Farley) and the conditions of women's labor are the "real stuff" around which many women's days and nights revolve.[14] Thus, Parton shares with Sarah Bagley and members of the Female Labor Reform Association a conception of "reality," born of particular historical circumstances, which makes visible class differences, the institutions and practices that enforce them, and the details of women's wage labor.

If one part of Parton's project is to redefine women's work in the literary marketplace as labor and not avocation, her strategy is to position a formerly middle-class protagonist on an economic plane with other women who were struggling week by week to survive by the work of their hands. She takes on, that is, a challenge similar to that announced in the *Voice of Industry* nine years before: eschewing the neutrality of showing only "the bright side of the picture," she collapses the dominant bourgeois cultural division between manual and mental labor. Parton places Ruth in a number of locations and situations from which the protagonist may not only learn of, but also share the same plight and "quarter of the city" with

> poor emigrants and others, who were barely able to prolong their lease on life from day to day, . . . a tailor, . . . cutting and making coarse garments for the small clothing store in the vicinity, . . . a pale-faced woman, with a handkerchief bound round her aching face, bent over a steaming wash-tub, . . . a young girl, from dawn till dark, scarcely lifting the pallid face and weary eyes—stitching and thinking, thinking and stitching. (90)

This is not the conventional "woman's story," outlined by Nina Baym, of the poor orphaned girl who learns self-control and strategic silence and ultimately reaps the narrative reward of economically and socially privileged marriage. Ruth is an adult widow whose efforts to seek employment in a factory fail because her former friends cannot imagine her "among those girls" and because she has children whose presence or needs might disrupt factory discipline (80). Ruth therefore is forced to take in piecework—one of the few sources of employment for which immigrant women, free-born African-American women, and unmarried and widowed Euro-American women could compete in northern cities in the 1850s and 1860s (Kessler-Harris 46, 65). When Parton herself had worked as a seamstress before turning to authorship, women were being paid approximately six cents for every shirt produced, with ten shirts as the maximum number it was possible to complete in a week (Warren, *Fanny Fern* 325). Making her novel a record of this ongoing exploitation, Parton has Ruth describe her efforts to pay room and board by sewing: "'Only fifty-cents for all this ruffling and hemming,' said Ruth, as she picked up the wick of her dim lamp, 'only fifty cents! and I have labored diligently too, every spare moment'" (96). To describe the manual labor of what would have been recognized by antebellum audiences as a "lady" and then to name the wage for which that work was done may seem now only a small addition to the content of one novel at mid-century; however, this passage and others like it represented a sharp departure from the bourgeois literary conventions of the sentimental novel in 1854. While Ruth's character and gentility continue to define her as heroic, Parton makes the issue of money visible as well. Like the "young girl" with "pallid face" and "weary eyes," whose home likely has always been filled with the "odor of cabbage" (81), Ruth stitches and thinks, thinks and stitches.

Ruth's body, like those of her fellow boarders, comes to bear the inscription of the working class when she "bend[s] over the washtub, and rub[s] out her clothes and her children's . . . till the blood started from her knuckles . . . looking so pale about the mouth, and holding her hand to her side" (82–83). Yet Parton does not restrict descriptions of the effects of work on Ruth's body to the work done with her hands. Rather, she draws a clear analogy between Ruth's physical labor and the work of writing depicted in the latter half of the novel:

> Scratch—scratch—scratch, went Ruth's pen; the dim lamp flickering in the night breeze, while the deep breathing of the little sleepers was the watchword, *On!* to her throbbing brow and weary fingers. One o'clock—two o'clock—three o'clock—the lamp burns low in the socket. Ruth lays down her pen, . . . leans faint and exhausted. . . . and the overtasked lids droop heavily over the weary eyes. (126)

Whether the means of survival is manual or mental, the conditions of labor (length of workday and sufficient monetary compensation) are revealed by Parton to be the bottom line. While her aim may be to communicate to readers that middle-class women's bodies are at risk, her transference onto Ruth's "nice form" of the marks also born by the other tenement dwellers recalls their needs to the attention of readers as well. The others too had pale faces, aching brows, weary eyes, and weary fingers (90). Parton takes the analogy between Ruth's labor as author and the work of seamstresses (and laundresses) further, when she has Ruth discover her "market value" (142) after overhearing her first editors discussing ways to pay her less than she is worth to them (132). These scenes echo an earlier discussion between a sewing factory owner and his wife about a Mrs. Slade, who said "she couldn't drive as good a bargain with [these persons who 'had seen better days,'] as she could with a common person, who was ignorant of the value of their labor" (81). It is clear that Parton seeks to establish in *Ruth Hall* the collective exploitation experienced by workers, whose labor may go unremunerated if its value is not publicized by those who know it. In the process she collapses a central figuration, the manual/mental binarity, of class difference accepted in the dominant culture. Like Bagley, she reveals the material obstacles, one of which is the body itself, that can deter or prevent even those with talent from performing either mental or manual labor. Parton's conscious depiction of the interests that employees in the literary marketplace have in common with other laborers is further evident in a number of scenes throughout the book: when Ruth imagines typesetters to be working as late and as hard as she, and with the same motives (125); when domestic servants articulate the ethical response to Ruth's distress that the wealthier characters refuse (e.g., 65, 82–83); when a male author (Horace Gates) is shown to live the garret existence of an exploited worker; and when Johnny Galt, farmer *cum* fireman, remains a support to Ruth until he finally is made the hero of the "hairbreadth escape" that Parton, in her preface, had denied she would provide (199).

Given the patterns of labor solidarity that inform Parton's novel, it is feasible to see the climactic illustration of Ruth's rewards for her work, one hundred shares of Seton Bank stock, as, in part, a triumph for labor against corrupt corporate interests as well as for a woman battling patriarchal oppression. It would be a mistake, however, to pretend that *Ruth Hall* is not a novel about possessive individualism or to fail to suspect that, by making Ruth a stockholder, Parton reinforces a socioeconomic and indeed a literary paradigm that identifies success and happy endings with capital, if not marriage. After all, Ruth's independence was won in the field of professional writing, where relatively few such opportunities were available.[15]

I would like to conclude with what therefore at first may seem a perverse discussion of Sara Parton's novel as an interrogation of collectivity in antebellum culture, despite its apparent rejection of even the potentiality of such a social model. In *Ruth Hall*, Parton rejects or, more accurately, redefines the formulation of the collective that had become conventional in women's fiction. According to Nina Baym, "In novel after novel, a network of surrogate kin gradually defines itself around the heroine, making hers the story not only . . . of a self-made woman but . . . of a self-made or surrogate family" (*Woman's Fiction* 38). In *Ruth Hall,* however, this network of surrogates does not appear. Parton's gesture toward this convention is the character John Walter, who is frequently described by Ruth as fulfilling the role of "brother." But Parton makes Mr. Walter Ruth's editor as well; his "brotherly" attentions always are conditioned, therefore, by the business relationship. In this way, Parton refuses to return Ruth to the bourgeois "dream" of the heterosexual familial ideal which would negate her need for financial independence. The novel does, however, discover successful collective action in an unlikely location—that is, in the collaboration, or collusion, of lower- and upper-middle-class males. Despite Tom Develin's individualist assertion that "a man must look out for No. 1 in this world" (76), he promotes the interests of Ruth's father-in-law in order to achieve this end. Fathers and fathers-in-law collude, husbands become "intimate" with asylum superintendents, male judges side with cruel fathers, all-male school committees vote with the most powerful member, and male publishers promote each other's books and magazines or carry out collaborative negative campaigns, as the angry Mr. Tibbets makes clear to Ruth: "I have many an editorial friend, scattered throughout the country, who will loan me their column [to 'spoil the sale of your book']" (157).

While Parton depicts privileged men and male arrivistes cooperating with each other to their mutual benefit, she reveals middle-class women to be generally isolated and competitive with each other—an irony surprising only in light of antebellum ideologies of gender that projected the reverse as the ideal *and* as the actual. Acting upon individualized self-interest, a number of women characters in *Ruth Hall* reproduce and facilitate the oppression of other women. Ruth's mother-in-law, for instance, consistently seeks to undermine her; Ruth's friends do not wish to "lose caste" by helping her when she is poor; and her female cousin chooses to take advantage of Ruth's poverty, rather than aiding her. Outside Ruth's "private" circle, one character illustrates women's acceptance of male-identified definitions of female insanity, which Parton shows to have, in actuality, social and legal causes. *Ruth Hall* thus stands as a record, critique, and partial analysis of the mechanisms by which bourgeois domestic ideology effected the in-group surveillance and policing that would ensure the continued identification of womanhood with certain narrowly defined activities and with a particular socioeconomic status. All women who fell, or were forced, outside these limits could be dismissed as deviant. It is with such examples of middle-class women's

complicity in patriarchal oppression that Parton's novel begins to suggest the difficulties faced by antebellum feminists and women labor leaders. At mid-century, *Ruth Hall* makes clear, American middle-class culture not only resisted, but actively and ideologically subverted, collective
responses to social inequity, particularly when those mistreated were
women.

It is not surprising, then, to find that a middle-class woman in such a
culture could not imagine collective action as a practical option for re-
solving the kinds of crises on which Parton's plot turns. Thomas Dublin
has argued that it was, in fact, the unprecedented living and working
conditions at the Lowell mills (and elsewhere) that made the Female
Labor Reform Association thinkable for antebellum American women like
Sarah Bagley:

> It would have been much harder to go to work as usual when one's
> roommates were marching about town, attending rallies, and circulat-
> ing strike resolutions as they did in 1834 and 1836. Similarly the ten-
> hour petitions of the 1840s benefited from the existence of a tight-knit
> community of women workers in the dense boarding-house neighbor-
> hoods. . . . Group pressure to conform, so important in the daily life of
> women in early Lowell, played a significant role in shaping their col-
> lective protests as well. (85)

In light of Dublin's hypothesis, I suggest that Sara Parton's fictional construction of woman-identified "individualism" differed from the masculine
model because the former was a pragmatic strategy for survival resulting
directly from Parton's lived immersion in the anticollective ideologies that
impeded the development of large-scale, unified action among middle-
class women in the first half of the nineteenth century. In her "Domestic
Tale of the Present Time," Parton does offer a resolution, partly compen-
satory and partly practical, to the "present" social dilemmas facing nineteenth-century women: the children for whom Ruth sacrifices and succeeds
are depicted as daughters of an unconventionally *surviving* mother; these
daughters already have inherited their mother's strengths (Harris 126)
and also act in support of each other. The terse and striking description
of Mary Leon's funeral represents, then, a utopian rupture in the text,
encapsulating the familial and gendered collectivity imaginable by an
antebellum middle-class author: "ONLY THREE MOURNERS — a woman
and two little girls" (112). It is this form of female association that motivates
action instead of submission in Parton's work. Less radical than the collective protest promoted by antebellum working-class women, Parton's focus
on female kinship is perhaps the most important of a number of shrewd
negotiations of the "political" and "literary" boundaries by which Parton

sought to "fan into flame, in some tried heart, the fading embers of hope" (3). That the novel did not, or, more precisely, *could not* go so far as to call for "united action," despite the other characteristics it shares with the literature of labor, serves as a historical marker of the material, commercial, and ideological conditions by which dominant definitions of literature are delimited. The politics of *Ruth Hall* may not easily be defined either as bourgeois, domestic liberalism, or as democratic collectivism, for the book describes a culture in which neither can ensure a woman author's survival—or the future of her daughters.

Notes

I am grateful to the Center for Twentieth Century Studies, University of Wisconsin–Milwaukee, where I finished this essay while holding a Center Fellowship. For helpful suggestions on the essay, I am indebted to Gregory S. Jay, Shelli Booth Fowler, and Gareth Evans.

1. As Tompkins observes in her inaugural reconsideration of the politics of nineteenth-century American women's fiction, "If the general charge against sentimental fiction has been that it is divorced from actual human experience, a more specific form of that charge is that these novels fail to deal with the brute facts of political and economic oppression" (160). Against these claims, Tompkins argues that, in fact, "domestic fiction is preoccupied . . . with the nature of power" (160) and that, at mid-century, middle-class women writers consciously reconceptualized power by identifying its source as divine and its location as the home rather than the arenas of commerce, industry, and legislature. Middle-class women novelists constructed submissiveness and self-control as vehicles and proof of women's spiritual empowerment, publicizing a "revolutionary" alternative to patriarchal power structures for the resolution of social conflicts and questions (163–64).

2. In *Woman's Fiction,* Baym identifies Parton's departure from literary and social conventions in *Ruth Hall* (252–53). See also: Douglas [Wood], "The 'Scribbling Women'"; Harris's analysis of Parton's creation of alternating narrative voices and reader resistance to sentimental convention in *Ruth Hall* (111–27); Berlant's examination of Parton's sketches and novels as evidence of the "collaboration between the commodity form and the stereotype on behalf of a feminine counterpolitics" (431) that promotes reader consensus via appeals to a "generic woman" (444).

3. Carby argues that African-American women authors "reconstructed the sexual ideologies of the nineteenth century [from which they were excluded by definition] to produce an alternative discourse of black woman-

hood" (6). Her conclusions and methodology have changed the ways I teach and write about Afro-American and Euro-American women's fiction, and have influenced here my understanding of the differences among working-class and middle-class Euro-American women's texts.

4.   Qtd. in Foner 60. I owe much of my initial interest in and understanding of the history of Massachusetts factory women to Eisler, *The Lowell Offering,* and Foner, *The Factory Girls.*

5.   In 1845–46, Sara Parton and her first husband, Charles Eldredge, resided in Boston, some 33 miles from Lowell, where Eldredge was struggling to win a lawsuit, the loss of which in May 1846 left the couple deeply in debt (Warren, *Fanny Fern* 67–76). Boston periodicals such as Orestes Brownson's *Boston Quarterly Review* brought before the public the disputed advantages and disadvantages of factory work for women. In her recent biography, Warren offers no evidence that Parton was familiar with the *Lowell Offering* or the *Voice of Industry.* It is unlikely, however, that Parton could have remained unaware of the *Offering* or of the issues that informed the public dialogue about factory labor while living in the Boston area.

6.   In the *Voice of Industry,* 25 Sept. 1845, Amelia Sargeant testifies to Harriet Farley's having been given time off:

> Farley remarked that she . . . had never asked or received
> any favors whatever. . . . How happens it then, that the
> Company employed another person to take charge of her
> looms one half of the time, while she remained absent ar-
> ranging matter for the same Offering; . . . it must have been,
> as many already said, because they saw in that work a me-
> dium, through which to defend and strengthen their darling
> system of slavery and oppression [*sic*]. (Qtd. in Foner 71–72)

7.   The anonymity of this author quite probably is another effect of the mill system omitted from such "wonderful stories" about the factory, since women thought to be active in the cause of labor reform could be dismissed and blacklisted in all the mills in the area (Eisler 38, Foner xxiii).

8.   For biographical factors that would have led Farley to feel conviction for her position, see Foner 26–29, 325–27; Douglas [Wood], *Feminization* 69–71; Eisler 40. For socioeconomic conditions that complicated Farley's strategy and its effects, see Kessler-Harris, chapter 2 and especially chapter 3; Foner xii–xxv, 19–20; Eisler, Introduction; Dublin. For historical analyses of the "rise of the [male] American working class," see Wilentz; Laurie.

9.   Farley's subject position obviously is conditioned by the bourgeois construction of gender difference as well. For Bagley's exposure and refusal of Farley's gendered subtext, see Foner 62.

10. For example, in 1853, Alice Cary defended her *Clovernook, Second Series* against critics who "objected" that her "former series of sketches . . . [were] of too sombre a tone" (140).

11. Editor of the *True Flag,* William Moulton is believed to have been the author of *The Life and Beauties of Fanny Fern.* See Warren, Introduction xvi–xvii; Warren, *Fanny Fern* 126.

12. See Brown 137–45; Douglas [Wood], "The 'Scribbling Women'"; Harris 111–27; Kelley; Warren, *Fanny Fern* 130–42.

13. My argument is informed by Williams's explanation of "structures of feeling" (131–32).

14. Wilson's novel *Our Nig* would, in 1860, incorporate economic issues into its plot, reconstructing womanhood to insist upon acknowledgment of African-American experience. See Carby, ch. 3; Gates, ch. 5.

15. It should be noted that Parton maintained a textual distinction between Ruth and her working-class "analogs" by adhering to conventional stereotyped use of dialect or vernacular speech to mark difference.

Works Cited

Bardes, Barbara, and Suzanne Gossett. *Declarations of Independence: Women and Political Power in Nineteenth-Century American Fiction.* New Brunswick: Rutgers UP, 1990.

Baym, Nina. *Novels, Readers, and Reviewers: Responses to Fiction in Antebellum America.* Ithaca, N.Y.: Cornell UP, 1984.

———. *Woman's Fiction: A Guide to Novels by and about Women in America, 1820–1870.* Ithaca, N.Y.: Cornell UP, 1978.

Berlant, Lauren. "The Female Woman: Fanny Fern and the Form of Sentiment." *American Literary History* 3 (1991): 429–54.

Bromell, Nicholas K. "'The Bloody Hand' of Labor: Work, Class, and Gender in Three Stories by Hawthorne." 42 *American Quarterly* (1990): 542–64.

Brown, Gillian. *Domestic Individualism: Imagining Self in Nineteenth-Century America.* Berkeley: U of California P, 1990.

Carby, Hazel V. *Reconstructing Womanhood: The Emergence of the Afro-American Woman Novelist.* New York: Oxford UP, 1987.

Cary, Alice. *Clovernook Sketches and Other Stories.* Ed. Judith Fetterley. New Brunswick: Rutgers UP, 1987.

Conrad, Susan Phinney. *Perish the Thought: Intellectual Women in Romantic America, 1830–1860.* New York: Oxford UP, 1976.

Douglas [Wood], Ann. *The Feminization of American Culture.* 1977. New York: Anchor, 1988.

———. "The 'Scribbling Women' and Fanny Fern: Why Women Wrote." *American Quarterly* 23 (1971): 3–24.

Dublin, Thomas. *Women at Work: The Transformation of Work and Community in Lowell, Massachusetts, 1826–1860*. New York: Columbia UP, 1979.

Eisler, Benita, ed. *The Lowell Offering: Writings by New England Mill Women (1840–1845)*. New York: Lippincott, 1977.

Foner, Philip S. *The Factory Girls*. Urbana: U of Illinois P, 1977.

Foster, Hannah W. *The Coquette*. Ed. Cathy N. Davidson. New York: Oxford UP, 1986.

Gates, Henry Louis, Jr. *Figures in Black: Words, Signs, and the 'Racial' Self*. New York: Oxford UP, 1987.

Halttunen, Karen. *Confidence Men and Painted Women: A Study of Middle-Class Culture in America, 1830–1870*. New Haven: Yale UP, 1982.

Harris, Susan K. *Nineteenth-Century American Women's Novels: Interpretative Strategies*. New York: Cambridge UP, 1990.

Kelley, Mary. *Private Woman, Public Stage: Literary Domesticity in Nineteenth-Century America*. New York: Oxford UP, 1984.

Kessler-Harris, Alice. *Out to Work: A History of Wage-Earning Women in the United States*. New York: Oxford UP, 1982.

Kirkland, Caroline. *A New Home—Who'll Follow?* Ed. Sandra A. Zagarell. New Brunswick: Rutgers UP, 1990.

Laurie, Bruce. *Working People of Philadelphia, 1800–1850*. Philadelphia: Temple UP, 1980.

Parton, Sara Payson Willis [Fanny Fern]. *Fern Leaves from Fanny's Port-folio*. New York: 1853.

———. *Ruth Hall and Other Writings*. Ed. Joyce W. Warren. New Brunswick: Rutgers UP, 1986.

Stowe, Harriet Beecher. *Uncle Tom's Cabin; or, Life Among the Lowly*. 1852. New York: Penguin, 1981.

Tompkins, Jane. *Sensational Designs: The Cultural Work of American Fiction 1790–1860*. New York: Oxford UP, 1985.

Warren, Joyce W. *Fanny Fern: An Independent Woman*. New Brunswick, NJ: Rutgers UP, 1992.

———. Introduction. *Ruth Hall and Other Writings*. By Sara Payson Willis Parton [Fanny Fern]. New Brunswick: Rutgers UP, 1986. ix–xxxix.

Welter, Barbara. "The Cult of True Womanhood: 1820–1860." *American Quarterly* 18 (1966): 151–74.

Wilentz, Sean. *Chants Democratic: New York City and the Rise of the American Working Class, 1788–1850*. New York: Oxford UP, 1984.

Williams, Raymond. *Marxism and Literature*. Oxford, England: Oxford UP, 1977.

Wilson, Harriet E. *Our Nig; or, Sketches from the Life of a Free Black*. 1859. New York: Vintage, 1983.

CHAPTER 6

"So Like Women!":

Louisa May Alcott's *Work*

and the Ideology of Relations

Mary Rigsby

Critical reassessments of Louisa May Alcott's writings have proliferated in recent years, but the political nature of her fiction has yet to be explored in its complexity. In her novel *Work: A Story of Experience* (1873), for instance, Louisa May Alcott challenges the glorification of individualism and condemns practices of capitalism that thrive on it. She presents an ambitious political agenda that becomes especially evident when we read *Work* in the context of Alcott's affiliation with Margaret Fuller's feminist transcendentalism—a utopian optimism with a corresponding microanalysis of social inequalities. Specifically, in Christie Devon, Alcott gives us a character who raises familiar genre and plot expectations but in the end uses them to defuse the powerful ideology with which they are usually complicitous. As a *Bildungsroman* character, Christie is most obviously an American ingenue who intends to claim her legacy as heir to the American Dream. However, as she tests the options available to women in capitalist society—moving from one job to another—the typical *Bildungsroman* trajectory from innocence to maturity is redefined. Individualism is self-delusion; self-interest is self-destruction; self-fulfillment follows the rejection of capitalist practices. In other words, the concept of a unified self, as it is defined within dominant American culture, is presented in this novel as an untenable ideal. Though we would have to stop short of claiming Alcott to be a nineteenth-century deconstructionist, it is not an exaggeration to say that she calls into presence the otherwise repressed social relations that make individualism possible. Christie Devon, by the novel's end, takes her place within a network of relations and commits herself to an American dream based on communitarian rather than capitalistic values.

My reading of *Work* relies on two assumptions about Alcott's writing context. First, Alcott was influenced by, and was sympathetic to, what I take to be Margaret Fuller's two-part model of human development, as it is expressed in *Woman in the Nineteenth Century* (1845). Second, nineteenth-century society was polarized in terms of gender, necessitating an approach to reading that acknowledges the historical reality of women's "outsider" status and grants theoretical credibility to their having to speak in what Carol Gilligan has characterized as "a different voice." The different voice, as manifested in Alcott's novel, is one that subverts the dominant ideology of capitalist individualism by manipulating powerful patriarchal images and narrative patterns to accomplish what Jane Tompkins in another context has called "cultural work"—in this case, the very reformation of the American Dream.

Before moving to a substantive analysis of *Work,* we need to address a major stumbling block interfering with efforts to read nineteenth-century women's fiction. Twentieth-century readers are faced with rhetorical traps of the same sort faced by Alcott. Much of our critical discourse begins with assumptions that turn our attention away from nineteenth-century women's writing, in the same way that the women writers themselves were confronted with a literary culture that failed to represent their experiences. There is a common judgment—still too pervasive even among willing readers—that, upon final analysis, the women we might like to champion really did not write very well. This assumption is typified by the opening comments in *The American Narcissus,* written by Joyce Warren, who otherwise has done much to enhance our appreciation of nineteenth-century writers. Warren writes:

> If I were a serious actress looking for a good strong role to play, I would be hard pressed to find such a part in nineteenth-century American fiction. There would be plenty of subordinate roles—ingenues, character parts (usually old ladies), or colorless romantic leads—but there would be no female Captain Ahabs, Huck Finns, or Natty Bumppos. . . . because most American female fictional characters are not people. (1)

We can wish all we want, this assertion tells us, but we can't find what isn't there; our desire to see a vigorous women's tradition in literature, if we are honest with ourselves, is blocked by the reality of women writers' failure to provide strong characters. That desire, however, is based upon a set of mostly unexamined assumptions about "strength"; about the importance of isolated individual characters; about the positive value of Ahab, Huck, and Hawkeye; and about hierarchical values in general (dominant versus subordinate, young versus old, masculinity versus femininity, competition versus cooperation). This rhetoric of "strength" is the very rhetoric that Alcott seeks to undermine and that we must transcend if we are to enter into the world of *Work.*

Feminists have theorized language to be inherently antagonistic to women's ontogeny. The most extreme proponents of this view—Kristeva,

Cixous, and Irigaray—warn us that phallogocentrism denies women even the possibility of speaking for themselves. Though I am not inclined to believe that women never can subvert language to their own agendas, the insight is invaluable to the project of (re)reading women's fiction. It alerts us to the insidious nature of masculinist discourse. In this light, the passage from Warren's book quoted above is instructive. Because it asserts a perceived limitation, it can become a passageway to a formerly secret annex of women's fiction. Opening the world of women's fiction requires demonstrating that blocked avenues are not really blocked.

First, the claim that female characters have had only "subordinate roles" or "colorless romantic leads" stands as a fairly accurate assessment of female characters who inhabit much of the fiction written by nineteenth-century male writers, as many feminist critics have pointed out.[1] But what about works by women writers? What if we refuse to accept the notion that women unilaterally accepted the patriarchal ideology that denied them their subjectivity? What if we assume that women did have "experiences" (of some sort) and did perceive themselves as having authority to speak (limited as that authority might be)? Even as the dominant ideology of the culture, as Joyce Warren describes it, imposed a climate of repression on those "experiences," women wrote about themselves. And within their self-representations exists the possibility of a competing feminist aesthetic.[2] We can imagine that "strong" characters like Ahab, Huck, and Hawkeye—characters who seemingly exemplify the ideal of the strong individual—had competition for cultural dominance. Recent studies by David Leverenz and Leland S. Person, Jr., make this supposition credible. It should come as no surprise, then, if some women writers failed to lend their support to the dominant concept of heroic individualism that traditionally denies women strong roles.

Second, what do we know about the characters created by women writers? In spite of the pervasiveness of negative judgments of fiction written by nineteenth-century women, most of these judgments in fact arise from examinations of very few texts. For example, Joyce Warren concludes, from an examination of relatively few works, that she knows of only two or three writers who create credible women characters.[3] Clearly the enthusiasm with which we accept (and promote) broad characterizations of women's writing ought to be tempered in accord with the range of texts supporting those characterizations.

Expanding our field of vision when considering the achievement of women writers is crucial, but what about the claim that there are "no female Captain Ahabs, Huck Finns, or Natty Bumppos"? The "lack" of such female counterparts is not necessarily a failure to live up to the standards set by high culture, but instead, I contend, may be a consequence of many women writers' inclination to use an alternate aesthetic strategy—one which underplays what Warren has termed the "inflated self" (17) that dominates the discourse of American individualism. It is the perception of "lack" that has kept women writers silenced, and it is here that we can best "listen to the silences," as Gayle Greene and Coppelia Kahn, following Adrienne Rich, suggest feminist literary criticism must do.[4]

Probably there are no female Ahabs, Huck Finns, or Natty Bumppos. This does not mean that there are no strong female characters or that the female characters in American novels have been, as Warren puts it, "uninteresting nonpersons" (2). Reading the works—and not simply the assessments of previous critics who have dismissed them as "not-literary"[5]—is absolutely necessary. My working hypothesis, tentatively offered here, not only is relevant to *Work* but potentially is useful for reading women's fiction generally: nineteenth-century women writers resist heroic individualism by positing social relations as inescapable. Instead of heroes who, as Shapiro observes, "leave civilization and domesticity to forge their own destinies, independent of social constraints" (1), we find characters who bond with others. These characters struggle to achieve freedom *within* the constraints of civilization and domesticity and, thus, struggle to *remold* them. Looking at Louisa May Alcott's *Work* with sensitivity to an alternative aesthetic and to alternative depictions of such concepts as strength, freedom, success, and self-fulfillment, then, will lead us to a rich vein of social and literary criticism.

Christie Devon of Alcott's *Work* functions to unravel the ideology of the strong individual who champions the single life outside of "civilization" and domesticity. Appropriately, she is a multilayered literary figure who initially promises a feminine version of the Emersonian-Jacksonian individual. Her character is a bouquet of several conventional literary types: the naive youth of the *Bildungsroman*, an American adventurer, the orphan-child of popular fiction, and a messianic figure who eventually leads others to a better life. Consequently she raises expectations in readers for familiar kinds of plot and character development. In contravening those expectations, Alcott delivers a narrative that radically revises the value of such conventions. The "American Adam" described by classic canon-forming studies of American literature is rendered an original sinner in the world of *Work*. Christie is a foil for traditional heroics. The very fact that Alcott names her *Christie* associates her with Christ, suggesting that Christie might seem—to the uninitiated—to be a patriarchal figure of salvation. But just as Christ himself was misunderstood by those who expected a traditional leader, we shall misunderstand Christie if we see her in conventional terms. Her "divinity," such as it is, can be found only in her eventual ability to "divine" a better life for women and men. Through Christie, Alcott offers a utopian vision of a reformed society, a new testament of American idealism.

Alcott's reformed American society grows out of a deep sympathy with the idealism of Margaret Fuller. Susan K. Harris has effectively pointed to the novel's Emersonian impulse, but her analysis stopped short of connecting the novel's social analysis to Emerson's intellectual sparring partner, Margaret Fuller. Fuller's significant influence on Emerson, and so on the Alcott household, has not been adequately acknowledged. Fuller echoes Emerson throughout *Woman in the Nineteenth Century,* insisting "that what the soul is capable to ask it must attain" and encouraging women to "unfold [their rule] from within" (40). Unlike Emerson, however, Fuller emphasizes an interdependence among individuals that demands a social conscience. She asserts that only a fraction of humanity's "purpose" can be accomplished in the life of any one individual. As she says, "[Humanity's] entire accomplishment is to be hoped only from the sum of the lives of men, or Man considered as a whole" (169). She carries this insight into an examination of women's condition in society and finds that there are numerous artificial barriers to women's ability to develop themselves. Furthermore, these barriers keep men and women from interacting harmoniously. The full depth of Fuller's gendered transcendentalism cannot be represented here, nor can the extent of her influence on the Alcott household. The traces of Fuller's idealism nevertheless are recognizable in Alcott's fiction.

Focusing on the concepts of liberty, work, love, and union, Alcott conceives liberty as the exhilarating release from isolation and the expansion of one's individual energies that occurs as a consequence of union with others. Liberty, thus redefined, challenges the value of American capitalism, heroic individualism, and the inequities of patriarchy. Alcott's promotion of liberty through union at first may seem paradoxical—like nineteenth-century doublespeak. It is, however, a concept of unity contingent on the equality of its members, calling for a program of personal and communal reform that inevitably results in greater liberty for women. The benefits extend beyond women, though, rippling across the boundaries of class, race, and sexual orientation. With Margaret Fuller, Alcott accepts that "union is only possible to those who are units" (119). Alcott's concept of liberty, following Fuller, then, depends upon a two-tiered process: (1) men's and women's equal access to opportunities for self-actualization; and (2) individuals' ability to join with each other in mutually supportive ways. In the spirit of an altered definition of liberty, Alcott invokes the American Declaration of Independence, suggesting by implication that it is union through love and the earnest pursuit of work that gives us satisfying life, true liberty, and long-lasting happiness. This alternative "Declaration" offers liberty to all members of society.

The repeated pattern of pairs that characterizes Fuller's *Woman in the Nineteenth Century* is present in Alcott's *Work* as well. Pairing underscores the significance of relationship because it insists on drawing attention to connections. Liberty, as a product of union, comes about through a pairing process. Love alone is not liberating, nor is work; but when work and love are combined, ordinary drudgery is transcended.

Good work, work which takes into consideration moral responsibilities, cannot be demeaning, because it contributes to communal well-being while maintaining the worker spiritually as well as financially. Work is essential to well-being. But work done exclusively for self-gain and profit is destructive. Likewise, Alcott portrays love as essential to well-being. Closely associated with the origins of life itself, its perfected manifestation is the love of a parent for the child. Though Alcott typically presents perfect love through the image of the mother, she does not assume that the feeling belongs exclusively to her. Within Alcott's fiction, fathers, too, have the potential for this best of all possible love. In this, Alcott again echoes Fuller, who saw parental love as the source of optimism in breaking the hierarchy between men and women. True love also occurs between friends and, of course, between lovers, insofar as it replicates concern for the well-being of the other in the spirit of parental (that is, nonmanipulative and nonoppressive) love.

Appropriately, emphasizing the importance Alcott places on work in this novel, the original title page of *Work* quoted Carlyle: "An endless significance lies in work; in idleness alone is there perpetual despair." The book, however, also included a dedication to Alcott's mother: "To My Mother, Whose Life has Been a Long Labor of Love." Love and work come together, in both the process and the product of this literary endeavor. Pairing complementary parts to achieve a whole—like Fuller's assertion that human growth is "two-fold, masculine and feminine" (169)—operates as the central mechanism of the novel. No one works effectively in isolation in the world of *Work*. This is the lesson learned by Christie as she attempts to claim the promise of American democracy.

The pattern of pairing is reinforced by the two-part organization of the novel itself. The first section is the story of Christie Devon's experience (as an isolated individual) in the capitalist and patriarchal marketplace outside of the home. The second section is the story of fulfillment through an alternate social organization that includes the home, but home redefined. This second section, in keeping with the duality governing other aspects of the novel, offers two possibilities for women's fulfillment: (1) the companionate marriage which includes an array of job options, and (2) the unmarried life devoted to work and integrated relations with others.[6]

In her redefined conceptions of liberty, work, love, and union, Alcott criticizes American society and suggests a utopian alternative. To do this, she has had to meet the challenge that all women writers have had to meet: the challenge of representing a feminine agenda within a literary culture that, as Sandra Gilbert and Susan Gubar have argued, is overtly and covertly patriarchal. Alcott resists patriarchal pressures in language and culture by co-opting dominant literary conventions for purposes not generally associated with those conventions. *Work* is a nineteenth-century American version of what Rachel Blau DuPlessis has named "writing beyond the ending"; that is, Alcott uses strategies of narration that "sever the narrative from formerly conventional structures of fiction and consciousness about women" (DuPlessis x). Among other things, Alcott prepares her audience for romance but delivers realism. She gives us heroes who are not heroic. Her women are neither angels nor demons. And her "heroine's" adventures go beyond courtship. Similar to twentieth-century feminist writers examined by DuPlessis, Alcott re-parents Christie in an adopted family; she involves Christie in a fraternal-sororal tie that temporarily reduces romance; and she emphasizes emotional attachments between women. In short, Alcott (mis)uses conventions in order to create the unconventional.

As the naive youth of a *Bildungsroman,* Christie is ready for the maturing experiences of life on her own. Typical of the *Bildungsroman* character, Christie begins as a central character, an individual whose maturation process will be the focus of the novel. By the end of the novel, however, she has been "decentralized" through her merger with a large network of characters, many of whom have matured in ways parallel to Christie's own. The *Bildungsroman* generally valorizes an *individual* character, but it is exactly the concept of the individual that Alcott deconstructs. In fact, Alcott's modification of the *Bildungsroman* conforms very neatly to Rita Felski's recent characterization of the twentieth-century feminist *Bildungsroman.*[7] Rita Felski points out that the feminist *Bildungsroman* differs in significant ways from its masculinist counterpart, arguing that, as women writers thematized gender as a central problem, they appropriated and reworked the form. In both the twentieth-century feminist reworking of the genre and in *Work,*

> the journey into society does not signify a surrender of ideals and a recognition of limitations, but rather constitutes the precondition for oppositional activity and engagement. . . . [Furthermore] the move from the sphere of the family into society, from the private into the public world, is a potentially far more liberating process than is the case for the male *Bildungsroman* protagonist. . . . [In the feminist *Bildungsroman,* marriage] is now explicitly revealed not as the endpoint of female *Bildung,* but as its very antithesis. . . . The goal . . . is an identity which is more or less explicitly defined in terms of a notion of broader female community, and it is this which can be said to identify the genre as distinctively feminist. (Felski 137–38)

Alcott's use of the convention undercuts the tradition in ways consistent with modern feminist strategies.

Similarly, *Work*'s opening allusion to the Declaration of Independence and the American Founding Fathers sets up reader expectations that are consequently redirected. In her reference to the Declaration, Christie claims kinship with American heroes, both historical and literary—taking on, for herself, the challenge of self-invention and self-reliance.

Work, then, aligns itself with those narratives of American literature that reenact an archetypal declaration of independence from oppression (whether religious persecution, taxation without representation, urban poverty, or European traditions) and proceed to articulate a better life (in America, in the wilderness, in the West). America emerged, in the nineteenth century, as a place perceived to be especially suitable for, and dedicated to, self-improvement.

Drawing on this familiar scenario, *Work* begins in a very *American* way. In her announcement of a new Declaration of Independence and her subsequent move away from a limiting life on the farm, Christie Devon behaves in the manner of American heroes before (and after) her, though she goes beyond the typical American adventurer. So our first impression of Christie is of a familiar character type, despite the fact of her being female. Her need to leave the farm is not so different from Ishmael's need in *Moby Dick* to "sail about a little and see the watery part of the world." Herman Melville, through Ishmael, asserts, "If they but knew it, almost all men in their degree, some time or other, cherish very nearly the same feelings" (23). What Ishmael claims for "almost all men" is true for Christie as well; Alcott concurs that experience is necessary for self-fulfillment.

In the same way that she "decentralizes" Christie through the latter's developing affiliations with other characters, Alcott redefines the significance of the Declaration of Independence. Christie's "new" Declaration of Independence is also the Declaration of Sentiments from the Seneca Falls Convention. Her bold move out of her aunt and uncle's home is an unambiguous, if initially understated, move in favor of greater liberty for women. Alcott never specifically mentions the Seneca Falls Convention, but Christie's prefacing her Declaration with the word "new" makes the allusion credible.[8] Gender is to be significant in this novel; Christie is not simply a female playing the conventional male role. Here the novel gives us another double line to observe: the narrative progress of a woman attempting to play out what has been the male prerogative (the role of hero), and the narrative of a woman who illustrates an alternative to the hero and promotes a different set of social relations as a result.

Alcott begins her critique of the hero by having Christie initially accept without question the idealization of the individual as gender-neutral.

Christie does not begin with what can immediately be defined as a feminist agenda. To the contrary, she sees herself first and foremost as a gender-neutral individual. Her femininity is secondary, not primary, to her self-identification. Because she sees herself as an individual, she accepts her differences from the others who inhabit the small farm community of her adopted home as part of her unique personhood rather than as evidence of her failure to be a proper woman. Consequently, she feels justified in rejecting this home for herself.

The rejection of her home on the farm operates metaphorically as a rejection of the Cult of True Womanhood. In place of patriarchy, Alcott traces Christie's heritage through her dead mother, who offers a role model outside of the prescribed life on the farm. It is her mother who provides a "beautiful example" of struggle against the degradation of dependence and drudgery, even though her success was shortened by an early death. As viewed through her Uncle Enos's eyes, Christie has inherited her mother's "highfalutin' notions" and is "discontented, and sot in her own idees" (8). She is "dis-contented," empty of the content of traditional femininity, and must, in postmodernist terms, re-write herself to be "content"—that is, "content" as both *cont*ent, meaning substance contained, and con*tent,* as in satisfied.

Appropriately for Christie, the symbolic representative of patriarchal authority is an uncle—a relationship subordinate to the filial one. Uncle Enos's commands can be questioned because he is not her real father; he does not represent the values of parental love as they are defined by Fuller and Alcott. Uncle Enos speaks for male domination and crass materialism. We are not surprised to find, then, that, as a new kind of female character and one who insists on rejecting the traditional expectations for women, Christie articulates for us that "Uncle doesn't love or understand me" (2). For similar reasons, Aunt Betsey is an inadequate surrogate mother. Aunt Betsey mistakenly accepts her husband as the rightful authority in her life; she had "a most old-fashioned and dutiful awe of her lord and master" (10). Christie rejects patriarchal oppression of women because it conflicts with her desire for self-determination. And, much like Huck Finn, Ishmael, and Natty Bumppo, in spite of her sex she sets out on her own to "earn at last, the best success this world can give us, the possession of a brave and cheerful spirit, rich in self-knowledge, self-control, self-help" (11).

As an orphan living in the household of an oppressive uncle, Christie has no familial obligation to stay. Her aunt is kind enough, but their natures are too different for Christie to be satisfied with the life Aunt Betsey has accepted for herself. Aunt Betsey's love is not enough to make up for the lack of satisfying work that the farm life offers Christie. This situation allows Alcott realistically to examine the consequences of a

woman's attempt to live out the American heroic ideal. And the first section of the novel illustrates the inherent difficulties and ultimate destruc-
tiveness of the heroic ideal for women who attempt it.

There is an additional significance to Christie's character. Christie's
status as an orphan ties her to two sets of literary orphans: the Jane Eyre
type and the Ragged Dick type. These two prototypical orphans, and
their many literary sisters and brothers, again reflect the dual concerns
of Alcott's novel: the female orphans tend to appear in novels concerned
with love and family, while the Ragged Dick stories are rags-to-riches
stories of the American work ethic and economic success. They echo
the themes of love and work announced on the original title page.

American literature of the 1800s is populated by numerous female
orphans, including Susan Warner's Ellen Montgomery in *The Wide Wide
World* (1851) and her Fleda in *Queechy* (1852), Maria S. Cummin's Gerty
in *The Lamplighter* (1854), and Augusta Evans Wilson's Edna in *St. Elmo*
(1867). These American orphan girls very likely were inspired by Charlotte Brontë's Jane Eyre, also well known among the reading public.
These orphans, though not without their subversive undertext, tended,
at least ostensibly, to support the traditional patriarchal attitude toward
women and woman's place in society—particularly her place in the
home. Even though they are characters who prove their integrity and
often overcome obstacles with admirable fortitude and intelligence, they
tend to be pushed into the "wide wide world" by circumstances beyond
their control. Their efforts usually reflect a desire to reintegrate themselves into properly loving families, either their own by birth, previously
hidden from them; or new, and better, adopted ones. Christie Devon
stands out as a different kind of American female orphan because she
chooses to leave her home and family, and, in the end, constructs family
for herself as quite different from that defined by patriarchal society.

Christie's literary affiliation with these other orphan girls is important
to our understanding of her significance. Jane Eyre is both Christie's inspi-
ration and her point of departure. It is at least partly because of Jane Eyre's
story that Christie resists the temptation to give up liberty for the security of
marriage and woman's "proper sphere." While working as a governess for
Mrs. Saltonstall, Christie receives the attentions of her employer's brother,
Philip Fletcher. The day on which Christie anticipates an offer of marriage
from him, she is reading *Jane Eyre* on the beach. Philip asks her opinion of
Rochester, and Christie replies derogatorily. Philip pursues:

> "Then you think Jane was a fool to love and try to make a saint of
> him, I suppose?"
> "I like Jane, but never can forgive her marrying that man, as I
> haven't much faith in the saints such sinners make." . . .

"What hard-hearted creatures you women are sometimes! Now, I fancied you were one of those who wouldn't leave a poor fellow to his fate, if his salvation lay in your hands."

"I can't say what I should do in such a case; but it always seemed to me that a man should have energy enough to save himself, and not expect the 'weaker vessel,' as he calls her, to do it for him," answered Christie, with a conscious look, for Mr. Fletcher's face made her feel as if something was going to happen. (80–81)

Philip proceeds to propose marriage but does so in a way that makes it clear to Christie that the price of her compliance would be the loss of her liberty and integrity as an individual. She declines the offer, altering the pattern established by *Jane Eyre*. In Christie's life, the governess will refuse to marry her employer (or her employer's brother, as the case may be). Philip, with his back appropriately "against the rock"—as Christie is firm in her refusal—expresses anger and incredulity at her refusal. In response, Christie delivers a speech much like Jane's to Rochester in the garden, though Jane speaks of her integrity as an individual *before* Rochester proposes. If we compare the two speeches, we find that Christie and Jane are sisters in spirit:

> [Jane:] . . . Do you think because I am poor, obscure, plain, and little, I am soulless and heartless? You think wrong! —I have as much soul as you,—and full as much heart! . . . I am not talking to you now through the medium of custom, conventionalities, or even of mortal flesh:—it is my spirit that addresses your spirit; just as if both had passed through the grave, and we stood at God's feet, equal,—as we are! (Brontë 318)

> [Christie:] . . . it is what we *are,* not what we *have,* that makes one human being superior to another. I am as well-born as you in spite of my poverty; my life, I think, has been a better one than yours; my heart, I know, is fresher, and my memory has fewer faults and follies to reproach me with. . . . (87)

In spite of the similarities between them, Christie insists on revising her part, refusing to sacrifice her liberty for anything less than a "fair bargain" (81).

Given her plans to go out and make her way in the world, we might expect Christie to prove to be a female captain of industry or a female Ragged Dick. This expectation remains unfulfilled, as Christie consistently discovers that work for wages is inconsistent with the principles of friendship and true love. As Sarah Elbert has pointed out, in this novel profit motives are shown to take destructive precedence over moral responsibility and charity. The dehumanization of a capitalistic work world affects both employer and employee. Christie is called "Jane" while in the employment of the Stuart household, simply because Mrs. Stuart prefers her maids to have that name. Christie's loss of her own name marks the dehumanizing process of a work relationship without mutual regard between employer and employee (and echoes Christie's identification with Jane Eyre). Even the manager of a "large and well-conducted mantua-making establishment" (128), Mrs. King, is not free to act according to her heartfelt impulses. She finds that she must dismiss an especially competent seamstress, Christie's good friend Rachel, because, at some time in her past, Rachel had committed a sexual indiscretion. As much as Mrs. King is inclined in her heart to overlook the woman's past, retaining a worker with a tarnished reputation would hurt business, and Rachel is let go. Beyond its significance as an illustration of one woman's difficulties, Elbert points out that readers at the time would have understood an additional message in this factory scene. The factory owner, Mrs. King, is dependent upon Miss Cotton, her forewoman and the one heartlessly insisting on Rachel's dismissal. Elbert tells us:

> Readers could hardly miss the irony of "King Cotton," an infamous phrase with double meaning for abolitionists. Cotton was indeed the king of American crops in the antebellum period, and as the country's leading export commodity, it led Northern factory and workshop owners to ignore the cruelty of slavery in the name of profits. Mrs. King fears losing Miss Cotton and so, although the owner knows better, she fires Rachel in order to validate the hypocritical sensibilities of Miss Cotton. (*Hunger* 246)[9]

Alcott harshly criticizes America's profit-oriented economic practices. In their place she offers the cooperative living arrangement that Christie establishes after her husband's death. Christie manages the greenhouse and shares the profits equally with Mrs. Sterling and Letty (known as Rachel in the first part of the book). Mrs. Sterling and Letty run the household and contribute to the care of Christie's daughter. Uncle Enos, as the voice of capitalism, does not approve of the women's arrangement because it runs counter to the individual accumulation of profit. He says to Christie: "That ain't a fair bargain if you do all the work. . . . So like women!" he grumbles (419). Uncle Enos, in the spirit of patriarchy, sees only the greenhouse business as "work"—the housekeeping and child care activities don't count. Alcott might say, "So like a man!"

Looking more closely at the pattern of Christie Devon's experience in the world of work, we find her ability to survive more or less depends upon the development of an emotionally close relationship with other people. In the first section of the novel, Christie finds work as a servant, an actress, a governess, a companion to an invalid, and a seamstress. Her work as a house servant for Mrs. Stuart is tolerable only because of the intimacy Christie develops with Hepsey, the black cook. Through her friend Lucy's encouragement and support, Christie achieves success as an actress. Furthermore, her loss of intimacy with Lucy convinces her that she is not strong enough to resist the pitfalls of vanity and competition that being an actress involves. As a governess, Christie develops a friendship with Philip Fletcher, but this friendship, unlike her previous friendships, is uneven and calls for her to give up her liberty in exchange for comfort and security. Her successful role as companion to Helen also hinges on her willingness to offer and accept friendship. And the choosing of her loyalty to Rachel over the relative security of work as a seamstress is the greatest testament of all to the importance of the relationship over all other considerations. Christie learns this lesson of relationship slowly but consistently. In *Work,* no one is "self-made," only "mutually-made." Everyone who succeeds in achieving a satisfying life does so because he or she recognizes the support of others. Those who pursue success in business through competition and the capitalistic reverence for profit fail as human beings, as Mrs. King and Miss Cotton demonstrate.

Clearly, Alcott offers a critique of the rhetoric of the self-made individual in the capitalistic world of work. Christie's romantic plans to go out on her own to make her fortune are unrealistic. But, in addition to undermining the promise of self-reliance and the romance of capitalism, Alcott criticizes dominant conventions of romantic love. Alcott does not end her story with Christie and David's successful romance. This is not a simple marriage plot. Instead she writes beyond the conventional ending. Consequently, the plot device acts as a necessary placeholder, allowing Alcott to make the point that women's lives (and women's fiction) need not center on, nor end with, successful courtship. One-fourth of the novel (five out of twenty chapters) occurs after Christie and David marry.

Throughout the novel, Alcott explicitly reveals strict Emersonian individualism to be unrealistic and ultimately dangerous to social relations. Instead, in the spirit of Margaret Fuller's version of transcendentalism, the highest satisfaction in life is achieved in a two-tiered process. Certainly, first of all, one must develop one's own character, become a whole person through experience in the world. And in this first step, Emerson's "Man Thinking" (the heroic intellectual man of action described in "The American Scholar") is also Alcott's ideal for women, as it was for Margaret Fuller. Women as well as men need, first, to be able to contemplate nature and their intimate connections to the natural world. Second, women as well as men need access to education; they, too, can be inspired by the geniuses of past times—though, as Emerson warns, the ideas of the past are not to be accepted to the detriment of new ideas and new ways of living. And third, the development of individual genius comes from "fit action," from getting out in the world and working.

Where Fuller and Alcott part company with Emerson is in their addition of another step. For them, individual self-development is not enough. Once self-fulfillment is achieved, the next goal is to experience the joy of fitting into the larger social group. Individuals experience the sublime when they join with each other in mutually supportive ways. Individuals must be allowed to explore and expand their own inherent talents, but, finally, the fullest expression of those talents is meaningful only as they contribute to the overall good of others. Realistically, this expression can only be achieved through the willing support of others. This formulation, of course, is another way of defining the feminine aesthetic of both Fuller and Alcott.

The second part of the novel works to elaborate a vision of a better society which has as its base a duality, bringing the pattern from the first part of the novel to its most positive expression. Contrary to Emerson's claim in "Self-Reliance," in Alcott's world it is not the "resolution of all into the ever blessed ONE" that is most important. Instead, as we saw with Margaret Fuller, it is the everlasting two, perhaps even the ever interchangeable two.

It is important to note that Alcott's promotion of a pair as the basic unit of human fulfillment is not the formulaic male-female pair of the married couple. *Work* is not a romance which reaches its denouement with the marriage of its lady to her knight in shining armor. Though Christie, in the course of the novel, does reject what she deems to be unsuitable suitors and continues her single life until she meets a man of "sterling" character (in the person of David Sterling), the point of the fiction is not to promote marriage as the only or even the most appropriate career choice for women. Alcott's rejection of such a plot is unambiguous. As she said about *Little Women*: "Girls write to ask who the little women marry, as if that was the only end and aim of a woman's life. I *won't* marry Jo to Laurie to please anyone" (Alcott, *Life* 201). Marriage is an option only when it involves mutual love between equals. Otherwise, useful work is the way to a successful life. Christie Devon's life both as a happily married woman in a companionate, and therefore an unconventional, union and as a working woman (before, during, and after marriage) drives home this rejection of traditional marriage as the only life for a woman. Other characters reinforce this idea as well. Mrs. Wilkins, for example, tells about her two younger sisters, who "both is prosperin' in different ways"; Gusty married the man she loved in spite of his poverty, and "they're happy as can be a workin' up together" (327). Her other sister didn't marry. Instead she "kep stiddy to her trade, and ain't never repented" (328).

Commitment to the isolation that heroic individualism implies is consistently regarded as naïve and self-destructive in the long run. In the final scene of the novel, all of Christie's women friends have come together: Hepsey, Mrs. Wilkins, Mrs. Sterling, Letty (Rachel) Sterling, Bella Carrol. Together they represent mothers, daughters, sisters, the rich, the poor, white, black, young, and old. They have just committed themselves to work for the betterment of women, each in her own way:

> With an impulsive gesture Christie stretched her hands to the friends about her, and with one accord they laid theirs on hers, a loving league of sisters, old and young, black and white, rich and poor, each ready to do her part to hasten the coming of the happy end.
>
> "Me too!" cried little Ruth, and spread her chubby hand above the rest: a hopeful omen, seeming to promise that the coming generation of women will not only receive but deserve their liberty, by learning that the greatest of God's gifts to us is the privilege of sharing His great work. (442–43)

This last scene is an expression of female unity. Like a larger version of the Three Musketeers, these women, pioneers of social reform, pledge all for one and one for all at a new kind of round table—a parlor table. Fuller believed that, until society was adjusted to meet the needs of its citizens, women would be their own "best helpers" (172). She urged women temporarily to separate themselves from men, not because men and women did not need each other, "but because in Woman this fact has led to an excessive devotion, which has cooled love, degraded marriage, and prevented either sex from being what it should be to itself or the other" (175).

Reading Alcott's *Work* through the lens of an alternative, feminine aesthetic thus enlarges the range and accomplishment of a book that otherwise has been seen only as the minor achievement of a minor writer. It shares the transcendental model established by Margaret Fuller in *Woman in the Nineteenth Century*. In David and Christie we have a brief encounter with the ideal couple envisioned by Fuller as "a youth and a maiden . . . both as yet uncontaminated; both aspiring, without rashness; both of strong nature and sweet feelings; both capable of large mental development" (155). If David had lived, their married life would have constituted the "palace home of King and Queen" (179) of Fuller's utopian vision. David, being an ideal, realistically was not available to all women. And so, Alcott, like Fuller, assumed that women would need to separate themselves from men for a while, "till they know what they need" (Fuller 172). And Alcott, like Fuller, urged women to help one another until the time of metamorphosis would revolutionize society. It may not be unreasonable to say that, with Christie Devon, Alcott answered Fuller's call for a woman who could "vindicate their birthright for all women; . . . teach them what to claim, and how to use what they obtain" (177).

Given this reading of *Work,* is it sensible to assume that there are no "good strong roles" for women in nineteenth-century American literature? That is, is Christie Devon only a subordinate character? an ingenue? a colorless romantic lead? To attempt to answer these questions is already to lose hold of the argument that I have made about Alcott's novel. None are relevant questions. They assume the valorization of the Masculine Achiever and the robust Emersonian hero. In contrast, Alcott presents us with a vision of inclusion rather than exclusion, where independence also means *in*-dependence. In Alcott's world, strength is the province of union and community—a place where all of us can find "good strong roles to play."

Notes

1.   The critics who have elaborated this observation have been of the so-called "images of women" school of feminist criticism. See, e.g., Cornillon.

2.   A feminist aesthetic, I would argue, takes as its goal the dismantling of patriarchal definitions of women. Not all feminist strategies are equally effective, but they share this common goal, regardless of their varying and sometimes conflicting practices. Alcott's aesthetic is supported by a feminist ideology that desires the integration of masculine and feminine activities. I do not mean to suggest that there is a homogenous and uniformly repressive patriarchal ideology or a homogenous "feminist" reaction. Given that class, race, and gender identities are acquired within the very culture that writers challenge, experience and self-representation already are suffused by dominant ideology. We can, however, usefully describe aesthetic features that are consistent with feminist ideologies.

3.   Warren mentions Harriet Beecher Stowe and Sarah Orne Jewett as exceptions among those nineteenth-century writers who created "complex female characters" and did not "lose their popularity" as a result. She also briefly mentions Charlotte Perkins Gilman and Fanny Fern in an extended footnote. For example, Warren claims that Fanny Fern's *Ruth Hall* was the "*first* (and the *only* nineteenth-century) [emphasis mine] American novel to portray a female protagonist who succeeds *wholly on her own*" (261n). This dismissing of all the other novels written by women in the nineteenth century and championing of one (who, significantly, was appreciated by Hawthorne, and thus sanctioned by an established member of the canon) unfortunately but effectively suppresses further exploration of women writers.

4.   Green and Kahn state: "Only the undermining of . . . opposition, the dismantling of the system that sanctions them, can undo the hierarchical opposition between men and women. . . . [W]e need to evolve a theory and practice true to the most radical implications of our positions. . . . Such criticism seeks out 'the lack in the work, what it is unable to say'—what is 'unspoken.' . . . Like the blank page in Dinesen's tale, it enables the 'silence to speak.' And 'listening for the silences' is, as Adrienne Rich suggests, difficult and essential in understanding women's experience" (26).

5.   See Shapiro. In a review of comments on Louisa May Alcott's work, the generally "curt dismissals" of Alcott's fiction, Shapiro argues, "raises questions about whether the critics really read the books or simply read each other" (66). I mean to suggest that this is a problem more widespread than simply regarding previous assessments of Alcott's work.

6.   Though this two-part construction of the second section of the novel may seem to replicate the nineteenth-century narrative pattern identified by DuPlessis in *Writing Beyond the Ending*, it differs significantly. DuPlessis has pointed out that, typically, nineteenth-century novels by women intertwine *Bildung* and quest narratives only to repress one or the other at the moment of resolution. Christie Devon's story includes a "successful" romance; she marries an exceptionally good man. However, during her period of courtship, engagement, and marriage, Christie continues to be active outside the home. She works with David in the greenhouse business and, after the outbreak of the Civil War, she enlists as a nurse. Certainly she shows more enthusiasm for domestic activities performed in the service of her future husband than modern readers might appreciate, but the consistency of her commitment to useful work outside the home, in spite of her relationship with David, marks her as atypical in the realm of fiction identified by DuPlessis. It is my contention that *Work* provides alternate choices rather than mutually exclusive conditions.

7.   See esp. Felski, "Novel of Self-Discovery" 122–53.

8.   Elbert, both in her introduction to the Schocken reprint of *Work* and in her discussion of the novel in *A Hunger for Home*, asserts without qualification that Christie Devon is using "the language of the Seneca Falls Convention to claim her rights" (*Hunger* 243). As the following discussion reveals, I believe the reference is more complex than Elbert allows.

9.   This is the second time Christie rejects a proposal of marriage. The first was her refusal to marry the young farmer Joe Butterfield, a neighbor of her Uncle Enos. Christie has a third proposal—a second offer from Philip Fletcher—but holds out for the single life until she falls in love with David Sterling. The marriage plot, then, is rejected three times in the first half of the novel. This is consistent with Felski's observations on the feminist *Bildungsroman*.

Works Cited

Alcott, Louisa May. *Life, Letters and Journals*. Ed. Ednah D. Cheney. Boston: Roberts Brothers, 1889.

————. *Work: A Story of Experience*. 1872–73. New York: Schocken, 1977.

Brontë, Charlotte. *Jane Eyre*. 1847. London: Clarendon P, 1969.

Chase, Richard. *The American Novel and Its Tradition*. New York: Anchor, 1957.

Cornillon, Susan Koppelman, ed. *Images of Women in Fiction: Feminist Perspectives*. Bowling Green, Ohio: Bowling Green U Popular P, 1972.

Cummins, Maria S. *The Lamplighter*. Boston: John P. Jewett & Co., 1854.

DuPlessis, Rachel Blau. *Writing Beyond the Ending: Narrative Strategies of Twentieth-Century Women Writers*. Bloomington: Indiana UP, 1985.

Elbert, Sarah. *A Hunger for Home: Louisa May Alcott's Place in American Culture*. New Brunswick: Rutgers UP, 1987.

————. Introduction. *Work: A Story of Experience*. By Louisa May Alcott. 1872–73. New York: Schocken, 1977. ix–xliv.

Emerson, Ralph Waldo. *The Collected Works of Ralph Waldo Emerson*. Gen. ed. Joseph Slater. 4 vols. Cambridge: Belknap P of Harvard UP, 1971–87.

Feidelson, Charles. *Symbolism in American Literature*. Chicago: U of Chicago P, 1953; abridged, 1959.

Felski, Rita. *Beyond Feminist Aesthetics: Feminist Literature and Social Change*. Cambridge: Harvard UP, 1989.

————. "The Novel of Self-Discovery." *Beyond Feminist Aesthetics: Feminist Literature and Social Change*. By Rita Felski. Cambridge: Harvard UP, 1989. 122–53.

Fuller, Margaret. *Woman in the Nineteenth Century*. 1844. New York: Norton, 1971.

Gilbert, Sandra M., and Susan Gubar. *The Madwoman in the Attic: The Woman Writer and the Nineteenth-Century Literary Imagination*. New Haven: Yale UP, 1979.

Gilligan, Carol. *In a Different Voice: Psychological Theory and Women's Development*. Cambridge: Harvard UP, 1982.

Greene, Gayle, and Coppelia Kahn. "Feminist Scholarship and the Social Construction of Woman." *Making a Difference: Feminist Literary Criticism*. Ed. Greene and Kahn. New York: Routledge, 1985. 1–36.

Harris, Susan K. *Nineteenth-Century American Women's Novels: Interpretative Strategies*. Cambridge: Cambridge UP, 1990.

Irigaray, Luce. *Speculum of the Other Woman*. Trans. Gillian C. Gill. Ithaca, N.Y.: Cornell UP, 1985. Trans. of *Speculum de l'autre femme*. 1974.

Kristeva, Julia. *The Kristeva Reader*. Ed. Toril Moi. New York: Columbia UP, 1986.

Leverenz, David. *Manhood and the American Renaissance*. Ithaca, N.Y.: Cornell UP, 1989.

Lewis, R. W. B. *The American Adam: Innocence, Tragedy, and Tradition in the Nineteenth Century.* Chicago: U of Chicago P, 1955.

Matthiessen, F. O. *American Renaissance.* New York: Oxford UP, 1941.

McNall, Sally Allen. *Who Is in the House?: A Psychological Study of Two Centuries of Women's Fiction in America, 1795 to the Present.* Westport, Conn.: Greenwood P, 1981.

Person, Leland S., Jr. *Aesthetic Headaches: Women and a Masculine Poetics in Poe, Melville, and Hawthorne.* Athens: U of Georgia P, 1988.

Reising, Russell J. *The Unusable Past: Theory and the Study of American Literature.* New York: Methuen, 1986.

Rich, Adrienne. *On Lies, Secrets, and Silence: Selected Prose 1966–1978.* New York: Norton, 1979.

Rotundo, E. Anthony. "Learning about Manhood: Gender Ideals and the Middle-Class Family in Nineteenth-Century America." *Manliness and Morality: Middle-Class Masculinity in Britain and America, 1800–1940.* Ed. J. A. Mangan and James Walvin. Manchester, England: Manchester UP, 1987.

Shapiro, Ann R. *Unlikely Heroines: Nineteenth-Century American Women Writers and the Woman Question.* Westport, CT: Greenwood P, 1987.

Warner, Susan. *Queechy.* New York: G. P. Putnam, 1852.

———. *The Wide Wide World.* New York: G. P. Putnam, 1851.

Warren, Joyce W. *The American Narcissus: Individualism and Women in Nineteenth-Century American Fiction.* New Brunswick: Rutgers UP, 1984.

Wilson, Augusta Evans. *St. Elmo.* New York: George W. Carleton, 1867.

CHAPTER 7

A World of Their Own:
The Separatist Utopian Vision
of Mary E. Bradley Lane's *Mizora*

Duangrudi Suksang

In her introduction to Charlotte Perkins Gilman's *Herland,* Ann J. Lane
admits that Mary E. Bradley Lane's *Mizora: A Prophecy* is "the only self-
consciously feminist utopia" published before Gilman's *Herland.* Even
so, the critic dismisses *Mizora* as "an utterly preposterous story" and its
author's vision of the Mizoran community as "something less than convincing, even as an imaginative creation" (xix–xx). In minimizing *Mizora,* Ann
J. Lane fails to consider its contribution to the feminist utopian tradition as
a whole, and specifically its status as precursor of the outpouring of twentieth-century American separatist feminist utopias. Many characteristics of
the Mizoran society anticipated those depicted in Gilman's more celebrated
Herland. While other nineteenth-century American women utopian writers—such as Mary Griffith, who wrote *Three Hundred Years Hence* (1836),
and Jane Sophia Appleton, author of "Sequel to the Vision of Bangor in
the Twentieth Century" (1848)—visualized an alternative society that was
a revision or restructuring of patriarchal society, Mary E. Bradley Lane
structured a totally new society in which patriarchy had been eradicated.
Placed in the context of nineteenth-century social practices, *Mizora* offers a unique and radical rethinking of the sociopolitical position of
women. Never before had a nineteenth-century woman writer presented
the public with an all-female society that was completely self-sufficient.

At the beginning of *Mizora: A Prophecy,* the narrator, Vera Zarovitch,
expresses her hope: "That wonderful civilization I met with in Mizora, I
may not be able to more than faintly shadow forth here, yet from it, the
present age may form some idea of that grand, that ideal life that is
possible for our remote posterity" (7). Implicit in her statement is a tension between the existing polity and the "ideal life that is possible." Vera's
hope is also the hope of nineteenth-century female American utopian
writers, who appropriated utopia, originally a male-created literary genre,
as a vehicle to express their displeasure at the present state of affairs

and as a tool for entering into serious political discussion and argument with patriarchy. Through her narrator Vera, whose name means "truth," Mary Lane criticizes nineteenth-century women's oppressive social and economic conditions and at the same time offers an alternative vision of a scientifically and technologically advanced matriarchal society. That Lane's matriarchy is born after the extinction of men suggests that patriarchal practices hinder women's progress.

After three decades of feminist scholars' examinations of nineteenth-century American culture, it is well recognized that women's existence in that culture was marginalized. Women were excluded not only from participating in education and politics but also from decision-making in familial matters. In marriage, women lost at once their identities, their property, and their earnings. Even though women often viewed themselves as morally superior to men, they still had to submit to men because of their economic dependence. A woman's alleged moral superiority gained her no support, but kept her isolated from the world outside the home. To uphold her virtuous womanhood, Barbara Welter points out in "The Cult of True Womanhood: 1820–1860," a woman was to possess "piety, submissiveness and domesticity" (152). Such a cult was a subtle strategy to oppress women and to safeguard society against any change in the relationships between the sexes.

Qualifying Welter's characterization of nineteenth-century middle-class women as being submissive and domestic, Frances Cogan argues in *All-American Girl* that there existed another popular ideal known as "the ideal of the Real Woman," which "advocated intelligence, physical fitness and health, self-sufficiency, economic self-reliance, and careful marriage" (4). Cogan also points out that the primary educational goal of the "Ideal of Real Womanhood" was to enable a woman to attract a man and prepare for marriage, so she could perform her roles as wife and mother efficiently (74). In this light, education was used to keep women confined within the world of domesticity and femininity. Accepting her culturally predetermined role obligations, however, a Real Woman remained stifled and relegated to a subordinate position, forever dependent on a man. While the advocacy of women's education and self-sufficiency were important, Cogan concedes that

> even under the criteria of the Real Womanhood ideal, the learned maiden or wife did operate under certain restrictions in regard to her conversation. She was expected to avoid the appearance of pedantry, for example, and cautioned against alluding excessively to the classics or "various departments of science" or making it painfully clear that she was better versed than her guests in any subject areas. (81–82)

Thus the Ideal of Real Womanhood qualified and complemented the Cult of True Womanhood; in the final analysis, women in either category remained trapped in patriarchy. "True" and "real" women alike operated in accord with the presumed distinctions between men and women, described by Welter as follows:

> The womanly virtues of wisdom and understanding have conclusions reached through intuition, while the male virtues of truth and knowledge come from the intellect. Man sins through ignorance, through "not knowing"; woman through folly, willful disregard of knowledge. Man labors and learns facts in history; woman is made for lighter tasks and responds emotionally to poetry. Man is a doer, an actor. Woman reacts, she reflects rather than creates, is the moon to his sun. He makes laws and she obeys commandments. Man's mind leads him to truth while woman's soul informs her of the higher wisdom. Man has skills and talents, but woman's gifts, like her knowledge, come from a deeper source and do not respond to training or practice since they are the product of genius. Man reasons and is just; woman loves and is merciful. ("Anti-Intellectualism" 265)

Such stereotypic and devaluing conceptions of women have been an integral part of American cultural and economic history. Nineteenth-century women authors were forced to contend with this long-established tradition of antagonism, and to find ways to liberate themselves and their characters from the social confinement instituted by patriarchal culture. To attain their goal, they often chose to create a utopian fiction that was open-ended and allowed limitless possibilities. By adopting a male-invented discourse, these women writers challenged the male literary tradition from which they had been excluded, for they dared to overstep conventional demarcations to offer their visions of women that were diametrically opposed to those developed by men. Their appropriation of the male-created genre of utopia was a significant point of departure for the birth of a utopian tradition that is uniquely women's; at the same time these women publicly announced that they would not allow their visions of women's future to be dictated by male-instituted conventions. Their action was indeed defiant and subversive, for they succeeded in reclaiming control of their future through language.

The open-ended nature of utopia has been postulated by the German philosopher Ernst Bloch (1885–1977). According to Bloch, utopia is the "Not-Yet-Conscious" and a "real and concrete final state which can be achieved politically" (*Principle* 1: xxviii). The "Not-Yet-Conscious" surfaces in a daydream which is progressive and anticipatory. The daydream, charged with hope and anticipation, projects into the future, giving meaning to life, which without it could become "triviality" (*Principle* 1: 145–46). To realize her or his utopian goal, a person must, to use Bloch's term, "overtake" the present existing order (Bloch, *Philosophy* 85). In order to do this, one must keep active "in order not to take things as they are, by resigning oneself to them instead of revolting against them and rejecting them when necessity demands" (86). Utopia, in other words, is by nature revolutionary, for it presupposes a subversive action.

Women, in order to be able to overtake and gain control of their lives, must maintain their fervent belief in the "Not-Yet," instead of letting themselves be victimized by the blind fate of patriarchy. Concerned about their oppressive existence and loss of identity in patriarchal society, they constantly daydream of something better, or utopia. If they feel only anger and despair, fantasizing but not taking action, they certainly will remain forever trapped in the status quo. On the contrary, if they employ their active and contemplative knowledge, together with their courage, they eventually will succeed in making the "Real-Possible" emerge as a "new Real" (Bloch, *Principle* 1: 196). They must invest their energy and efforts in breaking away from the "Not" state, or "the still empty, undefined, undecided," in pursuit of the "All," by putting their trust in the "Not-Yet" (*Principle* 1: 306).

Women utopian writers belong to the group of women who are working actively toward attaining their selfhood and independence. They take action through thinking and writing. In Blochian terms, "thinking means venturing beyond" (*Principle* 1: 4). Thinking is a contemplative and revolutionary act preceding writing; in and of itself, thinking can be perceived as a revolutionary undertaking. It stems from deprivation and oppression, of which we must be aware in order to liberate ourselves (*Principle* 1: 42). While thinking functions as an impetus, writing allows women utopianists to articulate their thoughts, feelings, and desires after having been silenced for a long time. In this respect, utopia as a literary genre becomes significant to women writers as they attempt to call the public's attention to the injustices done to them, and as they work toward social reconstruction, redefinition, and repositioning of their selves.

The increasingly popular literary genre of utopian fiction seemed to serve nineteenth-century reformist women writers' purposes well, for it is at once constructive and critical. Through their utopian narratives, these women writers transformed the rhetorical demands of their feminist activist sisters into a concrete image in a fictional dimension. Their utopias represent their efforts to break down the wall of prejudices culturally and historically erected by patriarchy. Indeed, these women utopian writers inscribed themselves, in the words of Hélène Cixous, "into the world and into history" (875), and into the history of women's struggle and the history of utopian literature in particular, liberating the genre from male hegemony.

In addition to reaffirming women's capability, *Mizora* contributes to the tradition of separatist feminist utopias which has flourished in the twentieth century. The indirect influence of the ideas of *Mizora* is most noticeable in Gilman's *Herland* (1915). Though there is no evidence that Gilman read *Mizora* (1880–81), her utopian novel, written approximately thirty-four years after *Mizora*, has an astonishing number of characteristics suggesting Lane's possible influence. Both novels glorify sisterhood, children, communitarianism, education, and motherhood, topics Gilman dealt with in her popular work *Women and Economics* (1898). The two utopias both depict homogeneously Caucasian separatist feminist societies, which have emerged as a result of women's revolt against men's oppression. Both utopias were designed to demonstrate that women could fare well without men. In fact, the female inhabitants of Mizora and Herland eschew religious orthodoxies and excessively formal governing structures to lead their lives peacefully and harmoniously under the guidance of the spirit of maternal love and cooperation. They enjoy equality, good health, prosperity, and a beautiful environment. Both solve the issue of reproduction, crucial for a separatist utopia, by postulating a process of female parthenogenesis. It is noteworthy that, while the Mizorans attribute their reproductive discovery to science, the Herlanders mystically regard parthenogenesis as a "natural miracle" (Gilman 71). Finally, both societies' firm belief in the inevitability of evolution and their knowledge of science enable them to prosper and look forward into the future. The past to them holds no significance.

Mary E. Bradley Lane's *Mizora: A Prophecy,* published in 1880–81 as a serial in the *Cincinnati Commercial,* depicts a scientifically and technologically advanced matriarchy in which men have been extinct for three thousand years. As we learn from the book's preface, Lane's work "attracted a great deal of attention." The full title of the first edition (1889) reads:

> *Mizora: A Prophecy.* A Mss. Found Among the Private Papers of the Princess Vera Zarovitch; Being a true and faithful account of her Journey to the Interior of the Earth, with a careful description of the Country and its Inhabitants, their Customs, Manners and Governments. Written by Herself.

Like many utopian writers, Lane attempts to establish authenticity for her projected vision as a realistic, detailed account of an actual place. A future that can be "seen" seems less an impossible fantasy than a concrete political agenda to be realized.

In her work, Lane offers a vision of a totally liberated society of women who are self-sufficient, capable, and intelligent. Through scientific education, they have full control of themselves and their environment. As with the Herlanders, education lies at the heart of the Mizorans' social reform; they believe strongly that only through increased understanding can their society remain free of social ills. Like the Mizorans, the Herlanders, to ensure that their citizens are "the best kind of people," focus their attention on educating their children (Gilman 59). Lane's emphasis on education—in particular, scientific education—suggests that technological and scientific knowledge could help free women from biological as well as economic and social predicaments. Through science, Mizorans have gained control of the natural processes in order to reproduce, preserve, improve, and continue their race and heritage. Moreover, strong maternal and sisterly bonds give rise to a harmonious society. *Mizora* reveals Lane's desire for women's intellectual emancipation from nineteenth-century conceptions of virtuous womanhood, which sought to suppress women's intellectual cultivation and selfhood. Mizoran women belong to a class by themselves, for they can survive and prosper without men.

Mizora recounts Vera Zarovitch's initiation process in Mizora. During the period between her arrival and her departure, Vera's nineteenth-century attitudes undergo drastic revision. To authenticate the existence of the Mizoran utopia, Vera, author-narrator of the book, writes:

> I have this consolation: whatever reception may be given my narrative by the public, I know that it has been written solely for its good. That wonderful civilization I met with in Mizora, I may not be able to more than faintly shadow forth here, yet from it, the present age may form some idea of that grand, that ideal life that is possible for our remote posterity. (7)

While some peoples have tried to liberate themselves from an imperfect materialistic life to attain spiritual perfection in a religious heaven, others, like the Mizorans, have achieved their utopia through science and technology. Through Vera, Lane expresses her convictions concerning the future.

Lane's book is typical of many nineteenth-century American utopias in its faith in the inherent beneficence of technological and scientific control of natural processes, and in its essentially eugenicist approach to the problems of reproduction. However, while Lane envisioned science and technology as means to liberate women from their domestically and biologically defined roles, most nineteenth-century male writers saw science and technology chiefly as means of promoting national interests and maintaining the stability of an industrialized patriarchy. For example, in Edward Bellamy's technologically "progressive" vision of twenty-first-century Boston in *Looking Backward* (1887), patriarchy remains strong and women still are regarded as inferior to men. Bellamy depicts women in his utopia as having no interest in cultivating themselves intellectually. They work in the industrial army, contributing solely to the economic security and prosperity of the nation. In the words of Bellamy's spokesperson, Dr. Leete, women should be content with "their power of giving happiness to men" (212).

Like many of the Russian revolutionaries associated with Continental anarchist and socialist thought, Vera Zarovich belonged to "a family of nobility, wealth, and political power" in Russia (8). While studying in Paris, she became acquainted with an American family, from whom she "acquired a knowledge and admiration for their form of government and some revolutionary opinions" (9). Instead of keeping silent, she expressed her opposition to the Russian government, contrasting it with the American system. Her critical attitude brought her under suspicion.

At the age of twenty, Vera married Alexis and bore him a son. Her troubles began when she visited a Polish friend on the "anniversary of the tragedy of Grochow" and joined a group of people gathering to mourn their relatives' death (9). Russian soldiers suddenly appeared to interrupt the ceremonies. Her friend was stabbed by a bayonet, and Vera was arrested and sent to work in Siberia for life. Her family tried to secure her a lesser sentence, but to no avail. Finally, bribing a jailer, Vera escaped to the frontier and headed for France to meet her husband. Boarding a whaling ship sailing toward "the Northern Seas," she began her journey hoping later to find a passage to the south. Unfortunately, the ship was caught "between ice floes" and wrecked (10). She and her fellow passengers sought refuge with the Eskimos. Vera remained with her hosts after having been deserted by crew members. Later she decided to leave the Eskimos and set out into an unknown sea in a rowboat. At this point, the actual action of the narrative begins.

During the voyage, Vera's rowboat is caught and carried by a whirling current to a place where "[a] rosy light, like the first blush of a new day, permeated the atmosphere" (14). She finds herself in a beautiful and enchanting environment; then she comes upon a pleasure boat full of "young girls of the highest type of blonde beauty" (15), who take her to what seems "a female seminary" (16), as she sees no man around. Vera is presented to the "Lady Supreme of the College" and given a new set of clothing (17). By putting on her new clothing, Vera symbolically shows her willingness to embrace new ideas, and this is the first stage of her initiation. In the dining hall, she is very impressed with the striking appearance of her hostesses, their luxurious environment, and the abundance of healthful food. Vera notices that fruit is the principal diet of the inhabitants; later she discovers that their meat is chemically prepared. Later she also learns that the Mizorans' dietary regimen reflects their effort to control and maintain their physical perfection.

This all-female society possesses its own unique language, which Vera quickly learns. "Mizoran" is a language solely for women, a new symbolic order representing the Mizorans' subjectivity. It is a language of the mother, who has displaced the father. After learning the Mizoran language, Vera discovers that the place is not a female seminary, as she has surmised, but a "College of Experimental Science" (19). The women she has met are "practical chemists" (19) who possess eternal youth. Knowing the language helps Vera learn new utopian realities and gain a deeper understanding of Mizorans' value system. Prior to her acquisition of language, Vera seems to focus on her hosts' physical characteristics. The first thing she notices is the Mizorans' beautiful physical appearance and voices. She also observes that, in contrast to nineteenth-century ideals of physical beauty, which value a slender woman, Mizorans consider a big waist beautiful, and physical health is measured by the size of the lungs (20). Vera's preoccupation with physical distinctions is characteristic of the initial stage of her educative journey in Mizora.

Coming from a nineteenth-century patriarchal society, Vera is extremely puzzled by the absence of men in Mizora. In her society, men occupied "all governmental offices" and functioned as "arbitrator[s] of domestic life" (20). At this point, she cannot even imagine how a country can survive "without his [i.e., male] assistance and advice" (20). In her view, this country, with its beautiful inhabitants, is perfect for men; Mizora would be "a paradise for man" (21). It is obvious that Vera's view reflects her stereotypically patriarchal beliefs, which influence her way of thinking at an early stage of her stay in Mizora. Her traditional conception of the relations between the sexes undergoes transformation as she comes to know the Mizorans better. In the meantime, she continues to reflect on the position of "man" in her society and finds the absence of men in Mizora an anomaly; "man," she has been taught, is an indispensable and superior being who "has constituted himself the Government, the Law, Judge, Jury and Executioner" (21). The question "Where are the men?" stays on Vera's mind throughout the first part of the book, revealing the profound patriarchal influence on her upbringing and her struggle with that influence as she tries to understand the new value system.

Education in Mizora is provided by the state and is free for all; every student is expected to attain a certain level of excellence. Since education is considered most important to the Mizorans, teachers are highly honored and respected. As one of the instructors points out, education is "the foundation of our moral elevation, our government, our happiness. Let us relax our efforts, or curtail the means and inducements to

become educated, and we relax into ignorance, and end in demoraliza-
tions" (24). A person's wealth and social status, then, are measured by
her intellectual excellence, not by material possessions.

Since nothing is hereditary, Vera learns, except for "the prosperity
and happiness of the whole people" (25), in order to earn a livelihood
each Mizoran is engaged in "some regular trade, business or profession"
in which she feels competent (27). There are no distinctions according
to birth or position; all belong to "one immense family of sisters" (28).
The Preceptress of the National College, who is the leading scientist of
the country, explains to Vera that work is highly valued: "We are all
born equal, and labor is assigned to all; and the one who seeks labor is
wiser than the one who lets labor seek her" (28). The Mizorans adhere
to the proverb "Labor is the necessity of life" (37), so all are socially
equal and work in a spirit of cooperation. The women whom Vera has
mistaken for servants in fact are "all highly-educated, refined, lady-like
and lovely" (37).

The Mizoran people are "gentle, tender, and kind to solicitude" and
are devoid of malice and envy (27). Mizorans regard everyone as members of the same family. Their way of life is guided by custom, not by
law; and they surround themselves with beautiful objects. Their love of
exquisite environments and ornaments is revealed in the artistic manner
in which they decorate their homes. Unlike the comfortless opulence
which supported patriarchal pretentiousness, their pattern of life emphasizes domestic comfort and beauty; it is a lifestyle that enhances happiness and harmony. Vera wishes to take such a model of happiness—
"this social happiness, this equality of physical comfort and luxury"
(41)—back to her country. The Preceptress suggests that education is
the only way to bring about such a change:

> Educate them. Convince the rich that by educating the poor, they are
> providing for their own safety. They will have fewer prisons to build,
> fewer courts to sustain. Educated labor will work out its own salvation
> against Capital. Let the children of toil start in life with exactly the same
> educational advantages that are enjoyed by the rich. Give them the same
> physical and moral training, and let the rich pay for it by taxes. (41–42)

Education will equalize the rich and the poor, and intellect will be, according to the Preceptress, the "only standard of excellence" (42). From
the Mizoran perspective, a tempered meritocracy based on education is
the solution to all social problems.

Even though people may differ intellectually, they do have a chance
to move upward in occupation by developing their minds to the fullest
(64–65). The Mizorans' social stratification does not rest upon a rigid,

inflexible foundation. Everyone is entitled to engage in whatever she finds interesting. Education is only a means to an end, never an end in itself, for it continues even after graduation. The Mizorans believe in improvement—in moving toward perfection. Wauna, the Preceptress's daughter, who has been assigned to be Vera's guide and companion, explains:

> It is a duty with us to constantly seek improvement. . . . My children will have intellects of a finer grade than mine. This is our system of mind culture. The intellect is of slower development than the body, and takes longer to decay. The gradations of advancement from one intellectual basis to another, in a social body, requires centuries to mark a distinct change in the earlier ages of civilization. . . . (67)

The Preceptress further emphasizes the significance of education as a social equalizer: "'Universal education is the great destroyer of castes. It is the conqueror of poverty and the foundation of patriotism. It purifies and strengthens national, as well as individual character'" (67–68). And such intellectual development can help eliminate any "'domestic miseries'" (68). In addition to serving as a social equalizer, education helps to ensure the nation's political well-being, for everyone, the Preceptress implies in her statement, is satisfied. Rather than the military might used by male rulers to guarantee their political success, the intellectual quality of their people is the Mizorans' guarantee of political stability. Since Vera has always been concerned about social and political issues, the Preceptress's reaffirmation of the beneficent social and political effects of education proves very convincing to her.

At this point, Vera's attitude begins to change, as her nineteenth-century values are being replaced with those of the enlightened Mizorans. After witnessing and hearing how the Mizorans regard education, Vera is resolved to "devote all my energies and ability to convincing the government of its importance" (32). However, she remains troubled by the absence of men. Finally, she asks Wauna about her "other parent" (29). Vera's curiosity increases after Wauna replies that she has only "one mother, one adorable mother" (29). Strikingly similar to Wauna's answer is Somel's response to Terry's question about the existence of men and children in Herland: "We are mothers—all of us—but there are no fathers" (Gilman 45). Without men, women in both Mizora and Herland reproduce parthenogenetically.

Despite her curiosity about the absence of men, Vera continues to learn whatever she can about this intriguing society. She is very impressed with the way infants are raised. Unlike those in her country, Mizoran babies are like "little angels" (31) because they are taken care of with kindness and affection (32). Mizoran mothers pay close attention to their babies' "diet and exercise, both mental and physical" (32). Vera observes:

> The love of Mizora women for their children is strong and deep. They consider the care of them a sacred duty, fraught with the noblest re-sults of life. A daughter of scholarly attainments and noble character is a credit to her mother. That selfish mother who looks upon her chil-dren as so many afflictions is unknown to Mizora. If a mother should ever feel her children as burdens upon her, she would never give it expression, as any dereliction of duty would be severely rebuked by the whole community if not punished by banishment. (33)

The narrator here seems untroubled by any of the darker implications of repression, even the silencing of hostile views by a well-intentioned com-munal female society. Striking a child is deemed the most serious crime in Mizora, for childhood is regarded as "the only period of life that is capable of knowing perfect happiness" (118). Like the Mizorans, the Herlanders' unbreakable bond with their children is remarkable. As Moadine of Herland explains to the male intruders, "The children in this country are the one center and focus of all our thoughts. Every step of our advance is always considered in its effect on them—on the race. You see, we are *Mothers*" (Gilman 66). They also take great pains in educating and caring for their children. Growing up in a loving and beau-tiful environment, these young Herlanders develop a "voracious appetite for life" (Gilman 103).

In both Mizora and Herland, the spirit of motherhood pervades all aspects of the inhabitants' lives. Their children are the focus of their de-votion, and their maternal love is extremely intense. Since their children embody the future of their heritage, these women make sure that all children are properly raised and carefully educated. Motherhood, which is necessary to the continuation of the race, is regarded by Mizorans as a "sacred duty fraught with the noblest results of life" (33) and by Herlanders as an integral part of life: "By motherhood they were born and by moth-erhood they lived" (Gilman 59).

This ideal matriarchy is upheld by a minimum of formal govern-ment. The "Federal Republic" of Mizora is headed by a president, whose term lasts five years (69). Candidates for government offices, including the presidency, must be qualified by their state colleges as well as by the National College. However, politics are not of great significance, for there is neither political debate nor political campaign. All inhabitants vote for candidates of their choice. Every politician works honestly and professionally for the good of the whole country (71). The Mizorans' disinterest in politics is shared by the later Herlanders, who are guided by their strong sense of community. As Van, the narrator of *Herland*, points out, "To them [Herlanders] the country was a unit—it was theirs. They themselves were a unit, a conscious group; they thought in terms of the community. As such, their time-sense was not limited to the hopes and ambitions of an individual life" (Gilman 79).

In Mizora, technology and science form an integral part of daily life. Telecommunication and transportation systems are highly efficient. The inhabitants invent rain and control other aspects of their environment, which is very clean; there are flowers and fruit trees and singing birds everywhere (48). In Mizora, neither "domestic fowls" nor any other kinds of animals exist (54). To cut the cost of production, machinery is used, and, as a result, all goods are affordable for everyone. Heavy and coarse domestic work is done by machines; cooking, which is considered an art, is carried out carefully and professionally (47). The union between sciences and arts, characteristic of the Mizoran lifestyle, plays an important role, too, in the lives of the scientifically and agriculturally progressive Herlanders (Gilman 64), whose goals in life are "Beauty, Health, Strength, Intellect, Goodness" (Gilman 59).

From where the country is located, "a hollow sphere, bounded North and South by impassable oceans" (25), Mizorans cannot see the sun, moon, or stars. The sole branch of science which is unrepresented is astronomy—for Mizora is, quite literally, not of this universe. By creating a geographical distance, Lane wants to separate herself from the nineteenth-century world and to emphasize the separatist nature of her utopian society.

Despite the ideal conditions Mizora has to offer, Vera remains puzzled by the absence of members of the male sex. Finally, she manages to elicit a question about men from the Preceptress: "Are there men in your country?" (89). In part 2, Vera's curiosity about men in Mizora is satisfied. The Preceptress informs her that Mizoran women have transcended the boundaries of Natural Law. That is, like the later Herlanders, the Mizorans are born through parthenogenesis. In the past, Mizora was a patriarchal society not different from Vera's world. Women then, Vera learns, "had known temptation and resistance, and reluctant compliance. They had experienced the treachery and ingratitude of humanity, and had dealt in it themselves" (91). Vera emphasizes the comparison with her own society: the Mizorans "had known joy as I had known it, and their sorrow had been my sorrows. They had loved as I had loved, and sinned as I had sinned, and suffered as I had suffered" (91). At this juncture, the experiences of women in the two worlds are conflated. Women in patriarchal society, no matter where it is located, have had to endure similar oppression. On the optimistic side, there is hope of overcoming the suffering, as shown by the history of Mizora.

Because Mizoran women took action to achieve what might have seemed to them unattainable, they reached their utopian goal, liberating themselves from miseries. However, their victory did not occur without struggle and conflict. The Preceptress tells Vera that men have been extinct in Mizora for three thousand years (93). Before their extinction, Mizoran men, like their nineteenth-century brothers, ruled and oppressed women, who were perceived as mentally and physically inferior. Women were treated unjustly; for example, they worked hard but received lower wages, a situation familiar to Lane's nineteenth-century readers. Patriarchy then was corrupt; the country was full of poverty, oppression, and wretchedness. Only very few enjoyed power and wealth. Women had no rights in the government, and "[t]heir privileges were only what the chivalry or kindness of the men permitted" (99). Subsequently, women decided to unite to struggle against male hegemony, and by a revolution even more significant than its late-eighteenth-century American predecessor, women seized control of the government in order to institute a truly female-centered republic. Those women remembered how they had been discriminated against, excluded, and deprived of educational and occupational opportunities. After the revolution, a republic was established, and men were excluded from the government for one hundred years. At the end of that period, not a single male existed (101). Having learned from the mistakes committed by men, the pioneering Mizoran women succeeded in making their nation prosperous by completely restructuring their political system.

While the republic controlled by men had been dependent upon military and naval dominance, the republic run by women was founded on morality, a trait traditionally distinguishing women from men. Instead of relying on military prowess and destructive technology, Mizoran women erected an academy of nature-oriented science. Under women's rule, the arts and sciences were encouraged, and "every branch of education now was open to women" (102). The political revolution carried out by Mizoran women represents a reversal of the nineteenth-century exclusion of women from education and various occupations. The emphasis on natural and social sciences has enhanced the nation's progress and the inhabitants' quality of life, as "science had revealed the Secret of Life" (103) and so has enabled them to continue and improve their health and longevity after the extinction of men. Mizorans deem education, especially scientific education, politically vital because such education has the power to change women's lives socially and biologically.

In accord with the book's fundamental "scientism," the Preceptress explains bioengineering techniques to Vera. In order to assist the preparation for "a higher development" of the next generation, Mizorans subscribe to the fashionable "science" of eugenics (104). Mothers are con-

sidered "the only important part of all life" (103). The Preceptress points
out that "[i]t is the duty of every generation to prepare the way for a
higher development of the next, as we see demonstrated by Nature in
the fossilized remains of long extinct animal life, a preparatory condition
for a higher form in the next evolution" (104). To improve their off-
spring, she says,

> We devote the most careful attention to the Mothers of our race. No
> retarding mental or moral influences are ever permitted to reach her
> [sic]. On the contrary, the most agreeable contacts with nature, all that
> can cheer and ennoble in art or music surround her. She is an object of
> interest and tenderness to all who meet her. Guarded from unwhole-
> some agitation, furnished with nourishing and proper diet—both mental
> and physical—the child of a Mizora mother is always an improvement
> upon herself. (104)

From childhood, Mizorans find themselves in a pleasant environment,
which enhances both their physical and their intellectual growth, keeping them free of diseases. But, in a projection of blame onto the victim,
they assume that disease causes immorality, so that a person's physical
health reveals the degree of her morality (108), and the physically and
mentally handicapped have no place in Mizoran society (104). Mizorans
consider disease to be the cause of crime. As its absence eliminates
crime, they place great emphasis on a healthy and pleasant life.

Vera fears that she will be unable to communicate what she has
seen in Mizora to her people, so that they may emulate the Mizoran
way. She suggests that she may use her knowledge only to improve her
own "kindred" and hopes that the rest of the world someday will find its
own way (111). Hearing Vera's words, the Preceptress rebukes her:

> What a barbarous, barbarous idea! Your country will never rise above its
> ignorance and degradation, until out of its mental agony shall be evolved
> a nature kindled with an ambition that burns for Humanity instead of
> self. It will be the nucleus round which will gather the timid but anxious,
> and then will be lighted that fire which no waters can quench. It burns
> for the liberty of thought. Let human nature once feel the warmth of its
> beacon fires, and it will march onward, defying all obstacles, braving all
> perils till it be won. Human nature is ever reaching for the unattained. It
> is that little spark within us that has an undying life. When we can no
> longer use it, it flies elsewhere. (111)

The Preceptress's statement recalls Ernst Bloch's affirmation of human
utopian consciousness—"that little spark within us that has an undying

life"—and human faith in our improved future which is not yet in existence. To reach that goal, women must keep "reaching for the unattained" and make sure that "that little spark" may stay lit.

Because science has enabled Mizorans to overcome biological limitations, it is highly revered. Nature is regarded as God and the Great Mother (120). Orthodox religion does not exist, and prayer has no place in this society. Instead, a faith in the prescriptions of science serves as a religion for the Mizorans, improving and ennobling their lives. Wauna, Vera's companion, explains that science is

> the goddess who has led us out of ignorance and superstition; out of degradation and disease, and every other wretchedness that superstitious, degraded humanity has known. She has lifted us above the low and the little, the narrow and mean in human thought and action, and has placed us in a broad, free, independent, noble, useful and grandly happy life. (121)

Vera is alarmed by what Wauna has to say about the Mizorans' beliefs. As a nineteenth-century Christian, she seeks to confirm her religion in Mizora and is disappointed and perplexed to learn that these people can be prosperous and happy without Christianity. To the inhabitants of Mizora, religion can neither solve problems nor make people moral. Instead, the power of enlightenment and education can transform and reform people. The Preceptress reaffirms her faith in education:

> Education will root out more sin than all your creeds can. Educate your convicts and train them into controlling and subduing their criminal tendencies by their own will, and it will have more effect on their morals than all the prayers ever uttered. Educate them to that point where they can perceive for themselves the happiness of moral lives, and then you may trust them to temptation without fear. (133)

Religions do not contribute to any progress, but rather obstruct true knowledge. They are compared to "beliefs in creeds and superstitions" which are "perversions of judgment, resulting from a lack of thorough mental training" (134). The Mizorans' intellectual preoccupation contributes significantly to the design of their nation's political system, in which science and education occupy the place held in other societies by religious institutions.

Wauna also instructs Vera in the Mizorans' view of death. To them there is no life after death, but instead they will return to the elements to become part of Nature, and "[w]hat our future is to be after dissolution no one knows" (122). Since Mizorans do not believe in an afterlife, they accept death, along with physical and mental decline, matter-of-factly. There is no mourning for those who die of old age, for they have lived a full life. The Mizorans' attitude toward death indicates that they have progressed "almost beyond the reach of sorrow" (137). Oblivion is a blissful state to these happy people. However, the untimely death of the young is a "cause for grief," because the dead one has been prevented from enjoying what life had in store for her (136).

After absorbing all that she learns and experiences in Mizora, Vera wishes to return home in order to change her society to accord with the Mizoran model. She visualizes an emergence of a utopia in her homeland:

> I pictured to myself my own dear land—dear, despite its many phases of wretchedness—smiling in universal comfort and health. I imagined its political prisons yawning with emptiness, while their haggard and decrepit and sorrowful occupants hobbled out into the sunshine of liberty, and the new life we were bringing to them. Fancy flew abroad on the wings of hope, dropping the seeds of progress wherever it passes.
>
> The poor should be given work, and justly paid for it, instead of being supported by charity. The charity that had fostered indolence in its mistaken efforts to do good, should be employed to train poverty to skillful labor and economy in living. And what a world of good that one measure would produce! The poor should possess exactly the same educational advantages that were supplied to the rich. In this one measure, if I could make it popular, I would see the golden promise of the future of my country. (142)

To carry out her plan, Vera asks Wauna to go back with her, hoping that Wauna will help change her people and transform her homeland into a Mizora, which to her is a "sweet ideal land of my Soul, of Humanity" (141).

After fifteen years in Mizora, Vera departs with Wauna, her reformer designate. They arrive in Russia, only to find no one in Vera's family there; her father and son have died, and her husband is in the United States (144). Subsequently, they decide to carry out their plan in the United States. On their way to the United States, Wauna's beauty, not the ideal humanity she represents, serves as her only attraction for men. Though she receives "a juster appreciation" in the United States, Wauna expresses dismay at what she experiences in Vera's "civilization" (145). The sight of a child being abused and other miserable conditions she witnesses sadden and discourage her greatly. She announces to Vera: "I cannot reform them. It is not for such as I to be a reformer. Those who need reform are the ones to work for it" (146). Wauna's words remind us of Bloch's notion that, to realize our utopian goal, we must keep wishing and wanting, for "without wishes we would be the dead bodies over which the wicked would stride on to victory" (*Principle* 1: 77); we must refuse to accept the status quo.

Despite the failure of her efforts to reform her nineteenth-century society under Wauna's influence, Vera remains optimistic. Wauna dies on her way home, leaving Vera still clinging to her faith in utopia, though knowing that its realization is going to take a long time. She reminds herself and the reader that "[t]hough we cannot hope to attain their [the Mizorans'] perfection in our generation, yet many, very many, evils could be obliterated were we to follow their laws" (147). Taught by the Mizoran example, she entrusts her hope for utopia to free universal education. She closes by reaffirming her belief in the "Not-Yet": "The future of the world, if it be grand and noble, will be the result of UNIVERSAL EDU-CATION, FREE AS THE GOD-GIVEN WATER WE DRINK" (147).

Vera's call for universal education echoes progressive reformist and anarchist belief in education as the basis for an equal and democratic society. It is also opposed to the anti-intellectual nineteenth-century Cult of True Womanhood, which idealized woman and isolated her at the same time, at least in theory, from the taint of social ills. Angelika Bammer suggests that Mizoran women are "perfect Victorian ladies" who represent "the very essence of the ideal true womanhood" (175), but Bammer's view of Mizorans is a misrepresentation. Though Mizorans possess feminine beauty, they do not by any means fit the image of either a nineteenth-century True Woman or Cogan's nineteenth-century Real Woman. Unlike Cogan's educated and self-sufficient Real Woman, whose main purpose in life is to serve her man, Mizorans are independent intellectuals. It is noteworthy that the Mizorans' intellectualism defies patriarchy's artificial demarcation between the sexes.

Lane's vision of an alternative society embodies her attempt to criticize and reconceptualize women's roles and condition in American society. Instead of maintaining the heterosexual social structure, she eliminates patriarchy altogether. Living in the age of industrial progress, Lane optimistically expresses her faith in the liberating force of technology and modernization, initiated by industrialization. Her Mizoran women no longer are burdened with the drudgery of domestic chores. Machinery, as well as trained professionals, relieve them of household responsibilities. Unlike many nineteenth-century women who lived their lives solely within domestic confines, a Mizoran woman, liberated from her traditional roles as wife and mother within the patriarchal nuclear family, can enjoy improving herself intellectually and culturally. In Mizora, matriarchy has brought down the walls created by patriarchal culture. Through her utopian narrative, Lane argues that women are competent and perfectly capable of governing a society that is technologically and scientifically progressive.

Ironically, industrial progress increased restrictions of women, as they shared unequally in the profits produced by the new technology. Nevertheless, like most Americans of her period, Lane was optimistic concerning the great potential and inherently liberating benefits of science and technology, which play a significant role in the life of Mizoran women. These woman have eradicated illnesses and transcended biological limits, to continue their race without men. Nineteenth-century women, lacking the reproductive alternatives only recently made available to twentieth-century women, were controlled by men sexually. Although twentieth-century women have more reproductive freedom than their nineteenth-century sisters, the former have not come very far in their struggle against patriarchal control of reproduction, championed by conservatives in the government and in religious organizations. What science has afforded today's women, living in such a politically and religiously hostile environment, is very limited and reactionary in comparison with Lane's vision of women's reproductive freedom. In this respect, Mizorans are much more radically advanced than twentieth-century women, for they have succeeded in eliminating the phallocentric culture altogether. Marriage, virtually the only alternative for nineteenth-century women, does not exist in Mizora. As a result, Mizoran women are able to prosper intellectually and, unlike their nineteenth-century sisters, are free to reap benefits from state-provided education. They live together in a spirit of love and cooperation, and they celebrate communitarianism, sisterhood, and motherhood.

Because science has given Mizorans reproductive independence and enabled them to attain perfect physical and moral character, the "science" of human progress, not militarism, has become their savior. Regrettably, their obsession with the power of science, particularly the then-fashionable pseudoscience of "eugenics," seems not to make them more civilized in all respects than their militaristically minded male predecessors; they disregard the value of other human beings who are handicapped and/or who do not belong to "a fair race" (92). The Mizoran attitude toward people who are not of "a fair race" or of Northern European descent is condescending and racist, and this society is unable to incorporate the physically unfit or handicapped. According to Lane, Mizorans have eliminated not only "the coarser nature of men" (104) but also people of "the dark complexions," who, in their view, possess "the elements of evils" (92). Here Lane's faith in eugenicism and white superiority echoes Francis Galton's statement in the introduction to the 1892 edition of his *Hereditary Genius,* reprinted in the 1914 edition:

> There is nothing either in the history of domestic animals or in that of
> evolution to make us doubt that a race of sane men may be formed, who
> shall be as much superior mentally and morally to the modern European,
> as the modern European is to the lowest of the Negro races. (Galton x)

Also, in instructing Vera concerning the Mizorans' ability to control "Nature's processes of development" (104)—that is, reproduction—the Preceptress echoes Galton's adamant belief that "the improvement of the natural gifts of future generations of the human race is largely, though indirectly, under our control. We may not be able to originate, but we can guide" (xxvi–xxvii). Lane's glorification of the "fair race" and her advocacy of eugenic priorities taints her otherwise radical feminist stance with elitism and racism.

Despite these limitations, Lane presented her nineteenth-century readers with a rather shocking alternative to gender inequality—a society without men. To most nineteenth-century minds, such a world probably was inconceivable. In that respect, Lane offered an innovative, optimistic view of the possibilities of a more enlightened science and technology. However, what seemed utopian for nineteenth-century women may not seem adequate to twentieth-century women. Since Mizora was born as a result of women's struggle, Lane implies that women could make a revolution happen if they took matters into their own hands. Women can rewrite their own history. Women can reposition themselves in society. *Mizora* represents the author's attempt to create, outside patriarchy, a new text, a new world order, a new history, in which women no longer are marginalized but are in complete control of their bodies as well as their social arrangements. Lane's women characters have gained full subjectivity. They are no longer defined as the "other"; they are bona fide individuals. The Mizorans' political efforts to redefine and reposition themselves recall the actions of the nineteenth-century feminist activists who in 1848 united at Seneca Falls, in the belief that, without the right to elect their representatives in government, women forever would remain excluded and disadvantaged.

In addition to its sociopolitical significance, Lane's utopia seems to have been the first in a long line of feminist separatist utopias, of which the most famous is Gilman's *Herland*. Though Lane and Gilman share a similar vision of women, Lane seems much more uncompromisingly separatist than Gilman, for she does not even suggest the possibility of a final reconciliation with patriarchy, as does Gilman. Vera's patriarchal world is totally separate from Mizora and cannot be reformed, as suggested by Wauna's loss of will power at the very outset of her mission. Unlike Lane's Mizorans, Gilman's Herlanders are willing to learn from their male intruders, Van, Terry, and Jeff. They even allow their citizens, Ellador, Alima, and Celis, to marry the outsiders, for they are hoping for "the New Tie with other lands—Brotherhood as well as Sisterhood, and, . . . Fatherhood" (Gilman 119). The marriages symbolize the remarriage between matriarchy and patriarchy. The Herlanders' optimism and their willingness to reestablish a connection with the outside world is expressed by Somel during the wedding ceremonies:

You see, it is the dawn of a new era. You don't know how much you
mean to us. It is not only Fatherhood—that marvelous dual parentage
to which we are strangers—the miracle of union in life-giving—but it is
Brotherhood. You are the rest of the world. You join us to our kind—
to all the strange lands and peoples we have never seen. We hope to
know them—to love and help them—and to learn of them. Ah! You
cannot know! (Gilman 119)

At the end, Ellador travels with Van to his land. While other Herlanders
await her return, the location of Herland will be kept a secret. Their
intention to conceal their location shows their apprehension and reser-
vations about the unknown. However, Herlanders are willing to leave
their options open, while Mizorans are very confident that their own
system is the only option for them. In this respect, Lane is more pre-
scriptively radical than Gilman.

As a nineteenth-century American woman, Lane viewed industrialization, technology, and science, though credulously, with trust, hope,
and optimism. Reflecting nineteenth-century faith in progress, she chose
not to look back nostalgically to a past of supposed pastoral tranquillity,
perhaps because past societies on record had dealt so harshly with
women. Rather, she projected unknown possibilities onto a distant land.
She could see clearly what she wished for women of her time, in contrast to the painful situation women then had to tolerate; regrettably, her
genuine boldness in projecting a solution to "the woman issue" ignored
prejudice toward nonwhite races and the handicapped. Lane did not
dwell on the past, which had nothing to offer her and her female contemporaries but the status quo of patriarchy. To reaffirm women's humanity and to reassure her women readers that there were other choices,
Lane emphasized women's vastly improved position in her realistically
presented alternative society, placed beyond the reach of patriarchy. In
this respect, her work encourages an expansion of women's consciousness, opening up an entirely new dimension of life for women as a
whole. At the same time, the sharp contrast between the real and the
ideal highlights women's issues. The success of Mizoran women reminds
us of Eliza Farnham's statement in *Woman and Her Era* (1865): "Only
Woman is sufficient to state Woman's claims and vindicate them" (1:
308). It also recalls Elizabeth Cady Stanton's assertion that "woman herself must do this work; for woman alone can understand the height, the
depth, the length and breadth of her degradation" (qtd. in Flexner 77).

Through her utopian fiction, Lane committed linguistic mutiny against
the patriarchal order. *Mizora* is a woman's text, anticipating a fall of patriarchy and envisioning a return of matriarchal values and a reestablish-
ment of women's language, or a language of the mother. The book's

prophetic stance remains politically defiant and subversive indeed. Lane, in essence, did exactly what Hélène Cixous, a century later, insists upon: "Woman must put herself into the text—as into the world and into history—by her own movement" (875).

Works Cited

Appleton, Jane Sophia. "Sequel to the Vision of Bangor in the Twentieth Century." 1848. Rpt. in *American Utopias: Selected Short Fiction*. Ed. Arthur O. Lewis, Jr. New York: Arno P, 1971. 243–65.

Bammer, Angelika. "Visions and Revisions: The Utopian Impulse in Feminist Fiction." Diss. U of Wisconsin, 1982.

Bellamy, Edward. *Looking Backward, 2000–1800*. 1887. New York: Modern Library, 1951.

Bloch, Ernst. *A Philosophy of the Future*. Trans. John Cumming. New York: Herder and Herder, 1970.

———. *The Principle of Hope*. Trans. Neville Plaice, Stephen Plaice, and Paul Knight. 3 vols. Oxford, England: Basil Blackwell, 1986.

Cixous, Hélène. "The Laugh of the Medusa." Trans. Keith Cohen and Paula Cohen. *Signs* 1 (1976): 875–93.

Cogan, Frances B. *All-American Girl: The Ideal of Real Womanhood in Mid-Nineteenth-Century America*. Athens: U of Georgia P, 1989.

Farnham, Eliza W. *Woman and Her Era*. 2 vols. New York: C. M. Plumb, 1865.

Flexner, Eleanor. *Century of Struggle: The Woman's Rights Movement in the United States*. New York: Atheneum, 1973.

Galton, Francis. *Hereditary Genius: An Inquiry into Its Laws and Consequences*. 1869. London: Macmillan, 1914.

Gilman, Charlotte Perkins. *Herland*. New York: Pantheon, 1979.

Griffith, Mary. *Three Hundred Years Hence*. 1836. Rpt. in *American Utopias: Selected Short Fiction*. Ed. Arthur O. Lewis, Jr. New York: Arno P, 1971. 9–92.

Lane, Ann J. Introduction. *Herland*. By Charlotte Perkins Gilman. New York: Pantheon, 1979. v–xxiv.

Lane, Mary E. Bradley. *Mizora: A Prophecy*. 1890. Boston: Gregg P, 1975.

Welter, Barbara. "Anti-Intellectualism and the American Woman: 1800–1860." *Mid-America* 48 (1966): 258–70.

———. "The Cult of True Womanhood: 1820–1860." *American Quarterly* (Summer 1966): 151–74.

CHAPTER 8

"A Goddess Behind a Sordid Veil":

The Domestic Heroine Meets the Labor Novel

in Mary E. Wilkins Freeman's

The Portion of Labor

Dorothy Berkson

In one of the defining moments in Mary E. Wilkins Freeman's 1901 novel, *The Portion of Labor*, Ellen Brewster, the heroine of the novel, leads a group of her fellow workers back to work in the shoe factory against which they have been on strike. The strike began largely because of an impassioned speech she delivered against the injustice of a cut in their wages. Convinced now that she is responsible for the suffering and privation of her friends as they struggle through a bitter winter without wages, Ellen, who has led the workers out of the factory, determines to lead them back in. Described as "a beautiful child, her light hair tossed around her rosy face, her eyes full of the daring of perfect confidence," Ellen walks defiantly past a crowd of picketing workers and cries out to them, "If you want to kill a girl for going back to work to save herself and her friends from starvation, do it. I am not afraid! But kill me, if you must kill anybody, because I am the one that started the strike" (257). It is a moment that reveals the complex and conflicting ideologies of work, class, and gender in the novel. Described here as a working-class heroine, risking her life to lead her friends back to work, Ellen is also, as the physical description of her suggests, a quintessential nineteenth-century child-woman, beautiful, delicate, and totally unsuited to the rough and physical world of the factory, a world her family and friends are determined she will rise out of. Born into the working class but not of it, Ellen is contrasted throughout the novel with the rough and vulgar women of her class (including her mother and her aunt), among whom she has been raised but to whom she bears as little resemblance as to animals of a different species. Like Stephen Crane's Maggie, she has blossomed in a mud puddle, an anomalous figure whose narrative arises out of and illuminates the conflicting and interdependent ideologies of class and gender that dominated nineteenth-century capitalist culture.

Two closely interwoven plot lines center on the figure of Ellen Brewster. The first is the story of a working-class community's clash with the owners of the shoe factory which provides work for most of them. In this plot line, Ellen is the working-class heroine who, when her father loses his job, refuses a wealthy benefactor's offer to send her to Vassar. She takes a job at the shoe factory instead and leads the workers out on strike when their wages are cut. The second plot line revolves around Ellen's love affair with the nephew of the factory owner and her eventual marriage to him, a classic rags-to-riches Cinderella story. The first plot emphasizes class solidarity and the dignity of labor; the second, the aspiration of the working class to attain the leisure, education, and taste of the upper classes. Those few critics who have discussed the novel at all have praised Freeman's gritty realism in depicting a nineteenth-century New England factory town and the hardships of the working classes, while deploring the novel's emphasis on Ellen Brewster, whom one critic describes as "tedious in her ecstasies of self-sacrifice, her commitment to perfection, her tense demand for happiness" (Foster 155).[1]

Yet it is precisely these qualities of Ellen's which link the two strains of the novel and reveal the complex connection between domesticity and industry, between private sphere and public sphere, and between nineteenth-century culture's constructions of gender and of class. Ellen mediates between these two spheres and two sets of values, which are cast as opposites but which her presence reveals to be mirror images of each other.

The novel is structured as a *Bildungsroman,* a coming-of-age narrative, in which Ellen's journey to knowledge and maturity tie together the disparate threads of the narrative. Part of the story of her coming of age is cast as the traditional female *Bildungsroman*—the courtship plot in which the young girl discovers that her destiny is marriage. Ellen's coming of age, however, is also marked by her developing class consciousness: her awareness of social injustice and of the economic gulf between the capitalists and the workers. Linking these two plots is a set of values which arises out of evangelical Christian ideology, which sees the poor as victims of the oppressive rich and which aligns women with the Christian virtues of compassion and concern for the weak and the oppressed. Thus, in the novel, Ellen plays the dual and not incompatible roles of traditional heroine and social reformer. Both roles are intimately linked to nineteenth-century constructions of womanhood.[2]

As the mediating figure between public greed and private morality, Ellen in many ways resembles the pure, noble young heroines of Stowe and Dickens, young women whose spirituality is tested and developed through their exposure to the suffering of others; it is the confrontation between their idealism and the suffering caused by social injustice that shapes their development. Stowe's Mara Lincoln, Dickens's Esther Summerson, and all of those heroines whose names are preceded by the adjective "little"—Little Eva, Little Nell, Little Dorrit—fill the pages of mid-nineteenth-century Anglo-American fiction. These are the childlike heroines who identify with the oppressed: slaves, prisoners, the orphaned, the poor. Ellen Brewster belongs in their company. Like them she feels she has been specially marked, that her duty requires her not only to strive against oppression, but to renounce opportunities that would provide her with privileges not granted to others of her class.

Like these nineteenth-century "angels in the house," Ellen is marked from childhood by her beauty and her sensitivity. Her working-class parents watch her anxiously, fearful that she is too good to live. Determined that she will not live the hard life they have endured, they scrimp and save in order to give her every luxury. Their obsession with her future reveals one of the significant links between gender and class in industrial cultures. They are determined that she will not work, for while it is "no social degradation for a man to work in a shoe factory . . . a woman who worked therein [had] hopelessly forfeited her caste" (8). Ellen's Aunt Eva (herself a worker) declares that she will burn the shoe factory down before she will see Ellen work there. Freeman illustrates vividly in this novel the way in which it is women who carry the primary markers of class. By definition, only middle- or upper-class women, whose lives were bounded by the domestic sphere, and who were not tainted by work or by exposure to the degraded and mercenary qualities of the public sphere, could aspire to the qualities of genteel womanhood. Freeman also makes it clear that working-class women deeply aspire to that role, and their failure to achieve it leaves many of them bitter and angry.

In a culture which automatically pronounced a woman who worked as déclassée, there were only a few ways in which she could move to a higher class. If a woman could not work her way up the class ladder— unlike a man, who could do so—she could be lifted up the ladder through adoption or marriage. By the end of the nineteenth century, these attitudes were beginning to shift, and education was beginning to provide a respectable route into a higher class for a few women. Ellen Brewster is presented with each of these opportunities, and the way in which the narrative treats them reveals a great deal about the relationship between class and gender ideology at the turn of the century.

The novel opens with a vivid description of the harshness of the Brewsters' lives. The entire family, grandmother, mother, father, and aunt, have displaced all of their own disappointed aspirations onto Ellen. But it is the women who feel the burden of class most passionately. Ellen's mother Fanny, who does piecework at home to supplement the family income, "had sunk her personal vanity further and further in that for her child. She brushed her own hair back from her temples, and candidly revealed all her unyouthful lines, and dwelt fondly upon the arrangement of little Ellen's locks, which were of a fine, pale yellow, as clear as the color of amber" (11). Fanny dresses Ellen like a young princess, cutting up her old clothes and those of her sister Eva to make Ellen beautiful clothes. When Fanny cuts up one of Eva's dresses without asking, a violent fight erupts between Eva and Fanny, in which Ellen becomes the contested object of everyone's rage. Terrified and bewildered by the violence of the family outburst, Ellen runs away.

Ellen's flight from home marks her as different from the rest of her family, as having more delicate and sensitive feelings. The description of Ellen as she makes her way through the winter landscape points particularly to her difference from her mother and aunt. When she falls down on the icy ground and skins her knee, she does not cry aloud "from a delicate sense of personal dignity, and a dislike of violent manifestations of feeling which had strengthened with her growth in the midst of the turbulent atmosphere of her home" (13). Ellen's horror of violence is further marked when she stops before the window of a butcher shop and recoils at the sight of the dead animals in the window. "Ellen was a woman-child," the text tells us here, "and suddenly she struck the rock upon which women so often wreck or effect harbor, whichever it may be" (19). The narrative has already made clear, however, that not all women are horrified by violence—working-class women live with violence all the time and become deadened to it. The association of Ellen with a loathing of violence is a marker of class as well as gender. And it is precisely at this moment, as if in a fairy tale, that Ellen is found by a truly genteel woman of the upper classes. Cynthia Lennox, sister of the owner of the factory where Andrew Brewster works, will become Ellen's link to the upper-class world of genteel womanhood; she comes upon the scene as if she were a fairy godmother destined to bring the worthy child (who has demonstrated her worthiness by her abhorrence of violence) to her proper estate. Cynthia Lennox is a wealthy, unmarried woman whose unsatisfied maternal longing fixes itself on Ellen. When Ellen refuses to tell her where she lives, Cynthia takes the child home with her and determines to adopt her.

Just as Freeman introduces the possibility of Ellen's magical rescue from working-class drudgery and her delivery into upper-class leisure, she deconstructs it. Cynthia Lennox is a fascinating figure. Although she is in many ways the model of genteel womanhood, in other ways she has jumped out of the narrow restrictions of that category. Unmarried by choice, she is a childless woman who desperately loves children. When her brother's wife died many years before, her young nephew, Robert Lloyd, was given to her to raise. When her brother remarried several years later, the child was taken from her, and her grief for him is unabated. Indeed, in the intensity of her frustrated mother-love, the fairy godmother has a dark side. Her love for Ellen is as devouring and frightening as Fanny's. When Cynthia picks Ellen up and carries her home, murmuring endearments to her all the way, Ellen "panted in bewilderment, and a terror which was half assuaged by something like fascination" (22). The working-class and upper-class woman are not that different, beneath the veneer of class difference. Just as Ellen is terrified of Fanny's violent love, she fears Cynthia's. Freeman goes further, however, in her deconstruction of gender and class differences. Ellen, faced with the opulence of Cynthia's clothes, is reminded of "the morning wrappers of dark-blue cotton at ninety-eight cents apiece" which her mother sews to supplement the family income, and the child is "filled with undefined apprehensions of splendor and the opulence which might overwhelm her simple grasp of life and cause her to lose all her old standards of value" (41). Young as she is, Ellen is aware of the difference between this woman's life and her mother's, and she is filled with "a bitter and piteous jealousy for her mother and home, and all that she had ever loved and believed in. . . . What right had this strange woman, dressed in a silk dress like that, to be leaning over her in the morning, and looking at her like that—to be leaning over her in the morning instead of her own mother, and looking at her in that way, when she was not her mother" (41). Thus, instead of becoming the means by which Ellen will be elevated into upper-class luxury and leisure, Cynthia Lennox represents Ellen's first lesson in class consciousness.

Even while Ellen is demonstrating her loyalty to her mother, however, she is provided with an opportunity to prove her sensitivity and selflessness in relationship to Cynthia Lennox herself. When Ellen overhears a conversation in which Cynthia hysterically claims she cannot give the child up and is told that she might be "lynched" if people discovered she had kept the child without trying to find the parents, Ellen once again runs away, this time to save the woman who wants to provide her with all the luxury and privilege of upper-class life, but who would alienate her from her parents to do so. Reunited with her parents, Ellen refuses to tell anyone where she has been. But Ellen's flight is not quite so simple and noble as it appears. When she leaves Cynthia Lennox's house, she takes with her the gifts the upper-class woman has given her: a gilt cup, some flowers from the hot house, and a large, beautiful doll that had once belonged to Cynthia Lennox's nephew, Robert Lloyd. If the working-class child chooses to go home to protect her benefactress and to be reunited with her working-class parents, she nonetheless takes with her tokens of upper-class luxury. The effect of Ellen's experience at Cynthia Lennox's is described as an initiation, a loss of innocence: "The breath of human passion had stained the pure crystal of her childish imagination." It is as if "the evergreen trees in the west yard, and the cherry-trees on the east had found out that they were not in the Garden of Eden" (84).

Yet another lesson concerning class and gender awaits Ellen, however. One night she hears some of the workers from the factory talking bitterly about the owners' temporarily closing down the factory and throwing all of the hands out of work during the bitter winter. In the midst of the angry talk, Cynthia Lennox's name is mentioned as one of the rich parasites whose luxuries are bought "by the sweat of [the workers'] brows" (103). Nahum Beals, one of the most outspoken of the workers, angrily denounces her: "Cynthia Lennox and all the women like her are the oppressors of the poor. They are accursed in the sight of the Lord, as were those women we read about in the Old Testament, with their mantles and cripsing-pins. Their low voices and their shrinkin' from touchin' shoulders with their fellow-beings in a crowd don't alter matters a mite" (104). Women are here singled out by Nahum as symbols of class oppression. Not even his anger at the bosses has quite the virulence of his anger at Cynthia Lennox and "all the women like her." When Ellen goes to bed, distraught at all that she has heard, she takes the doll Cynthia Lennox has given her and puts the doll in the closet "face to the wall." Before putting the doll away, she shakes her and tells her, "You have been naughty . . . dreadful naughty. . . . What right had you to be livin' with rich folks, and warin' such fine things, when other children don't have anything?" (107). Later, in a curious reversal of her parents' desire to dress her in fine clothes and raise her status, Ellen takes the doll from "the closet of vicarious penance," and dresses her "like a very cullion among dolls, in the remnant of a dress in which Fanny Brewster had done her house-work all summer" (111). Ellen has learned more than the unjustness of the bosses and the dreadful consequences of the factory closing. She has learned that women are the emblematic bearers of class status and class shame. This is a moment of crisis and maturation for Ellen. When she awakens the following morning, she had "aged." It is as if "she were blinded by the glare of many unsuspected windows. . . . She had lost something out of her childhood" (109).

Ellen's school days reinforce both her class consciousness and her growing radicalism, even while they set her apart as in some innate way different, better, more privileged than her working-class friends. Freeman's description of these years reveals another structural and ideological aspect of gender relations in nineteenth-century culture. As Carroll Smith-Rosenberg has argued so brilliantly, the separation of the private and public spheres and the construction of genteel womanhood as asexual resulted in a homosocial, even homoerotic, culture in which women's primary relationships were with one another. Even though Ellen and her friends are working-class women whose lives are not rigidly proscribed by the public/private split, they clearly aspire to the conditions and values of middle-class gentility. Indeed, Ellen's attachments to her female friends and to other women are far more intense and fully realized in the novel than are her more abstract and emotionally unconvincing relationships with her father and her male suitors. Particularly interesting, however, is the way in which class informs and eroticizes these female bonds. Two relationships in particular illustrate the way in which one woman is drawn erotically to another by her marks of superior class and breeding.[3]

Ellen's friendship with her working-class schoolmate, Abby Atkins, is the most interesting, both in its intensity and in the way in which Abby acts as a working-class foil for Ellen's genteel model of womanhood. When Ellen meets Abby on the first day of school, she sees a "grimy little face, looking out at her from a jungle of coarse, black locks" with an expression that "was fairly impish, almost malicious" (141). They are contrasted in the imagery of fair and dark heroines, with all the class connotations that this imagery often carries. Although both are from the working class, Ellen, as the petted only child of indulgent parents, already dresses and acts as if she were a member of the genteel upper classes, and Abby's initial animosity is aroused in terms which Freeman marks as class conflict. Abby sits beside Ellen in school and spitefully picks out one strand after another of Ellen's blonde hair until she is chastised by the teacher. Freeman's account of Abby's hostility is quite telling:

> She was really brilliant in a defiant, reluctant fashion. However, though she did not again disturb Ellen's curls, she glowered at them with furtive but unrelaxed hostility over her book. Especially a blue ribbon which confined Ellen's curls in a beautiful bow fired her eyes of animosity. She looked hard at it, then she pulled her black braid over her shoulder and felt of the hard shoe-string knot, and frowned with an ugly frown of envy and bitterest injury, and asked herself the world-wide and world-old question as to the why of inequality, and, though it was based on such trivialities as blue ribbons and shoe string, it was none the less vital to her mind. She would have loved, have gloried, to pull off that blue ribbon, put it on her own black braid, and tie up those yellow curls with her own shoe-string with a vicious yank of security. But all the time it was not so much because she wanted the ribbon as because she did not wish to be slighted in the distribution of things. Abby Atkins cared no more for personal ornament than a wild cat, but she wanted her just allotment of the booty of the world. (143–44)

Here class is marked by commodity fetishism, and, as Freeman makes clear in her description of Abby, it is not the thing itself that she wants, but the status it confers. Even more interesting is the scene that follows, in which Abby confronts Ellen in the playground and "pulled that blue ribbon off her head so cruelly and fiercely that she pulled some of the golden hairs with it and threw it on the ground and stamped on it" (145). Ellen, who is here described as not having "come of her ancestors for nothing," picks Abby up, sets her on the ground, retrieves her ribbon, and walks away. Having expressed her class antagonism and been bested by Ellen, Abby's envy turns to admiration, and she offers Ellen "the good half" of her apple and asks, "Say, didn't you never have to tie up your hair with a shoe-string?" (146) Ellen promptly offers Abby the ribbon, and "it ended in the two girls, with that wonderful and inexplicable adjustment of childhood into one groove after harsh grating on different levels, walking off together with arms around each other's waist" (147).

Abby, having identified with Ellen, sublimates all her class resentment and unfulfilled longing into vicarious aspirations for her friend. The relationship is frequently and explicitly cast as an alternative to marriage and heterosexual bonding. Abby begs Ellen in one scene not to marry her working-class suitor, Granville Joy: "I think more of you than any man ever will, I don't care who he is. I know I do, Ellen Brewster. . . . I tell you, Ellen Brewster, you ain't the right sort to marry a man like that, and have a lot of children to work in shops. No man, if he thinks anything of you, ought to ask you to; but all a man thinks of is himself" (228–29). Here Abby's longing for class privilege and status is eroticized through her identification with and adoration of her friend. Ellen answers her in similar language, saying, "I think more of you than any man I know," and promising that they will live together if they outlive their parents. In the language Carroll Smith-Rosenberg has defined as that of "the female world of love and ritual" (53–79), Freeman tells us that "Abby felt Ellen's warm round arm against hers with a throbbing of rapture, and glanced at her fair face with adoration. She held her in a sort of worship, she loved her so that she was fairly afraid of her. As for Ellen, Abby's little, leather-stained, leather-scented figure, strung with passion like a bundle of electric wire, pressing against her, seemed to inform her farthest thoughts" (230). Later in the novel, when Abby herself becomes engaged, she tells Ellen, "I don't love him a mite better than I do you. . . . so there! You needn't think you're left out, Ellen Brewster" (558). While the erotic content of such descriptions may seem clear to modern readers, Freeman describes these girlhood crushes as "the inexpressibly pure love of one innocent girl for another" (551), confirming Smith-Rosenberg's thesis that the erotic component of such relationships was possible precisely because no one thought of them as sexual.

Class appears to eroticize yet another of Ellen's relationships with women, but in this case the situation is reversed; it is Ellen who is drawn to Cynthia Lennox, after Cynthia reenters her life in the role of benefactor.[4] After hearing Ellen's valedictory address, Cynthia Lennox offers to send Ellen to Vassar—not, curiously enough, because she still harbors a lingering passion for the child she once tried to kidnap, but because she identifies so strongly with Ellen's mother, Fanny. By sending Ellen to college, she will expiate the guilt she has felt over the years for the suffering she caused Fanny. When Fanny "had gone almost hysterical with delight" upon hearing Cynthia's plan, Cynthia "found it almost impossible to keep her tears back. She knew so acutely how this other woman felt that she almost seemed to lose her own individuality" (140). Having protected Cynthia for years by not revealing where she had been during the three days of her absence, Ellen's ambivalent feelings about class and status become fixed upon Cynthia, and she finds herself "more in love than she had ever been in her life, and with another woman. She thought of Cynthia with adoration; she dreamed about her; the feeling of receiving a benefit from her hand became immeasurably sweet" (253). The erotic nature of her fascination with Cynthia is startlingly explicit in such passages as the following, describing a time when Ellen finds an excuse to visit Cynthia at her home:

> She had so hoped that she might find Cynthia alone. She had dreamed as a lover might have done, of a tête-à-tête with her, what she would say, what Cynthia would say. She had thought and trembled at the thought, that possibly Cynthia might kiss her when she came or went. She had felt, with a thrill of spirit, the touch of Cynthia's soft lips on hers, she had smelt the violets about her clothes. (268)

It is Lyman Risley, Cynthia's suitor of twenty years, who recognizes the symptoms of Ellen's passion and explains to Cynthia that Ellen "worships" her. She has, according to Risley, "one of those aberrations common to her youth and her sex. She is repeating a madness of old Greece, and following you as a nymph might a goddess. . . . But don't be alarmed, it will be temporary in the case of a girl like that. She will easily be led into her natural track of love" (270–71). Risley's use of the words "alarmed" and "natural" suggests that Ellen's feelings toward Cynthia are of a somewhat different and more problematic sort than Ellen's and Abby's feelings toward one another. Here, too, the novel seems to be caught between ideologies. Both Carroll Smith-Rosenberg (245–96) and Lillian Faderman (178–90, 233–79) have argued that changing attitudes toward female sexuality in the late nineteenth century made these intense bonds between women increasingly problematic. Finally, under the influence of sexologists such as Krafft-Ebing, Havelock Ellis, and Freud, such bonds were labeled deviant and driven underground. These changes accompanied women's increasing activity in the public sphere, and the shift in women's roles which Smith-Rosenberg describes as a conflict between the mid-century ideal of the "true woman" and the emergence of the "new woman." Increasingly, as the novel advances, Ellen seems caught between these two paradigms. Perhaps nowhere is this more evident than in the scene in which she delivers the high school valedictory address.

In being chosen to deliver this speech for her class, Ellen has demonstrated that she is a better scholar than any of her classmates, female or male, a most unwomanly position to be in. Her accomplishments, her appearance in the public sphere as a speaker, and the radical and political content of her speech all mark her as of the type of the emerging "new woman." Indeed, the content of her speech is radical:

> She had written a most revolutionary valedictory. . . . she might have had the inspiration of a Shelley or a Chatterton. . . . She had hesitated at nothing, she flung all castes into a common heap of equality with her strong young arms, and she set them all on one level of the synagogue. She forced the employer and his employee to one bench of service in the grand system of things; she gave the laborer, and the laborer only the reward of labor. (192)

But, if the content of the speech suggests that Ellen is a burgeoning "new woman," nothing else about her presence or her attitude does. Her small stature, the virginal white graduation dress, her modesty, and her embarrassment at being singled out all are traits associated with the "true woman." The radical nature of her speech is linked to her compassion and concern for social justice—characteristics that position her, ironically but securely, within the older tradition of womanly traits. Even more important, Freeman reveals her to be quite unconscious of her power or her affect: "She was quite innocently throwing her wordy bomb to the agitation of public sentiment. She had no thought of such an effect. She was stating what she believed to be facts with her youthful dogmatism. She had no fear the facts would strike too hard" (192). By speaking publicly and by speaking potentially inflammatory political rhetoric, Ellen steps outside the boundaries prescribed for genteel women, but her unconsciousness of the radicalism of her speech (she believes she is simply reiterating basic American republican ideology about equality and work), and her almost spiritual convictions about justice and fairness reincorporate her into that tradition of nineteenth-century womanhood which is concerned with the plight of the oppressed and the poor. The working-class members of her audience go wild with applause at the end: "Many of them were of foreign blood, people who had come to the country expecting the state of things advocated in Ellen's valedictory,

and had remained more or less sullen and dissenting at the non-fulfill-
ment of their expectations" (193). The factory owners and upper-class
members of the audience are less sure how to take the speech. Lyman
Risley half-jokingly remarks, "She may have a bomb somewhere concealed
among those ribbons and frills" (194), suggesting through his jesting image
the anomaly of the genteel woman (signified by ribbons and frills) deliver-
ing a speech which calls into question both the class basis of gentility and
the very nature of genteel womanhood, which shuns the public sphere
and all forms of conflict (signified by the bomb). Interestingly, the working-class members of the audience respond primarily to Ellen's message,
the upper-class members to her beauty and genteel image.

Ellen's valedictory sets in motion the events of the last third of the
novel, in which all of the issues of class and gender are intensified and
placed in conflict with one another. It is the valedictory which brings
Ellen to Cynthia Lennox's attention again and brings Robert Lloyd into
Ellen's life. Once again, Freeman plays with narrative possibilities for
rescuing Ellen from her working-class background. Like the adoption
strategy, the college option gives Ellen access to upper-class culture. The
day after she learns she is going to college, Ellen walks down the street
and looks "at the homeward stream of dingy girls from the shops, and
thought with a sense of escape that she would never have to join them"
(247). This perfectly natural response to her good luck is seriously at
odds with nineteenth-century ideology concerning women's roles and
nature. Ellen cannot benefit at the expense of her class and family—to
do so would be unwomanly. Furthermore, to send Ellen to college at
this point would work against the novel's class ideology. Once again,
Ellen's demonstration of class solidarity is linked to her "womanly" instincts, as another crisis gives her an opportunity to prove her selfless
devotion to her family. When her father loses his job and the family is in
desperate need of money, Ellen decides to give up her college education and go to work in the shoe factory to help support her parents. "I
will never be lifted out of the grind as long as those I love are in it"
(303), she tells herself.

By going to work in the factory, however, Ellen has *ipso facto* removed herself from the category of genteel womanhood, and it is this
tension between manual labor in the public sphere and gender ideology
that much of the rest of the novel tries to resolve. Here, Freeman's undeniable sympathy with socialist ideology becomes evident. On her first
day of work, Ellen "moved with this rank and file of the army of labor,
and all at once a sense of comradeship seized her. She began to feel
humanity as she had never felt it before. . . . Suddenly it seemed to her
that the greatest thing in the whole world was work and that this was
one of the greatest forms of work" (349–50). She is struck by "the dignity

of labor," which, in a remarkable metaphor, "had revealed itself to her like a goddess behind a sordid veil" (350). There is an almost Carlylean sense of the mystical and religious significance of work mixed here with images of class and labor solidarity, merging finally in the remarkable image of labor as "a goddess behind a sordid veil," which conflates labor and gender imagery. The image suggests the way in which the novel will bring together, albeit uneasily, the issues of genteel womanhood and labor, in the figure of Ellen Brewster as a working-class goddess. By spiritualizing labor as a goddess and by representing work as a sacrificial act, the text aligns Ellen with the image of the goddess, who, regardless of the appearance of the sordid, is still, behind that veil, a genteel woman motivated by selfless, nurturing motives. It is an image which prepares for Ellen's role as catalyst of the strike; and it explains why, in the image that forms the main title of this paper, there is so much emphasis on Ellen's childlike, pure, virginal innocence. She may be leading the workers out on strike, but she is doing so for purely selfless reasons, for reasons of compassion and pity, and not to gain anything for herself. It is important here that Ellen already has been seen to have sacrificed her own self-interest by refusing to go to college: no taint of self-interest will be associated with her impassioned speech to the workers.

Woven together with the story of Ellen's renunciation of a college education and her employment at the shoe factory is the story of her love affair with Robert Lloyd. On the face of it, this love story is the most improbable aspect of the plot, not least because it lacks the emotional intensity that would make it believable. It must be seen, therefore, as part of the dialogic tension between class and gender in the novel. Just as many female characters serve essentially symbolic functions in male narratives, Robert Lloyd serves such a function in this female-centered novel. It is Ellen's relationship with Robert Lloyd that allows the tangled issues of class and gender to play themselves out. From the beginning, it has been clear that Ellen and Robert are linked through Cynthia Lennox, who has tried to adopt each as a young child. Ellen does not actually meet Robert, however, until she graduates from high school and he attends the graduation dance. Then, in terms which deliberately evoke the Cinderella myth, Fanny Brewster watches her daughter dance with the young scion of capitalism; "immediately she married Ellen to young Lloyd, and the next moment she went to live in a grand new house built in a twinkling in a vacant lot next to Norman Lloyd's residence, which was the wonder of the city" (198). But, again Freeman confounds our expectations, for it is the upper-class "prince" who must prove himself worthy of the working-class "princess." And this is where *The Portion of Labor* joins earlier nineteenth-century fiction in presenting its heroine as a spiritual guide—an "evangelist," to use Harriet Beecher Stowe's term for little Eva—whose role is to open others' eyes to the corruption and injustice of society.

Robert is scarcely a fairy-tale prince; full of indecision and class bias, he is a singularly unattractive suitor. In his first visit to Ellen's home, he is struck primarily by the vulgar taste of its furnishings and is alarmed that Ellen seems unaware of her ugly surroundings. His eye catalogues every offensive detail: "The lamp was hideous, the shape was aggressive, a discordant blare of brass, and the roses of the globe were blasphemous" (209). Worse yet, he begins to revise his impression of Ellen, who "sat in the full glare of this hideous lamp, and Lloyd considered that she was not so pretty as he had thought last night . . . suppose she liked it? Lloyd, sitting there, began to speculate if it were possible for one's spiritual nature to be definitely damaged by hideous lamps" (209). Ellen is completely unaware of his assessment of her mother's cherished parlor. In fact, "Ellen at that age could have had no possible conception of the sentiment with which the young man viewed her environment. She was sensitive to spiritual discords which might arise from meeting with another widely different nature, but when it came to material things, she was at a loss" (211). Once again the text reveals its indecision, for, even while Freeman appears to condemn Robert for the materialism of his judgments, she suggests in the following passage that, due to her working-class upbringing, Ellen in fact may be lacking in precisely these finer aesthetic judgments:

> She was innocently glad that she had such a nice room into which to usher him. She felt that the marble-top table, the plush lambrequin on the mantle-shelf, the gilded vases, the brass clock, the Nottingham lace curtains, the olive-and-crimson furniture, the pictures in cheap gilt frames, the heavily gilded wall-paper, and the throws of thin silk over the picture corners must prove to him the standing of her family. She felt an ignoble satisfaction in it, *for a certain measure of commonness clung to the girl like a cobweb*. She was as yet too young to bloom free of her environment, her head was not yet over the barrier of her daily lot; her heart never would, *and that was her glory*. (210; my emphasis)

The detailing of the vulgar furnishings, and the emphasis on Ellen's "commonness," juxtaposed with the statement "that was her glory" suggest the same sort of ambivalence the text has demonstrated throughout about Ellen's rise from her working-class roots. It is Ellen's point of view, and not Robert's, however, that the novelist prefers. Robert proves to be a vacillating lover who finds suspect Ellen's decision to go to work in the shoe factory instead of going to Vassar. He does not visit her for several months after she begins working in the factory, and, even though he sees her every day at the factory, he scarcely speaks to her. When he does visit her again, he tells her that he thought she might have "deliberately preferred a lower life to a higher one." She asks him if "Vassar College [is] any higher than a shoe factory. . . . Instead of being benefited by the result of labor, I have become part of labor. Why is that lower?" (389) Clearly these exchanges are designed as tests for Robert, tests which he continually fails.

This is not a simple reversal of the fairy-tale plot, however, because it is the prince who still has the power—both the power of class and money and the power of gender. He controls the wages of the workers (including Ellen's), and he controls the terms of their relationship. He comes to her, she cannot come to him. Most of the time he is completely indifferent to her opinion of him, as he "does not concern himself in the least as to what the employees in his uncle's factory thought of him" (222). This, to play off a phrase of Elaine Showalter's, is the single-voiced discourse of the dominant. Power allows him to be blind and deaf to those who are his subordinates—he assumes that they share his point of view; if they do not, he is free to dismiss them (both figuratively and literally).

In this section of the novel, increasingly it is things, commodities, which signify the differences between the Lloyds and the factory workers and which spur class resentment. The day that Robert Lloyd reduces wages, it is his Russian sleigh that Abby Atkins seizes on as a symbol of injustice: "I wish Robert Lloyd had to get up at six o'clock and trudge a mile in this snow to his work. . . . He'll be driven down in his Russian sleigh by a man looking like a drum-major, and cut our poor little wages, and that's all he cares. Who's earning the money, he or us, I'd like to know? I hate the rich" (450). The cut in wages causes Floretta Vining to put off her marriage to Ben Simmons, because he won't be able to pay for the ribbons and finery she longs for. When Ellen delivers her impassioned speech to the workers and urges them to go out on strike, Sadie Peel is distressed because she will not be able to buy the near-seal cape she had her heart set on. The workers are being constructed as consumers whose conceptions of work, class, and loyalty more and more are tied to the things they can buy.

Ellen's role in leading the workers out on strike and then leading them back to work raises some of the most complex issues in the novel. When she urges the men to strike, she is convinced that the need for justice overrides all other issues, including her love for Robert Lloyd:

> She said to herself, here was this rich man, this man with accumulation of wealth, not one dollar of which he had earned himself, either by his hands or by his brains, but which had been heaped up for his uncle by

the heart and back breaking toil of all these poor men and women; and now he was going to abuse his power of capital, his power to take the bread out of their mouths entirely, by taking it out in part. (452)

The ambiguity imbedded in Ellen's role in the novel is nowhere more evident than here. Forced to choose between her lover and her friends and family, Ellen must choose between her own self-interest and the welfare of others. The womanly woman must, of course, act selflessly, but in this case that also requires her to act in the public sphere, a distinctly unwomanly choice. The ambiguity in Ellen's role also infects the narrative structure here—for a resolution in favor of the domestic plot. Initially, as Ellen delivers her impassioned speech to the workers, the labor plot seems to gain the upper hand. She tells them, "If you men will do nothing, and say nothing, it is time for a girl to say and act" (477). As in her valedictory, Ellen's speech to the workers is an appeal to class solidarity, rooted in a socialist economic analysis:

> What if times are hard? What is that to you? Have you made them hard? It is the great capitalists who have made them hard by shifting the wealth too much to one side. They are the ones who should suffer, not you. What have you done, except come here morning after morning in cold and heat, rain or shine, and work with all your strength? Those who have precipitated the hard times are the ones who should bear the brunt of them. Your work is the same now as it was then, the strain on your flesh and blood and muscles is the same; your pay should be the same. (477)

The result of the workers' appeal to Lloyd, of course, is negative: most of the workers strike, management brings in scabs, and the cold, harsh winter begins to take its toll on those who are now out of work. Another consequence of the strike is that Robert Lloyd, after years of vacillation, decides that he must convince Ellen of the justice of his own position and persuade her to marry him. He is dumbfounded when she refuses to accept either his version of the injustice of the strike or his proposal of marriage. When he tells her that he must cut wages or close the factory in order to avoid losing money, and she asks him, "What if you do lose money?" He can scarcely comprehend the questions, so fundamentally at odds is it with his capitalist ideology. Even his argument that she is refusing to let him act for the "final good" (495) of the workers, who are suffering from having been thrown out of work in midwinter, has no affect on her at this point.

Yet it is precisely the suffering of her friends and fellow workers that creates the next crisis of conscience and of role for Ellen Brewster, who holds herself responsible for the suffering of her friends and who begins to doubt the wisdom of the strike. Once again the crisis reveals the fault lines in the apparently seamless and coherent ideologies of class and gender in a capitalist culture. In her first outrage at the injustice of the wage cut, Ellen insisted that the workers must think only about "whether we are doing right or not, whether we are furthering the cause of justice and humanity. . . . There have always been martyrs" (485). Faced with the desperate reality of the workers' deprivation after months without wages, however, Ellen can think of nothing but how to stop the suffering: one girl has been forced into prostitution to earn a living, children are starving, and Abby's family is forced to spend most of the day in bed because they have no money for a fire, much less for food or clothing. "All winter . . . Ellen had been wondering, not whether the principle of the matter was correct or not, that she never doubted; she never swerved in her belief concerning the cruel tyranny of the rich and the helpless suffering of the poor . . . but she doubted more and more the wisdom of it" (519). Here, in an even subtler way, gender and class ideologies clash. Caught in the kind of ethical dilemma described by Carol Gilligan in her groundbreaking work, *In a Different Voice*, Ellen must choose between principle and individual need. Focusing on individual suffering, on "those hungry little children . . . the possible death . . . the ruin of another girl" (521), Ellen chooses an ethic of care over an ethic of justice. In doing so, however, she all but concedes the class struggle. Finding herself powerless to change the structure of the capitalist workplace, Ellen chooses food, shelter, and life over a principle which she now believes can create only suffering, not change.

It is at this point that the novel shifts toward a resolution that favors the domestic narrative. After the workers have returned, Robert Lloyd experiences conflicting emotions. He "knew what it was to have a complete triumph of his own will over his fellowmen. He had gotten his own way. All this army of workmen, all this machinery of labor, was set in motion at his desire, in opposition to their own. He realized himself a leader and a conqueror" (536). Robert here constructs himself not merely as the victorious capitalist, but as the victorious and dominant male. When he considers rewarding the workers for returning, he checks himself with the thought that "after all he was not a woman, to be carried away by a sudden wave of generous sentiment and enthusiasm, for his business instincts were too strong" (541). Business instincts and masculinity are synonymous; hierarchical structures of command, competition, profit, and self-interest are inscribed as masculine, just as their opposites—domestic and family values, egalitarian structures, compassion, and selflessness—are inscribed as female. Here Freeman suggests that the public, masculine sphere lacks a moral ideology that allows it to care for the oppressed. The doctrine of fair play which presumably governs the masculine ideology of competition clearly is inadequate in a system in which the workers and the owners begin at such unequal steps on the hierarchical ladder. Nahum Beals, Andrew Brewster, and Robert Lloyd do not begin at the same starting line in the capitalist race. Robert's clear equation of generosity and compassion with the female, private sphere suggests, however, both the interdependence of the two spheres and their dialogically opposed ideologies. Having won the battle, Robert Lloyd walks out onto the floor of the factory. There, simultaneously, he sees "Ellen's fair head before her machine" and sees "as if by some divine revelation, in his foes his brothers and sisters" (540). It is the conflation of Ellen's image with those of the workers that brings Robert to his epiphany. Having won the battle and proved his superior masculine strength, he now can prove his generosity, inspired by his love for Ellen, and raise the workers' wages. And, having inspired Robert's change of heart, Ellen now can marry him and become, without guilt, the genteel upper-class woman she has been destined to become from the first pages of the novel.

Ellen Brewster is in many ways a descendant of mid-century heroines such as Little Eva and Little Dorrit; yet, unlike her fictional predecessors, she is more than just a spiritual influence, for she works and acts in the public political arena. Even as Freeman draws upon the archetypal heroine of the past, the author deconstructs her. These women, defined by their roles in the domestic sphere, are key examples of what Barbara Welter has called the Cult of True Womanhood. Such heroines constantly are confronted by, *and are expected to mediate,* the problems created by the public sphere—industrialization, the legal system, slavery—even though they have neither the power nor the position actually to solve these problems. The presence of these heroines in novels that seem to be about the evils of capitalism, industrialism, and the public sphere reflects the deep schism in nineteenth-century culture between the roles of men and women and between the values of the public and the private spheres. The fact that it is the heroine who so often is called upon to mediate the problems of the public sphere suggests, on the part of Victorians, a deep loss of faith that the public sphere could resolve its ethical problems. Having relegated morality, virtue, compassion, and community feeling to women and to the private sphere, nineteenth-century culture had nowhere to turn *but* to the private sphere and to women for help in solving the social problems created by capitalist bourgeois ideology. But, of course, in turning to the private sphere, the culture could secure only private solutions; problems between labor and management are no more solved in *The Portion of Labor* than they are in *Hard Times.* Acts of private charity do not solve the structural problems of capital and labor, any more than they resolve the structural problems of slavery in *Uncle Tom's Cabin* or an unprincipled legal system that benefits no one other than the lawyers and clerks who feed upon it in *Bleak House*. These novels reveal the ways in which nineteenth-century bourgeois society's ideology *prevents* solutions that might be structural. The dialectic between public greed and private morality is constructed precisely to make such structural changes impossible. Thus, without a profound change in the ideology itself, change is unlikely. Yet these novels constantly reinforce this ideology, even as they reveal its inadequacy. The language of mediation used by these heroines is the private language of grace, of the redemption of sins: as Victorian "angels in the house," the Little Evas and Little Dorrits speak the language of evangelical piety; they are the saints who bring sinners to grace. But grace is a private act of individual transformation which leaves the structure of capitalism, industry, and slavery intact. Even though Ellen Brewster goes farther than these earlier heroines in using the language of socialist reform to criticize Robert Lloyd and the factory owners, she is essentially the same kind of "angel in the house" who acts privately to change the heart and soul of one individual capitalist. The solution to the problems of the workers in this novel is no more radical than the solutions provided in *Uncle Tom's Cabin*, *Bleak House*, or *Little Dorrit*. The structures that created the problems remain unchanged.

Notes

1.   Both Edward Foster and Perry D. Westbrook, authors of the only book-length studies of Freeman's life and fiction, take the condescending tone toward her work typical of mainstream criticism of women writers like Jewett and Freeman, whom they relegate to "local color" tradition. Westbrook also criticizes Freeman's characterization of Ellen Brewster, while praising her more realistic characterization of the other working-class characters. The most provocative treatment of the novel appears in Donovan 119–38. Donovan recognizes that the novel, "ostensibly . . . about factory conditions and working-class miseries, is really on another and deeper level a work about a young woman's ambivalence about her proper role." She calls Ellen Brewster "one of the first 'modern' women to appear in local color fiction" (124). Although neither discusses *The Portion of Labor*, two of the most perceptive critics of Freeman's fiction are Elizabeth Meese and Leah Blatt Glasser. Meese very perceptively locates the tension and interest in Freeman's work in the way in which "the interplay of feminism and antifeminism are textually inscribed" (21), while Glasser quite movingly describes her own

efforts to "rewrite beginnings and reshape endings of her stories or to manipulate details to fit my notion of a feminist book" and her realization that instead of being "wholly a rebel," Freeman was "a divided self" (188).

2. There has been a vigorous debate recently about how to define the competing ideologies of womanhood in nineteenth-century America. Cogan's excellent study, *All-American Girl,* calls into question the monolithic appeal of the passive, domestic-centered ideal of the Cult of True Womanhood, as defined by Welter. Cogan argues for a category which she calls the Real Woman, which mediates between the ideal of the True Woman and the image of the New Woman, which emerges in the last decades of the nineteenth century. The New Woman is more assertive, athletic, and at home in the public sphere. Cogan's Real Woman is intelligent, physically fit, self-sufficient, and self-reliant, and she marries carefully but remains securely within a separate female sphere. According to Cogan, this model competed with the ideal of the True Woman during the middle of the nineteenth century but then "vanished as an identifiable entity sometime after 1880 and has never been seen again." The reason for its disappearance, she suggests, is that individuals "could no longer resist the contradictory tensions pulling them either into the conservative camp of True Womanhood or into the growing tide of turn-of-the-century feminism" (257). It is precisely this latter tension that seems to control *The Portion of Labor.* Without any mediating ideal of Real Womanhood, Ellen Brewster is caught between conflicting ideologies. I have chosen to call the image of womanhood to which Ellen aspires "genteel womanhood" to emphasize its class basis, which is much closer to Welter's Cult of True Womanhood than to Cogan's ideal of Real Womanhood. *The Portion of Labor* seems to confirm Cogan's thesis that the Ideal of Real Womanhood had succumbed to the competing tensions of the Cult of True Womanhood and the more feminist cult of the New Woman by the end of the century.

3. I thank Deborah Heath for suggesting how class differences create an erotic sense of otherness.

4. Donovan is the only critic to comment on the intense relationship between Ellen and Cynthia, although she does not place it within the context of nineteenth-century women's culture and somewhat ahistorically calls it a "lesbian" relationship (125).

5. In her influential article, "Feminist Criticism in the Wilderness," Showalter describes women's writing as "a 'double-voiced discourse' that always embodies the social, literary, and cultural heritages of both the muted and the dominant" (263). The muted must be able to speak in two voices, while the dominant need speak only in one.

Works Cited

Cogan, Frances B. *All-American Girl: The Ideal of Real Womanhood in Mid-Nineteenth-Century America*. Athens: U of Georgia P, 1989.

Donovan, Josephine. *New England Local Color Literature: A Woman's Tradition*. New York: Frederick Ungar, 1983.

Faderman, Lillian. *Surpassing the Love of Men: Romantic Friendship and Love Between Women from the Renaissance to the Present*. New York: William Morrow, 1981.

Foster, Edward. *Mary E. Wilkins Freeman*. New York: Hendricks House, 1956.

Freeman, Mary Wilkins. *The Portion of Labor*. Ridgewood, N.J.: Gregg P, 1967.

Gilligan, Carol. *In a Different Voice: Psychological Theory and Women's Development*. Cambridge: Harvard UP, 1982.

Glasser, Leah Blatt. "'She Is the One You Call Sister': Discovering Mary Wilkins Freeman." *Between Women: Biographies, Novelists, Critics, Teachers and Artists Write About Their Work on Women*. Ed. Carol Ascher, Louise De Salvo, Sara Ruddick. Boston: Beacon P, 1984. 186–211.

Meese, Elizabeth. "Signs of Undecidability: Reconsidering the Stories of Mary Wilkins Freeman." *Crossing the Double-Cross: The Practice of Feminist Criticism*. Chapel Hill: U of North Carolina P, 1986. 21–38.

Showalter, Elaine. "Feminist Criticism in the Wilderness." *The New Feminist Criticism: Essays on Women, Literature and Theory*. Ed. Elaine Showalter. New York: Pantheon, 1985. 243–70.

Smith-Rosenberg, Carroll. *Disorderly Conduct: Visions of Gender in Victorian America*. New York: Knopf, 1985. 53–76.

Welter, Barbara. "The Cult of True Womanhood: 1820–1860." *American Quarterly* 18 (Summer 1966): 151–74. Rpt. in *Dimity Convictions: The American Woman in the Nineteenth Century*. Athens: Ohio State UP, 1976. 3–20.

Westbrook, Perry D. *Mary Wilkins Freeman*. Boston: Twayne, 1988.

CHAPTER 9

"Race" and Identity in Pauline Hopkins's
Hagar's Daughter

Claire Pamplin

In *Hagar's Daughter* (1901–2), the African-American novelist Pauline Hopkins uses the very system of legal codes that perpetuated racism in late-nineteenth-century America to expose the biases and illogical bases of the legal system. It is not skin color that proves Hagar to be a Negro; her "race" is not found in the skin color of her family members, nor is it revealed by her character, behavior, or language. It is, instead, a long-forgotten bill of sale in the hands of a slave trader that proves Hagar is black. Hagar has lived most of her life in freedom, as a white, and her white, slave-owning husband pays the price asked by the slave trader, so that the family may remain intact. But he says that he would willingly pay twice the price, if the transaction did not prove that his wife was "of Negro blood" (56).

Hagar's race, in the days just before Emancipation, is located not in her skin color, not in her character, but in the record of a monetary transaction between a slave seller and a slave buyer. In Hopkins's turn-of-the-century American novel, race can be defined only through slave records, and Hopkins uses this fact to undermine the notion that race can be defined according to physical or moral characteristics. Showing that racial status resides strictly and most reliably in the records of slavery, an illegal and outdated institution, Hopkins syllogistically exposes racist thinking as outdated, making skin color, character, and "culture" inadequate signifiers of race. In having Hagar's husband wish aloud that he could simply double Hagar's price, to obliterate her identity as black, Hopkins emphasizes the absurdity of racist thinking.

Hopkins made a logical appeal for compassion between whites and blacks, and for legal and social equality. She demonstrates that any definition of race is undesirable, because definition inevitably leads to discrimination, segregation, and race hatred. Her purpose is to demonstrate that the color line is so unreliable as to be no definer of race, no line at all, and thereby to expose the injustice of social and economic discrimination based on race. In Hopkins's view, the "line" to be drawn was the line between those who aspired to education, hard work, and morality, and those who did not.

White racists, by the time Hopkins was writing *Hagar's Daughter,* had already invented a locus of race other than skin color: character. Mississippi's state supreme court approved the Second Mississippi Plan for black disfranchisement, drafted by a state constitutional convention in 1890. The state's supreme court acknowledged the illegality of racial discrimination by asserting that the convention did not discriminate against the Negro race, but "against its characteristics." The United States Supreme Court upheld Mississippi's decision, ruling that "'the peculiarities of habit, of temperament and of character' that distinguished blacks from whites were acceptable targets of legislation in a way that skin color was not" (Michaels 191).

The Second Mississippi Plan was designed for a legal identification of, and resistance to, the invisible, internalized Negro race. Hopkins's novel attempts to bring this invisible Negro out of the racial closet, so that it can no longer serve society as a force to be resisted. Hopkins used the slippage between race and color to deconstruct the color line and to emphasize the need for racial justice. But, for Hopkins, racial justice entailed not only the elimination of prejudice against blacks but also their inclusion in the white American mainstream.

Pauline Hopkins's aspiration for African Americans was that they be given full opportunities as Americans, that those who demonstrated intelligence and energy be permitted their rightful place in middle-class American life. Hopkins believed—hoped—that the true integration of the middle class was inevitable. She has a white southerner in *Hagar's Daughter* say: "Black blood is everywhere—in society and out, and in our families even; we cannot feel assured that it has not filtered into the most exclusive families. We try to stem the tide but I believe it is a hopeless task" (160). She recognized the "mainstream" as white, and her characters embrace what were often regarded as "white" values, but Hopkins knew that blacks must not deny their true identities or wear the white disguise of "passing." To be whole, to live fully as human beings and as American citizens, African Americans must acknowledge their blackness, and America must acknowledge and accept its black citizens.

The "invisibility of race," in Walter Benn Michaels's phrase, explicitly recognized in *Williams v. Mississippi,* reinforced the idea of a white "American race" by defining race in terms of character instead of skin color or physical qualities. As Michaels observes, the idea that the racial identity of Americans was white—that there was a white American race— received new support in the 1890s; in 1907, Teddy Roosevelt used the phrase "the American Race." Michaels suggests that the very idea of American citizenship is a racial and even racist idea, not because it embodies a "preference for white skins but because it confers on national identity something like the ontology of race" (192). In other words, *race* is the biologizing equivalent of *nation*.

The notion of the black as a separate and possibly lower species had its proponents in post-Reconstruction racist thinking, but the dominant mode of distinguishing between the races became quality of character. White supremacists such as Thomas Nelson Page believed that anyone not purely "white" was naturally "lazy, thriftless, intemperate, insolent, dishonest, and without the most rudimentary elements of morality." The qualities so admired by whites in "old-time darkies" were not inherent in the Negro character; they had been brought out through strict white control (qtd. in Fredrickson 260). Senator John Daniel of Virginia said in 1899, "You may change the leopard's spots, but you will never change the different *qualities* of the races" (qtd. in Michaels 191). Hopkins frames her story with demonstrations of the political and legal ramifications of such attitudes. In the beginning of the novel, she depicts Jefferson Davis as defending slavery and separating it from questions of physical racial traits by suggesting that its basis "does not depend upon differences of complexion" but upon some natural inherent weakness. Davis suggested that a slave would be better off with a single master, rather than be the slave of a whole society, and that, in light of such a concept, a slave could be black or white (15–16). As Hopkins demonstrates, if "blacks" can be "white," and if slaves can be black or white, then the grounds for racist thinking and racist laws become extremely unsound. In the courtroom scene near the end of the novel, Hopkins exposes the association of dubious character with race and the prejudice that in some states prohibited blacks from testifying in court against whites. The "Attorney-General" says, "Would you impugn the honor of a brilliant soldier . . . by the idiot ramblings of an ignorant *nigger* brought here by the defense to divert attention from the real criminal . . ." (257). It is within this framework that the story challenges the prevailing racist ideologies of late nineteenth-century American culture.

In the 1890s, the majority of the black population was poor, and nearly half was illiterate (Carby, "Introduction" xxxiii). Thus, in the age of self-help, when poverty and ignorance were viewed as signs of laziness and lack of willpower, black poverty and poor education were interpreted in racist discourse as evidence of bad character. Self-help ideology dominated white social attitudes in the latter part of the nineteenth century and led to the "root, hog, or die" approach to the Negro problem. As Horace Greeley put it in 1865, "Freedom and opportunity—these are all that the best government can secure to White or Black." Blacks were granted equality before the law and were left in a self-regulating South to "fight out the question of predominance," in Albion Tourgee's words—in essence, to fend for themselves or to "root, hog, or die" (Fredrickson 196, 182). But the self-help ideology also was embraced by some African Americans. "No one will [create and preserve a record of customs, manners, and social conditions of black culture] for the race," writes Pauline Hopkins, calling for a literary expression of the ideology of work and self-determination in the United States at the turn of the century. "The black man was expected to make his own way and find his 'true level' with a minimum of interference and direct assistance," observes George M. Fredrickson (197). It was un-American to be poor.

Still, the question of personal race identity was crucial. As Thomas Dixon wrote in his first novel, *The Leopard's Spots* (1902), "There could be but one issue—are you a White man or a Negro?" (161). So, when Venus Johnson, a black servant, answers that question for the Bowens by proclaiming them "white right through," she is affirming their Americanness and therefore their character, which is, as she says, "mos' *too* good for this world" (62). The Bowens' character is good because they are hard-working, decent, honest, and well-mannered. Perhaps Venus believes they are too good for this world because "this world" happens to be Washington, D.C., the center of a government that permits profound injustices against individuals on the basis of their race; a government, as Hopkins's narrator states earlier in the novel, "whose excuse for existence is the upbuilding of mankind" (62)! On the other hand, Washington apparently can be a good place to hide one's past. Hopkins has one of her characters say, "We do not inquire too closely into one's antecedents in Washington, you know; be beautiful and rich and you will be happy here" (114).

Hagar's Daughter originally was published in serial form in *Colored American Magazine* in 1901 and 1902. The periodical had political aims from the beginning; an editorial in the first issue, in May 1900, named black unity as its utmost goal. The September 1900 issue announced that *Colored American Magazine* was to be "a monthly magazine of merit . . . which shall be a credit to the present and future generations." The advertisement of purpose further stated, "This magazine shall be devoted to the higher culture of Religion, Literature, Science, Music, and Art of the Negro, universally. Acting as a stimulus to old and young, the old to higher achievements, the young to emulate their example" (*Colored American Magazine* 1: 267). The magazine was a product of the Colored Cooperative Publishing Company of Boston, which also published Hopkins's novel, *Contending Forces*. Hopkins's literary output, and *Colored American Magazine* itself, were a part of the magazine "revolution" that started in the 1880s, when periodicals gained mass audiences and large advertising revenues. But it also was a product of the enormous burst of activity by black literary and political writers that erupted after the demise of Radical Reconstruction, in response to increasing race prejudice. Regularly featured were articles by prominent educators, ministers, and sociologists (such as Kelly Miller of Howard University). *Hagar's Daughter* and *Colored American Magazine* were products of an

African-American literary ground swell that arose in response to the white-dominated magazine industry and the white Genteel Tradition.

Colored American was little different from other magazines in many ways, but it was distinguished from white magazines by two features: it was a part of a publishing cooperative, in which both readers and contributors became full members; and it tried to define and create a reading public for African-American periodicals (Carby, Introduction xxxiii). In early editorials, Hopkins argued that northern black intellectuals must revive the New England tradition of radical politics, once dominated by white abolitionists. Hopkins wanted Boston to become again the center of black and white political agitation. *Colored American Magazine* was a response to northern political apathy, and to the hostile political climate at the turn of the century (Carby, Introduction xxxii). An editorial statement in the first issue, of May 1900, established black unity as the magazine's primary goal:

> Above all, [the magazine] aspires to develop and intensify the bonds of that racial brotherhood, which alone can enable a people, to assert their racial rights as men, and demand their privileges as citizens. . . . A vast and almost unexplored treasury of biography, history, adventure, tradition, folk lore, poetry and song, the accumulations of centuries of such experiences as have never befallen any other people lies open to us and to you. (*Colored American Magazine* 1: 64)

Hopkins, as a strong editorial influence at *Colored American*, saw in 1900 a burgeoning African-American literary culture. Blacks had published a handful of novels before the end of the Civil War; Negro newspapers and periodicals had existed in significant numbers since the 1820s and 1830s; and a number of slave narratives and autobiographies had been written. Over one hundred exslaves had written book-length "slave narratives" before the end of the Civil War (Gates, *Classic* ix). But beginning in the 1890s, black literature was being produced in unprecedented quantities. African Americans wrote novels, magazine articles, newspapers, nonfiction books. They wrote more than they ever had, more than they had in the first days of freedom after the Civil War. Between the end of the Civil War and the year 1909, eighty-five African-American periodicals were founded, twenty-eight in the 1890s alone (Bullock 2). The first association of black journalists was founded in 1890. Paul Laurence Dunbar was "discovered" in 1896 by William Dean Howells, and Charles Chesnutt's stories began to appear in mainstream American publications in the nineties. During Radical Reconstruction, blacks published only two novels, but in the 1890s they published many more than that. This, Hopkins believed, was only the tip of the iceberg, an indication of "a vast and almost unexplored treasury."

Hopkins insisted that Negro writers look to the richness of African-American heritage and culture for material. An advertisement in the September 1900 issue of *Colored American Magazine* for an upcoming series by Hopkins, entitled "Famous Men of the Negro Race," reads:

> To the Negro is denied the stimulus of referring to the deeds of distinguished ancestors, to their valor and patriotism. He is distinguished only as the former slave of the country. Truth gives him the history of a patriot, a brave soldier, the defender of the country from foreign invaders, a "God-fearing producer of the nation's wealth." (*Colored American Magazine* 1: 259)

The racial climate in the 1890s was one of fear and paranoia on all sides; aggression toward blacks reached a new high (Campbell 19). The death of Frederick Douglass in 1895 resulted in at least a partial abandonment of agitation for civil rights. That year marked the beginning of an era of accommodation and conciliation, for it was also in 1895 that Booker T. Washington delivered his famous accommodationist Atlanta Exposition Address. Anti-Negro hysteria continued into the early twentieth century, which was its most intense period in history (Friedman 89). The lynching of blacks reached a nadir in 1892, and newspapers reported that southern mobs were beginning to torture and burn their victims instead of simply hanging them (Fredrickson 273). Deportationist thinking—the notion that American blacks must be expatriated to Africa—experienced a major revival from 1887 to 1891. President Benjamin Harrison, in his speech accepting the Republican nomination in 1888, said that the nation had a duty to exclude or expel "alien races" that could not be assimilated (Fredrickson 263, 265). Many whites feared that blacks harbored contagious diseases, and their fear helped to facilitate the full implementation of Jim Crow laws, which the Supreme Court found Constitutional in 1896, in *Plessy v. Ferguson* (Friedman 122–23).

To combat race prejudice and racism, African Americans wrote. They wrote for a national community of black readers, and they wrote so that the community would continue to create itself and to grow. Dickson D. Bruce interprets the emphasis that blacks themselves placed on their own literary achievement as indicative of their belief that, through writing, they could prove their capability to handle the highest levels of thought and culture, and thus dispel the notion that they were inferior to and dependent upon whites (2).

In 1892, for example, the year that the number of lynchings of Negroes reached an all-time peak, Ida B. Wells, a black, twenty-three-year-old newspaper editor and former schoolteacher from Memphis, Tennessee, published *Southern Horrors: Lynch Law in All its Phases;* Anna Julia

Cooper published *A Voice from the South;* and Frances Ellen Watkins Harper published *Iola Leroy; or, Shadows Uplifted.* They composed what they called "race-works," as Hopkins called *Contending Forces,* "dedicated to the best interest of the Negro everywhere" (*Colored American Magazine* 1, May 1900, 65). As Frances Ellen Watkins Harper stated in a note at the end of *Iola Leroy,* African-American literature should "add to the solution of our unsolved American problem."

In the September 1900 issue of *Colored American Magazine,* an advertisement appeared for *Hagar's Daughter* (written under the name Sarah A. Allen, a pen name frequently used by Pauline Hopkins). It read, in part:

> Southern caste prejudice has grown stronger year by year for thirty-five years, and the determination of the South to dominate or annihilate the Negro, has grown world famous, and to all human seeming is but in its inception. Read the fate of Hagar's daughter, an outcast in the wilderness, like Ishmael of old. . . .

Hopkins compares her black characters with the Biblical Ishmael and Sarah. Ishmael, son of Abraham of the Old Testament, was born not of Abraham's wife Sarah but of her Egyptian maidservant. Ishmael and his mother, the maidservant Hagar, were cast into the desert by Abraham. In Hopkins's novel, Hagar and her infant daughter are cast out into slavery, and then again into the social and political wilderness of Jim Crow America—a white wilderness of segregation and prejudice.

Not since slavery had blacks been subjected to such stringent segregation and racial discrimination as in the 1890s and early l900s. Indeed, C. Vann Woodward has argued that the immediate post-Reconstruction period was a transitional period in southern race policy and social practice, a time during which blacks, for example, were free to go to the theater and were served at bars and soda fountains with whites (*Strange Career* 37). This relaxation of racial tensions in the 1870s was replaced, by 1900, by rigid segregation practices (Fredrickson 202n). The North was hardly less to blame than the South. Perhaps because of her keen disappointment at Boston's failure to become a center for racial activism at the turn of the century, as it had been at the height of the abolitionist movement, Hopkins has her character Ellis Enson take a jab at the North. He says, "Caste as found at the North is a terrible thing. It is killing the black man's hope there in every avenue; it is centered against his advancement. We in the South are flagrant in our abuse of the Negro but we do not descend to the pettiness that your section practices" (159). In Hopkins's view, prejudice and discrimination against any Negro were wrong, but prejudice against Negroes who sought what she believed was their rightful entry into the American middle class was absolutely intoler-

able. Many Negroes, simply by virtue of having had Caucasian ancestors, Hopkins believed, had the right to claim their white legacy. In addition, many, regardless of parentage or the shade of their skin, exemplified what Hopkins recognized as middle-class values and habits: they
worked hard, were educated, and were clean and decent.

A majority of Hopkins's contemporaries, black writers of the post-
Reconstruction period, were clearly committed to middle-class virtues.
Many were ministers or educators; many were college-educated. Hopkins
and other writers like her, such as Frances Ellen Watkins Harper and
nonfiction writer Anna Julia Cooper, were members of what sociologist
E. Franklin Frazier later called "the black bourgeoisie" (Bruce 5). For
Hopkins, commitment to middle-class, mainstream aspirations meant accepting, to a degree, the cultural hegemony of whites. Hagar's response
to having her Negro identity exposed betrays Hopkins's reliance on the
rhetoric of gentility and Anglo-Saxon superiority. As the narrator tells it:

> Here was a woman raised as one of a superior race, refined, cultured,
> possessed of all the Christian virtues, who would have remained in this
> social sphere all her life, beloved and respected by her descendants,
> her blood mingling with the best blood of the country if untoward cir-
> cumstances had not exposed her ancestry. But the one drop of black
> blood neutralized all her virtues, and she became, from the moment of
> exposure, an unclean thing. (62)

Hopkins does not assume simply that Caucasian blood is superior to
others; she believes it "the best blood of the country." The novel's white
slave trader, Walker, is described as "uncouth, *ill-bred,* hard-hearted, illiterate . . . repulsive-looking . . ." (8; emphasis added).

Undeniably, Hopkins attributes the desirable characteristics in mul-
attos to their "white" blood. Perhaps difficult for readers to understand,
nearly one hundred years after Hopkins wrote, is how she could have
admired white ideals and supported African-American pride at the same
time. Hopkins's white ideals and her black pride, in a delicate balance,
defy the truism that the colonized subject desires to assume the identity
of the colonizer. Unlike Frantz Fanon's colonized subject, who "becomes
whiter as he renounces his blackness" (Fanon 18), Hopkins's subjects, colonized *within* the nation, reclaim their blackness by acknowledging its existence, while at the same time they attain the "whiteness"—the social, economic, and political status—to which they have a legitimate claim. She
presents the picture whole, as complex and contradictory as it is.

As Hazel V. Carby points out, Hopkins does not offer her readers a
traditional nineteenth-century "passing" narrative. She reconstructs the
fictional formula of disguises and hidden identities by making the "white-

ness" of her heroines their disguise (Introduction xxxix). As an author, Hopkins was politically and pedagogically motivated to disguise her black characters as white. She believed that fiction could be used to teach readers, black and white, about blacks' contributions to American history and culture. Through this kind of education, the readers could be made more sensitive politically. She had expressed her motives for writing in the preface to *Contending Forces* (1900), seeking the public's "approval of whatever may impress them as being of value to the Negro race and to the world at large" (13). In *Hagar's Daughter,* the author reverses the popular fictional device of allowing a white character to darken his skin in order to enter the Negro community undetected. Her "black" characters, with white skin, move in the white community undetected. For black characters, there was no means of doing this except "passing" (Carby, *Reconstructing* 147). By disguising many of the "black" characters as "white," Hopkins is able to place them in a high-society setting, bringing the racial injustices they suffer into stark focus. The "white" setting also allows Hopkins to demonstrate blacks' capacity for refinement, education, grace, and gentility—a capacity that was constantly called into question by anti-Negro rhetoric in the nineteenth century. Through disguise, irony, and mild subversion, Hopkins achieves her political aims.

The author's goal for *Hagar's Daughter* was the same as for *Contending Forces:* she wanted to tell a story that crossed class and color lines. In *Hagar's Daughter,* Hopkins not only crosses the color line, she deconstructs it. She uses "passing" as disguise, and disguise as metaphor for slippage in identity. In a sense, the novel itself is disguised, as a sentimental romance complete with "noble heroes and virtuous heroines, melodramatic situations, unsavory villains, . . . highly emotional scenes," and "amazing coincidences" (Yarborough xxxi). But the novel's true identity is as an indictment of the prejudice against African Americans that prohibited them at once from positively affirming their race and heritage and from entering the American cultural mainstream.

When *Hagar's Daughter* opens, in late 1860 on the eve of the Civil War, Hagar is married to Ellis Enson, master of Enson Hall, and is living with him and their baby daughter at his Maryland plantation. A slave trader named Walker and Ellis Enson's brother, St. Clair Enson, plot to destroy Ellis and Hagar's marriage by the revelation of her "true identity." St. Clair, who, at the birth of Hagar's daughter, has lost his place in line for the family inheritance, then will have access to the family fortune. Walker tells the story: fourteen years earlier, he purchased Hagar when she was a small child, but, because of her "white complexion," was unable to find a ready buyer for her. He lent her to a Mr. Sargeant, who brought her up as his own child; she passed as white and behaved as if the Sargeants were her parents (52). Walker extorts six thousand dollars from Ellis as the value of the mother and child, by claiming that Hagar and her infant daughter are "stolen property" (53).

St. Clair's part of the plan is nearly foiled when Ellis decides that he cannot forsake his wife and child and begins to make plans for the three of them to live abroad, where "the shadow of this crime could not come," but St. Clair overhears the plot (61–62). Some time later, a mutilated body is found on the plantation grounds that is identified as Ellis. Apparently the death was a suicide, although Hagar believes that Ellis was murdered, and she accuses St. Clair of the deed. In retribution, St. Clair and Walker sell Hagar and her daughter to a New Orleans slave trader, but mother and child flee. Hagar, baby in her arms, throws herself off a bridge into the icy Potomac River to avoid enslavement (73–75). Here ends the introductory section of the novel, eight chapters long. The main body of the novel opens "twenty years later" in Washington, D.C.

This new narrative at first appears to have no relation to the first. Hopkins uses the same structure, however, in *Contending Forces,* which opens in slavery days and then jumps to post-Reconstruction, to make blatant the comparison between the bondage of slavery and the legally restrictive and inhumane conditions at the end of the nineteenth century. The second part of *Hagar's Daughter* opens with the introduction of General Benson, Major Madison, and the Bowen family, all living in Washington, D.C. in 1880. The patriarch of the Bowen family is Senator Zenas Bowen of California, "many times a millionaire," newly elected to his position. His wife is Estelle, his daughter Jewel. Estelle had married him, become stepmother to his small daughter, and guided him into politics, where, thanks to her cleverness and his "rugged good sense," he was successful. Estelle is a "grand woman," and Jewel is beautiful and "happy hearted" (82–83). Hopkins establishes Zenas Bowen as a man of goodness and integrity: he is rich, self-made, mild-tempered, unpolished, "one of those genial men whom the West is constantly sending out to enrich society" (80). He is an American.

In a plot paralleling the introductory narrative, General Benson and the slave trader Walker, along with Walker's beautiful quadroon daughter Aurelia, scheme to break up Jewel's engagement to rich young Cuthbert Sumner, using their knowledge of Estelle's and Jewel's "black" blood. While Aurelia lures Cuthbert and his family's money away from Jewel, General Bowen hopes to charm Jewel into marriage with him so that he can get at her family fortune. The narrative involves disguises of varying degrees of complexity. In a dramatic courtroom scene near the end of the book, aliases, disguises, and more complex changes in identity are unveiled, and the reader learns the fates of all the original characters, most of whom have been in one form of disguise or another. Hagar's new identity is as Estelle Bowen, the second wife of Senator Zenas Bowen. She had met Zenas while she was a waitress in San Francisco, using the name Estelle Marks. Zenas was a widower with a small "daughter," Jewel. The evil St. Clair Enson has become General Benson; Walker the slave trader is now Major Madison. Ellis Enson, long presumed dead, enters the story near the end, as Mr. Henson, chief of the United States Secret Service and a celebrated "detective." And Jewel Bowen, "disguised" as Estelle's stepdaughter, actually is her real daughter, the child she held in her arms as she jumped into the Potomac years ago. Mother and daughter became separated in the water; Zenas discovered the baby, rescued her, and raised her as his own. Jewel is Hagar's daughter.

All of the victims are ignorant of the true identities of Benson, Madison, and Aurelia until the end of the story. The plot eventually is foiled by Henson, who reveals his identity to Estelle, and they are reunited. (Senator Bowen has died by this time.) But Jewel and Cuthbert do not live happily ever after. Cuthbert Sumner already has made clear his position on racial intermarriage while Aurelia Madison was earnestly trying to fulfill her part in the corrupt plot of General Benson and her father. He rejects Aurelia, asserting, "if you were pure as snow, and I loved you as my other self, *I would never wed with one of colored blood, an octoroon*" (238). Sumner, like the proclamations of the Mississippi Constitutional Convention of 1890, privileges race above skin color.

Sumner and Ellis Enson have an informal debate common in turn-of-the-century race literature. Ellis tells Cuthbert that he plans to remarry Hagar, in spite of the fact that her Negro heritage has been made public. Cuthbert worries about public opinion, but Ellis answers that "nature was stronger than prejudice" and that

> race prejudice is all right in theory, but when a man tries to practice it against the laws which govern human life and action, there's a weary journey ahead of him, and he's not got to die to realize the tortures of the damned. This idea of race separation is carried to an extreme point and will, in time kill itself. Amalgamation has taken place; it will continue, and no finite power can stop it. (270)

Ellis posits that, if Aurelia Madison's moral development had equaled her beauty, Sumner would not have rejected her, but Sumner says that the mere knowledge of her origins would have killed all desire in him for her:

> The mere thought of the grinning, toothless hag that was her foreparent would forever rise between us. I am willing to allow the Negroes edu-

cation, to see them acquire business, money, and social status within a certain environment. I am not averse even to their attaining political power. Farther than this, I am not prepared to go. (270–71)

Cuthbert Sumner fears that Ellis is countenancing "wholesale union between whites and blacks" and that "our refinement and intelligence" will be linked to "such black bestiality as we find in the slums" (270). Cuthbert's image of the black as bestial and unrefined is juxtaposed with the image of his wife as the perfect representative of a female. Emphasizing the language of the Cult of True Womanhood, Hopkins describes Jewel's kiss (Cuthbert does not yet know that his wife has Negro blood): "The wife's lips touched his softly, lovingly—true woman to the core—as a 'ministering angel'" (268). Even a "black" woman can be a true woman. In the last pages of the novel, when he is faced with the truth about his wife and, significantly, the fact that the truth has been made public, he hesitates. His hesitation proves tragic. The Enson family takes Jewel abroad for a year, and, by the time Sumner tracks them down, Jewel is buried on the Maryland estate, dead of "Roman fever."

Sumner is grief-stricken and questions "wherein he had sinned and why he was so severely punished"; then he realizes that "the sin is the nation's. It must be washed out" (283). Responding to the oppression of blacks and using her fiction as a tool for teaching, Hopkins has Cuthbert Sumner manifest the national sin of race hatred and prejudice.

Hopkins explains Sumner's racism as an inevitable reflection of his upbringing and background: he had been born "with a noble nature" but had been corrupted by "environment and tradition." While Sumner was a good man and had been "born and bred in an atmosphere which approved of freedom and qualified equality for the Negro, he had never considered for one moment the remote contingency of actual social contact with this unfortunate people" (265).

Cuthbert Sumner is New England-born and Harvard-educated. Through Sumner, Hopkins illustrates that race prejudice is found not only in the South. (She condemns the North's record in race relations a number of times in the novel.) She adds irony to her emphasis of this point by having a former slave owner, Ellis Enson, favor racial tolerance and intermarriage; he debates the issues with Sumner and puts his beliefs into practice when he remarries Hagar. Sumner had heard the "Negro question" debated all his life and had considered himself to be a liberal; he had championed the Negro cause in a local paper. But "so had he championed the cause of the dumb and helpless creatures in the animal world about him." Hopkins describes him further:

He gave large sums to Negro colleges and on the same principle gave liberally to the Society for the Prevention of Cruelty to Animals, and endowed a refuge for homeless cats. Horses, dogs, cats, and Negroes were classed together in his mind as of the brute creation whose sufferings it was his duty to help alleviate. (265–66)

Sumner's classing black people with animals reflects the extremes of polygenesis theories from the antebellum period, which survived well into the twentieth century. Just a year before *Hagar's Daughter,* a book was published entitled *The Negro A Beast,* which argued that blacks actually are apes rather than humans. Also, in 1896, ironically the year in which the U.S. Supreme Court affirmed the status of black people as separate but equal, *Race Traits and Tendencies of the American Negro* by Frederick L. Hoffman was published. A principal source of information for anti-Negro writers for many years thereafter, this text actually helped to convince insurance companies not to insure blacks because race itself constituted an unacceptable actuarial risk. George M. Fredrickson calls this book "the most influential discussion of the race question to appear in the late nineteenth century" (249–50).

Hagar's life serves as Hopkins's central example of slippage in identity, an idea that is crucial support for her belief that there is no justification for racial prejudice. Race itself is a very slippery form of identification. Hagar's life story is a pattern of disguise and exposure. She has "black" blood, but she has "white" skin and lives in "white" society most of the time. Hagar and two other central female characters are what Vashti Lewis calls "near white" females. According to Hazel V. Carby, the mulatto figure in literature became a literary convention used frequently for exploring close relations between black and white, which had been proscribed by Jim Crow laws (*Reconstructing* 89). Hopkins had used the mulatto figure in the way Carby describes in *Contending Forces,* a novel about the "white" branch and the "black" branch of the same family. Hagar's life as a "white" Negro metaphorically suggests conflicts in racial self-identity rather than race relations. Hagar deliberately hides her blackness, even from herself. When the slave trader Walker confronts her and her husband with the truth, Hagar is sincerely, utterly humiliated:

Could it be true, or was it but a hideous nightmare from which she would soon awake? Her mother a slave! She wondered that the very thought did not strike her dead. With shrinking horror she contemplated the black abyss into which the day's events hurled her, leaving her there to grovel and suffer the tortures of the damned. . . . Was she, indeed, a descendant of naked black savages of the horrible African jungles? Could it be that the blood of these unfortunate ones flowed through her veins? (57)

Hagar's humiliation stems from fear not simply of "black" blood, but also of Africa itself. Negroes long had been criticized for their failure to develop a "civilized" culture in Africa, and Africa was seen as the scene of savagery, cannibalism, sexual license, cultural stagnation, inefficiency, and superstition (Fredrickson 49, 253). In 1902, the same year that the latter installments of the novel appeared, Joseph A. Tillinghast published his extremely influential study, *The Negro in Africa and America,* in which he argued that the Negro's African background was responsible for his lack of industrial capacity. Hagar's humiliation reflects white America's fear of discovering that the Negro character had become a part of the American character, that Africanness was merging with Americanness.

Finally, at the novel's end, Hagar faces herself and the world as a "black" woman, coming out of the race closet. Hagar's life story—a text of slippage between her "race" and her "color," and between her hidden racial identity and her social condition—invokes important cultural and political questions: What is race? How is our identity decided? How can a person be both a Negro and an American? When the "white" Hagar accepts her inner Africanness, she sends Hopkins's answer clearly: the question of race is not answerable. The question of equality is answerable, and of justice and inclusion. Hopkins believed that the answers begin with the fact that "white" America must accept and embrace its own inner Africanness.

Works Cited

Allen, Sarah A. [Pauline Hopkins]. *Colored American Magazine.* 1 (Sept. 1900). [Advertisement.]

Bruce, Dickson D., Jr. *Black American Writing from the Nadir: The Evolution of a Literary Tradition, 1877–1915.* Baton Rouge: Louisiana State UP, 1989.

Bullock, Penelope L. *The Afro-American Press, 1838–1909.* Baton Rouge: Louisiana State UP, 1981.

Campbell, Jane. *Mythic Black Fiction: The Transformation of History.* Knoxville: U of Tennessee P, 1986.

Carby, Hazel V. Introduction. *The Magazine Novels of Pauline Hopkins.* Ed. Hazel V. Carby. New York: Oxford UP, 1988. xxix–l.

———. *Reconstructing Womanhood: The Emergence of the Afro-American Woman Novelist.* New York: Oxford UP, 1987.

Cooper, Anna Julia. *A Voice from the South.* 1892. New York: Oxford UP, 1988.

Dixon, Thomas, Jr. *The Leopard's Spots.* Ridgewood, N.J.: Gregg P, 1967.

Fanon, Frantz. *Black Skin, White Masks.* Trans. Charles Lamm Markhmann. London: Pluto, 1986.

Frederickson, George M. *The Black Image in the White Mind: The Debate on Afro-American Character and Destiny, 1817–1914.* 1971. Middletown, Conn.: Wesleyan UP, 1987.

Friedman, Lawrence J. *The White Savage: Racial Fantasies in the Postbellum South.* Englewood Cliffs, N.J.: Prentice-Hall, 1970.

Gates, Henry Louis, Jr. Introduction. *The Classic Slave Narratives.* Ed. Henry Louis Gates, Jr. New York: New American, 1987. ix–xviii.

———. "The Trope of a New Negro and the Reconstruction of the Image of the Black." *Representations* 24 (Fall 1988): 129–55.

Harper, Frances Ellen Watkins. *Iola Leroy; or, Shadows Uplifted.* 1893. New York: Oxford UP, 1988.

Hoffman, Frederick L. *Race Traits and Tendencies of the American Negro.* 1896.

Hopkins, Pauline. *Contending Forces: A Romance Illustrative of Negro Life North and South.* 1900. New York: Oxford UP, 1988.

———. *Hagar's Daughter: A Story of Southern Caste Prejudice.* In *The Magazine Novels of Pauline Hopkins.* Ed. Hazel B. Carby. 1901–2. New York: Oxford UP, 1988. 3–284.

Michaels, Walter Benn. "The Souls of White Folk." *Literature and the Body.* Ed. Elaine Scarry. Baltimore: Johns Hopkins UP, 1988. 185–209.

Tillinghast, Joseph A. *The Negro in Africa and America.* 1902.

Wells, Ida B. *Southern Horrors: Lynch Law in All its Phases.* 1892. New York: Arno P, 1969.

Woodward, C. Vann. *Origins of the New South, 1877–1913.* Baton Rouge: Louisiana State UP, 1951.

———. *The Strange Career of Jim Crow.* 3rd ed. New York: Oxford UP, 1974.

Yarborough, Richard. Introduction. *Contending Forces: A Romance Illustrative of Negro Life North and South.* New York: Oxford UP, 1988.

Selected Bibliography

Alcott, Louisa May. *Life, Letters and Journals*. Ed. Ednah D. Cheney. Boston: Roberts Brothers, 1889.

———. *Work: A Story of Experience*. 1872–73. New York: Schocken, 1977.

Allende, Isabel. "Writing as an Act of Hope." Zinsser 39–63.

Ammons, Elizabeth. Introduction. *How Celia Changed Her Mind and Selected Stories*. By Rose Terry Cooke. American Women Writers Series. New Brunswick: Rutgers UP, 1986.

Appleby, Joyce. "Republicanism in Old and New Contexts." *William and Mary Quarterly* 43 (1986): 20–43.

Bardes, Barbara, and Suzanne Gossett. *Declarations of Independence: Women and Political Power in Nineteenth-Century American Fiction*. New Brunswick: Rutgers UP, 1990.

Baym, Nina. *Feminism and American Literary History: Essays*. New Brunswick: Rutgers UP, 1992.

———. "Melodramas of Beset Manhood: How Theories of American Fiction Exclude Women Authors." *The New Feminist Criticism*. Ed. Elaine Showalter. New York: Pantheon, 1985.

———. *Novels, Readers, and Reviewers: Responses to Fiction in Antebellum America*. Ithaca, N.Y.: Cornell UP, 1984.

———. *Woman's Fiction: A Guide to Novels by and about Women in America, 1820–1870*. Ithaca, N.Y.: Cornell UP, 1978.

Bell, Michael Davitt. "History and Romance Convention in Catharine Sedgwick's *Hope Leslie*." *American Quarterly* 22 (1970): 213–21.

Berlant, Lauren. "The Female Woman: Fanny Fern and the Form of Sentiment." *American Literary History* 3 (1991): 429–54.

Blotner, Joseph L. *The Political Novel*. Garden City, N.Y.: Doubleday, 1955.

Brown, Gillian. *Domestic Individualism: Imagining Self in Nineteenth-Century America*. Berkeley: U of California P, 1990.

Brown, Herbert Ross. *The Sentimental Novel in America, 1789–1860*. Durham, N.C.: Duke UP, 1940.

Bruce, Dickson D., Jr. *Black American Writing from the Nadir: The Evolution of a Literary Tradition, 1877–1915*. Baton Rouge: Louisiana State UP, 1989.

Buell, Lawrence. *New England Literary Culture: From Revolution Through Renaissance*. Cambridge, England: Cambridge UP, 1986.

Bullock, Penelope L. *The Afro-American Press, 1838–1909*. Baton Rouge: Louisiana State UP, 1981.

Campbell, Jane. *Mythic Black Fiction: The Transformation of History*. Knoxville: U of Tennessee P, 1986.

Carby, Hazel V. Introduction. *The Magazine Novels of Pauline Hopkins*. Ed. Hazel V. Carby. New York: Oxford UP, 1988. xxix–l.

———. *Reconstructing Womanhood: The Emergence of the Afro-American Woman Novelist*. New York: Oxford UP, 1987.

Cixous, Hélène. "The Laugh of the Medusa." Trans. Keith Cohen and Paula Cohen. *Signs* 1 (1976): 875–93.

Cogan, Frances B. *All-American Girl: The Ideal of Real Womanhood in Mid-Nineteenth-Century America*. Athens: U of Georgia P, 1989.

Conley, Verena Andermatt. *Hélène Cixous: Writing the Feminine*. Expanded ed. Lincoln: U of Nebraska P, 1984.

Conrad, Susan Phinney. *Perish the Thought: Intellectual Women in Romantic America, 1830–1860*. New York: Oxford UP, 1976.

Cornillon, Susan Koppelman, ed. *Images of Women in Fiction: Feminist Perspectives*. Bowling Green, Ohio: Bowling Green U Popular P, 1972.

Davidson, Cathy N. Introduction. *The Coquette; or, The History of Eliza Wharton*. By Hannah Webster Foster. New York: Oxford UP, 1986. vii–xx.

———. "Mothers and Daughters in the Fiction of the New Republic." *The Lost Tradition: Mothers and Daughters in Literature*. Ed. Cathy N. Davidson and E. M. Broner. New York: Ungar, 1980. 115–27.

———. *Revolution and the Word: The Rise of the Novel in America*. New York: Oxford UP, 1986.

de Lauretis, Teresa. *Alice Doesn't: Feminism, Semiotics, Cinema*. Bloomington: Indiana UP, 1984.

———, ed. *Feminist Studies/Critical Studies*. Bloomington: Indiana UP, 1986.

Devereaux, Mary. "Oppressive Texts, Resisting Readers and the Gendered Spectator: The *New* Aesthetics." *Journal of Aesthetics and Art Criticism* 48 (Fall 1990): 337–347.

Donovan, Josephine. *New England Local Color Literature: A Woman's Tradition*. New York: Ungar, 1983.

———, ed. *Feminist Literary Criticism: Explorations in Theory*. 2nd ed. Lexington: U of Kentucky P, 1989.

———, ed. "Women and the Rise of the Novel." *Signs* 16 (Spring 1991): 441–62.

Douglas [Wood], Ann. *The Feminization of American Culture*. 1977. New York: Anchor, 1988.

DuPlessis, Rachel Blau. *Writing Beyond the Ending: Narrative Strategies of Twentieth-Century Women Writers*. Bloomington: Indiana UP, 1985.

Elbert, Sarah. *A Hunger for Home: Louisa May Alcott's Place in American Culture*. New Brunswick: Rutgers UP, 1987.

———. Introduction. *Work: A Story of Experience*. By Louisa May Alcott. 1872–73. New York: Schocken, 1977. ix–xliv.

Elliott, Emory. *Revolutionary Writers: Literature and Authority in the New Republic, 1723–1810.* New York: Oxford UP, 1986.

Erkkila, Betsy. "Revolutionary Women." *Tulsa Studies in Women's Literature* 6 (1987): 189–223.

Faderman, Lillian. *Surpassing the Love of Men: Romantic Friendship and Love Between Women from the Renaissance to the Present.* New York: William Morrow, 1981.

Farnham, Eliza W. *Woman and Her Era.* 2 vols. New York: C. M. Plumb, 1865.

Felski, Rita. *Beyond Feminist Aesthetics: Feminist Literature and Social Change.* Cambridge: Harvard UP, 1989.

Fetterley, Judith. Introduction. *Provisions: A Reader from Nineteenth-Century American Women.* Ed. Judith Fetterley. Bloomington: Indiana UP, 1985.

———, and Marjorie Pryse. Introduction. *American Women Regionalists, 1850–1910: A Norton Anthology.* Ed. Judith Fetterley and Marjorie Pryse. New York: Norton, 1992. xi–xx.

Flexner, Eleanor. *Century of Struggle: The Woman's Rights Movement in the United States.* New York: Atheneum, 1973.

Foster, Edward Halsey. *Catharine Maria Sedgwick.* New York: Twayne, 1974. 68–69.

———. *Mary E. Wilkins Freeman.* New York: Hendricks House, 1956.

Foster, Hannah Webster. *The Coquette; or, The History of Eliza Wharton.* 1797. New York: Oxford UP, 1986.

Foucault, Michel. *Discipline and Punish: The Birth of the Prison.* Trans. Alan Sheridan. New York: Viking, 1979.

Fraser, Nancy. "The Uses and Abuses of French Discourse Theories for Feminist Politics." *boundary 2* 17 (Summer 1990): 82–101.

Frederickson, George M. *The Black Image in the White Mind: The Debate on Afro-American Character and Destiny, 1817–1914.* 1971. Middletown, Conn.: Wesleyan UP, 1987.

Freeman, Mary Wilkins. *The Portion of Labor.* Ridgewood, N.J.: Gregg, 1967.

Friedman, Lawrence J. *The White Savage: Racial Fantasies in the Postbellum South.* Englewood Cliffs, N.J.: Prentice-Hall, 1970.

Fuller, Margaret. *Woman in the Nineteenth Century.* 1845. New York: Norton, 1971.

Gates, Henry Louis, Jr. *Figures in Black: Words, Signs and the 'Racial' Self.* New York: Oxford UP, 1987.

———. Introduction. *The Classic Slave Narratives.* Ed. Henry Louis Gates, Jr. New York: New American Library, 1987. ix–xvii.

———. "The Trope of a New Negro and the Reconstruction of the Image of the Black." *Representations* 24 (Fall 1988): 129–55.

Gilbert, Sandra M., and Susan Gubar. *The Madwoman in the Attic: The Woman Writer and the Nineteenth-Century Literary Imagination.* New Haven: Yale UP, 1979.

Gilligan, Carol. *In a Different Voice: Psychological Theory and Women's Development*. Cambridge: Harvard UP, 1982.

Glasser, Leah Blatt. "'She Is the One You Call Sister': Discovering Mary Wilkins Freeman." *Between Women: Biographies, Novelists, Critics, Teachers and Artists Write About Their Work on Women*. Ed. Carol Ascher, Louise De Salvo, and Sara Ruddick. Boston: Beacon, 1984. 186–211.

Gossett, Suzanne, and Barbara Ann Bardes. "Women and Political Power in the Republic: Two Early American Novels." *Legacy: A Journal of Nineteenth-Century American Women Writers* 2, no. 2 (Fall 1985): 13–30.

Haight, Gordon. *Mrs. Sigourney: The Sweet Singer of Hartford*. New Haven: Yale UP, 1930.

Hale, Sarah. *Woman's Record*. 2nd edition. New York: Harper, 1855.

Halttunen, Karen. *Confidence Men and Painted Women: A Study of Middle-Class Culture in America, 1830–1870*. New Haven: Yale UP, 1982.

Hamilton, Kristie. "An Assault on the Will: Republican Virtue and the City in Hannah Webster Foster's *The Coquette*." *Early American Literature* 24, no. 2 (1989): 135–51.

Harris, Sharon M. *Rebecca Harding Davis and American Realism*. Philadelphia: U of Pennsylvania P, 1991.

———. Rev. of *Second Stories: The Politics of Language, Form, and Gender in Early American Fictions,* by Cynthia S. Jordan. *Pennsylvania Magazine of History and Biography* 116 (Jan. 1992): 90–92.

Harris, Susan K. *Nineteenth-Century American Women's Novels: Interpretive Strategies*. New York: Cambridge UP, 1990.

Heilbrun, Carolyn G. *Writing a Woman's Life*. New York: Norton, 1988.

Herrmann, Claudine. *The Tongue Snatchers*. Trans. Nancy Kline. Lincoln: U of Nebraska P, 1989.

Herzog, Kristin. *Women, Ethnics, and Exotics: Images of Power in Mid-Nineteenth-Century American Fiction*. Knoxville: U of Tennessee P, 1983.

Hopkins, Pauline. *Contending Forces: A Romance Illustrative of Negro Life North and South*. 1990. New York: Oxford UP, 1988.

———. *Hagar's Daughter: A Story of Southern Caste Prejudice*. In *The Magazine Novels of Pauline Hopkins*. Ed. Hazel V. Canby. 1901–2. New York: Oxford UP, 1988. 3–284.

Howe, Irving. *Politics and the Novel*. New York: Avon, 1957.

Irigaray, Luce. *Speculum of the Other Woman*. Trans. Gillian C. Gill. Ithaca, N.Y.: Cornell UP, 1985. Trans. of *Speculum de l'autre femme*. 1974.

Johnson, Jean O. Introduction. *Crumbling Idols*. By Hamlin Garland. Cambridge: Belknap P of Harvard UP, 1959–60.

———. "The American Political Novel in the Nineteenth Century." Diss. Boston U, 1958.

Jones, Kathleen B., and Ann G. Jónasdóttir, eds. *The Political Interests of Gender: Developing Theory and Research with a Feminist Face.* London: Sage Publications, 1988.

Jordan, Cynthia S. *Second Stories: The Politics of Language, Form, and Gender in Early American Fictions.* Chapel Hill: U of North Carolina P, 1989.

Karcher, Carolyn. Introduction. *Hobomok and Other Writings on Indians.* By Lydia Maria Child. American Women Writers Series. New Brunswick: Rutgers UP, 1986.

Kelley, Mary. *Private Woman, Public Stage: Literary Domesticity in Nineteenth-Century America.* New York: Oxford UP, 1990.

Kerber, Linda. "Separate Spheres, Female Worlds, Woman's Place: The Rhetoric of Women's History." *Journal of American History* 75 (1988): 9–39.

———. "The Republican Ideology of the Revolutionary Generation." *American Quarterly* 37 (1985): 474–95.

———. *Women of the Republic: Intellect and Ideology in Revolutionary America.* Chapel Hill: U of North Carolina P, 1980. Rpt. New York: Norton, 1986.

Kessler-Harris, Alice. *Out to Work: A History of Wage-Earning Women in the United States.* New York: Oxford, UP, 1982.

Kirkland, Caroline. *A New Home—Who'll Follow?* Ed. Sandra A. Zagarell. New Brunswick: Rutgers UP, 1990.

Kristeva, Julia. *The Kristeva Reader.* Ed. Toril Moi. New York: Columbia UP, 1986.

Lander, Dawn. "Eve Among the Indians." *The Authority of Experience: Essays in Feminist Criticism.* Ed. Arlyn Diamond and Lee Edwards. Amherst: U of Massachusetts P, 1977. 194–211.

Lane, Mary E. Bradley. *Mizora: A Prophecy.* 1890. Boston: Gregg P, 1975.

Lebsock, Suzanne. "Women and American Politics, 1880–1920." *Women, Politics, and Change.* Ed. Louise A. Tilly and Patricia Gurin. New York: Russell Sage Foundation, 1990. 35–62.

Leverenz, David. *Manhood and the American Renaissance.* Ithaca, N.Y.: Cornell UP, 1989.

McNall, Sally Allen. *Who Is in the House?: A Psychological Study of Two Centuries of Women's Fiction in America, 1795 to the Present.* Westport, Conn.: Greenwood, 1981.

Meese, Elizabeth A. "Signs of Undecidability: Reconsidering the Stories of Mary Wilkins Freeman." *Crossing the Double-Cross: The Practice of Feminist Criticism.* Chapel Hill: U of North Carolina P, 1986. 21–38.

Miller, Nancy K. "Emphasis Added: Plots and Plausibilities in Women's Fiction." *The New Feminist Criticism: Essays on Women, Literature and Theory.* Ed. Elaine Showalter. New York: Pantheon, 1985. 339–60.

Milne, Gordon. *The American Political Novel.* Norman: U of Oklahoma P, 1966.

Moi, Toril. *Sexual/ Textual Politics: Feminist Literary Theory.* New York: Methuen, 1985.

Norton, Mary Beth. *Liberty's Daughters: The Revolutionary Experience of American Women, 1760–1800*. Boston: Little, Brown, 1980.

Parton, Sara Payson Willis [Fanny Fern]. *Fern Leaves from Fanny's Port-folio*. New York: 1853.

———. *Ruth Hall and Other Writings*. Ed. Joyce W. Warren. New Brunswick: Rutgers UP, 1986.

Piercy, Marge. "Active in Time and History." *Paths of Resistance: The Art and Craft of the Political Novel*. Ed. William Zinsser. Boston: Houghton Mifflin, 1989. 89–123.

Rowson, Susanna Haswell. *Reuben and Rachel; or, Tales of Olden Times*. 2 vols. London: Minerva, 1798.

Sedgwick, Catharine Maria. *Hope Leslie; or, Early Times in the Massachusetts*. New York: Harper & Bros., 1842.

Shapiro, Ann R. *Unlikely Heroines: Nineteenth-Century American Women Writers and the Woman Question*. New York: Greenwood, 1987.

Shockley, Ann Allen, ed. *Afro-American Women Writers, 1746–1933: An Anthology and Critical Guide*. New York: New American Library, 1988.

Showalter, Elaine, ed. *The New Feminist Criticism: Essays on Women, Literary and Theory*. New York: Pantheon, 1985.

Sigourney, Lydia Huntley. *Letters of Life*. New York: D. Appleton, 1866.

———. *Letters to Young Ladies*. Hartford, Conn.: P. Canfield, 1833.

———. *Lucy Howard's Journal*. New York: Harper, 1858.

———. *Moral Pieces, in Prose and Verse*. Hartford, Conn.: Sheldon & Goodwin, 1815.

———. *Myrtis, with Other Etchings and Sketchings*. New York: Harper, 1846.

———. *Pocahontas, and Other Poems*. New York: Harper, 1841.

———. *Poems*. Boston: S. G. Goodrich, 1827.

———. *Select Poems*. Philadelphia: E. B. & J. Biddle, 1847.

———. *Sketch of Connecticut, Forty Years Since*. Hartford, Conn.: Oliver D. Cooke & Sons, 1824.

———. "Traits of the Aborigines of America. A Poem." Cambridge, Mass.: "from the University Press," 1822.

———. "The Western Home." *The Western Home and Other Poems*. Philadelphia: Parry & McMillan, 1854.

———. *Zinzendorff, and Other Poems*. New York: Leavitt, Lord, 1835.

Smith-Rosenberg, Carroll. *Disorderly Conduct: Visions of Gender in Victorian America*. New York: Knopf, 1985.

———. "Domesticating Virtue: Coquettes and Revolutionaries in Young America." *Literature of the Body: Essays on Populations and Persons. Selected Papers from the English Institute, 1986*. Ed. Elaine Scarry. Baltimore: Johns Hopkins UP, 1988. 160–184.

Speare, Morris E. *The Political Novel: Its Development in England and America.* New York: Oxford UP, 1924.

Stanton, Elizabeth Cady; Susan B. Anthony; and Matilda Joslyn Gage, eds. *History of Woman Suffrage.* 1881. New York: Arno, 1969.

Tompkins, Jane. *Sensational Designs: The Cultural Work of American Fiction, 1790–1860.* New York: Oxford UP, 1985.

Warren, Joyce W. *Fanny Fern: An Independent Woman.* New Brunswick: Rutgers UP, 1992.

————. *The American Narcissus: Individualism and Women in Nineteenth-Century American Fiction.* New Brunswick: Rutgers UP, 1984.

Weil, Dorothy. *In Defense of Women: Susanna Rowson (1762–1824).* University Park: Pennsylvania State UP, 1976.

Welter, Barbara. "Anti-Intellectualism and the American Woman, 1800–1860." *Mid-America* 48 (1966): 258–70.

————. "The Cult of True Womanhood: 1820–1860." *American Quarterly* 18 (Summer 1966): 151–74. Rptd. in *Dimity Convictions: The American Woman in the Nineteenth Century.* Athens: Ohio UP, 1976. 3–20.

————. *Dimity Convictions: The American Woman in the Nineteenth Century.* Athens, Ohio: Ohio UP, 1976.

Westbrook, Perry D. *Mary Wilkins Freeman.* Boston: Twayne, 1988.

Woloch, Nancy. *Women and the American Experience.* New York: Knopf, 1984.

Yarborough, Richard. Introduction. *Contending Forces: A Romance Illustrative of Negro Life North and South.* New York: Oxford UP, 1988.

Zinsser, William, ed. *Paths of Resistance: The Art and Craft of the Political Novel.* Boston: Houghton Mifflin, 1989.

Contributors

NINA BAYM, Professor of English at the University of Illinois, is the author of *Novels, Readers, and Reviewers: Responses to Fiction in Antebellum America*; *Woman's Fiction: A Guide to Novels by and about Women in America, 1820–1870*; *The Shape of Hawthorne's Career*; and numerous articles on American literature, including the classic essay "Melodramas of Beset Manhood: How Theories of American Fiction Exclude Women Authors" in *American Quarterly*.

DOROTHY BERKSON, Associate Professor of English at Lewis and Clark College, is the editor of an edition of Harriet Beecher Stowe's *Oldtown Folks* for Rutgers University Press's American Women Writers series. Professor Berkson has published articles in several collections, and she is currently completing a study of *The Voices of Women and Men in American Literature: 1820–1920*.

CHRISTOPHER CASTIGLIA has taught at Yale University, Bowdoin College, and Colorado College. He is currently completing *Bound and Determined: Captivity and Women's Writing from Mary Rowlandson to Patty Hearst* for the Women in Culture and Society series, University of Chicago Press.

KRISTIE HAMILTON, Assistant Professor in the Department of English and Comparative Literature at the University of Wisconsin–Milwaukee, has published in *Early American Literature* and is currently completing a genre study entitled *The Promise of Privacy: A Cultural Theory of the Literary Sketch in Antebellum America*.

SHARON M. HARRIS, Associate Professor of English at the University of Nebraska–Lincoln, is the author of *Rebecca Harding Davis and American Realism*. She has published articles in several journals, including *American Literary Realism, Women's Studies*, and *Legacy: A Journal of American Women Writers*. Professor Harris is the editor of *Selected Writings of Judith Sargent Murray* (forthcoming) and is currently completing an anthology of American women's writings before 1800.

CLAIRE PAMPLIN has presented numerous papers on American literature and culture and on authors ranging from Pauline Hopkins to James Joyce. She is currently completing a study of the race crisis in the works of post-Reconstruction writers.

Mary Bortnyk Rigsby, Assistant Professor of English at Mary Washington College, is currently completing *An American Feminist Aesthetic,* a study of nineteenth-century American women novelists' critiques of Emersonian idealism.

Duangrudi Suksang, Associate Professor at Eastern Illinois University, has published papers on female utopias in *Utopian Studies* and elsewhere. She is currently completing a book-length study on the subject, *"Reaching for the Unattained": Nineteenth-Century Utopias by Women.*

Sandra A. Zagarell, Professor of English at Oberlin College, has edited Caroline Kirkland's *A New Home, Who'll Follow?* and Elizabeth Stoddard's *"The Morgesons" and Other Writings* (with Lawrence Buell). She is author of the forthcoming *Configuring of "America": Narratives of Community and Literary Nationalism in Nineteenth-Century American Literature.*

Index